Andrew MacLaren

Urban unemployment

Local labour markets and employment initiatives

Chris Hasluck

Longman
London and New York

Longman Group UK Limited,
Longman House, Burnt Mill, Harlow,
Essex CM20 2JE, England
and Associated Companies throughout the world.

Published in the United States of America
by Longman Inc., New York

First published 1987

British Library Cataloguing in Publication Data
Hasluck, Chris
    Urban unemployment: local labour markets
    and employment initiatives.
    1. Unemployment   2. Urban economics
    I. Title
    331.13'791732   HD5707

ISBN 0-582-29668-4

Library of Congress Cataloging-in-Publication Data
Hasluck, Chris, 1947–
    Urban unemployment.
    Bibliography: p.
    Includes index.
    1. Unemployment—Great Britain.   2. Great Britain—
Full employment policies.   I. Title.
HD5765.A6H374   1987   331.13'7941   86-10323

ISBN 0 582 29668 4

Produced by Longman Group (FE) Limited
Printed in Hong Kong

Contents

Introduction

The publication of the book coincides with a period of intense public debate about the most appropriate policies to regenerate Britain's declining cities and their inner areas. The scale of the problem to be tackled is enormous and extremely serious; in a number of inner-city areas more than half of the resident labour force is unemployed. One consequence of this has been a rapid proliferation of government schemes to aid the jobless and, most interestingly, the introduction of local economic initiatives.

The reasons for the decline of the urban economies and the rise of spatial concentrations of unemployment are controversial and hotly debated. The debate has generated a large literature in recent years but this is not always in a form best suited to students of urban and labour issues, to practitioners in planning, training, and the caring professions, or to the general reader who is interested in understanding the issues. Much of the recently published material consists of political rhetoric, polemical journalism, or else takes the form of academic monographs of considerable technical complexity. This book makes a timely and valuable contribution to the debate by providing a thorough, rigorous, and objective examination of the causes of, and possible remedies for urban unemployment.

The text draws together the theoretical and empirical aspects of urban labour markets. Using concepts and models drawn from the fields of labour and urban economics and industrial geography, the author examines the nature and operation of the urban labour market. The approach is much more than a simple synthesis of existing ideas, with competing or alternative perspectives on the urban labour market being fully explored. These alternative theoretical frameworks (a mixture of concepts, theories, and ideology) influence the way in which the local labour market and the processes within it are perceived. These differences in perception in turn lead to alternative strategies for dealing with economic problems. The notion of competing theoretical perspectives is therefore a unifying theme which runs throughout the book and is particularly valuable when attempting to make some sort of order out of the confusing and often conflicting array of manpower and urban policy strategies.

Having developed the concepts and analysis of the urban labour market, the remainder of the book is concerned with the crucial questions of why there has been such a marked decline in the economies of the metropolitan and city economies and a corresponding rise in urban unemployment and what, if anything, can be done to reverse these trends. A picture of the patterns of change in employment and unemployment in urban areas is built up by a simple presentation of recent empirical evidence. Again the issue of alternative perspectives emerges in the discussion, with different interpretations being placed upon these changes by competing theoretical frameworks. One issue which is revealed as being important is whether the ultimate cause of the rise in urban unemployment is to be found within or outside the local economy. It may be argued that the scope for spatial or local policy initiatives will be much reduced if the latter is the case.

The 1980's will probably be regarded in retrospect as a decade of experimentation with alternative economic policies. This is particularly true in the field of urban policy and employment initiatives. The major developments in urban policy since the beginning of the decade have been spatially selective and local in character. On the one hand central governments have introduced such initiatives as Urban Development Corporations, Enterprise Zones and Free Ports, and City Action Teams, reflecting their commitment to a private enterprise and competitive market based perspective. In contrast a number of Labour-controlled local authorities have developed and implemented more radical local employment initiatives, reflecting their different perspective on urban problems. These testbeds of economic ideas and policies are so recent that there has been little academic discussion of them at all, a situation which this book seeks to remedy. The distinctive features and objectives of these local strategies are examined and an attempt made to evaluate both their achievements so far and their prospects of success.

The questions raised in this book do not always have simple answers. However, anyone interested in the question of why unemployment is disproportionately concentrated in the urban areas and the inner cities, or of why such unemployment persists despite being the focus of much economic policy, or what scope exists for local employment initiatives, should find valuable and thought provoking material in this book. Students of labour and urban economics, as well as those studying geography, public administration and the social sciences in general, will find the book useful as an introduction to a particular application of economic ideas. Post graduates and researchers may also find such an introduction of interest (the author developed the original idea of the text while teaching students of differing academic and professional backgrounds on an M.A. in Urban Processes, Problems, and Policies at Leicester Polytechnic). Given the rapid growth in recent years of the so-called 'unemployment industry' the text may provide useful material for those professional workers concerned with urban unemployment from a different perspective, namely, those concerned with training and job-creation schemes and people involved with social policy who wish to place their work within some kind of context. Although an acquaintance with elementary economic ideas (not uncommon these days) is an advantage, the analysis have been kept to a minimum.

In summary, the book provides a comprehensive and up-to-date introduction to a very important and rapidly developing topic. It is a measure of this rapidity that of the references cited in this book more than two thirds were published after 1980. For the specialist and non-specialist alike this work should remain a useful reference for some time to come.

Jo Campling

Acknowledgements

It is of course impossible to acknowledge all of the debts which are incurred during the writing of a book such as this. I must, however, thank my colleagues at Leicester Polytechnic especially Clive Harrison and Gary Cook for their helpful discussion and comment on various drafts of the manuscript. Some credit must also be given to students on the M.A. Urban Processes, Problems, and Policies and on the labour economics and urban economics options of the B.A.(Hons) in Economics. These groups of students have acted as guinea pigs for my experimentation with different methods of presenting my ideas; despite this most of them survived to obtain the degree to which they aspired, and I, for my part, also learnt quite a lot.

Finally, I must acknowledge the help and support of Sharon, my wife, who not only assisted with the presentation of the manuscript, but also together with our daughters bore the hidden costs of writing a book, namely the frequent absence of the author and his ill temper when things were not proceeding as they should. This book could not have been written without their support (I know this to be so because they keep telling me!)

We are indebted to the following for permission to reproduce copyright material:

Edward Arnold (Publishers) Ltd for table 2.3 from fig 3 (Cooke 1983); Association of District Councils for table 5.1 (Association of District Councils 1985); Cambridge University Press for figs 1.5 from figs 10 & 11 (Owen et al 1984) and 5.3 from fig 1 (Martin 1985); Charter for Jobs for fig 1.1 from p 2; The Economic and Social Research Council for tables 1.1, 1.2, 3.4 (Hausner & Robson 1986) Copyright The Economic and Social Research Council; the Controller of Her Majesty's Stationery Office for fig 1.2 from fig 1 (NEDC 1985), fig 1.4 from fig 2, fig 3.2 from fig 1 (c) Crown Copyright 1984; London Strategic Policy Unit for fig 1.3(b) (Greater London Council 1985); Methuen & Co Ltd for table 2.2 from table 3.1 (Lloyd & Dicken 1983), (Goddard & Champion 1983); Pergamon Press for fig 3.1 (Spence 1982) Copyright 1982 Pergamon Press; Pion Ltd for table 3.6 from table 10 (Healey & Clark 1985) Copyright Pion, London, 1985; Joint Planning & Transportation Data Team for fig 1.3(a) (West Midlands County Council 1983).

To Sharon, who is both friend and wife, and to my daughters Rachel and Katie for whom I wish a better future than that currently offered to young people.

1
Unemployment: an urban problem

It has never been more true to say that 'the problem of unemployment lies, in a very special sense, at the root of most other social problems' (Beveridge 1909: 1). Loss of employment and the consequent loss of income, status and self-esteem, brings in its wake a host of personal and domestic difficulties and communal problems. What is surprising is that this fundamental insight is still being denied nearly eighty years after Beveridge's original comment. Following the outbreak of rioting in Handsworth and Tottenham in 1985, the Prime Minister and members of the cabinet campaigned vigorously to deny that unemployment and poverty had any causal connection with violent disturbances. Yet it can surely be no coincidence that these and earlier incidents in Brixton and Toxteth during 1981 have taken place in the economically declining and physically decaying areas of Britain's urban core, primarily but not exclusively inner city areas, where unemployment is acute and often exceeds 50 per cent of the resident workforce.

Of course, riots and crime represent an exceptional response to urban deprivation and it would be absurd to suggest a single or simple causal relationship between such events and urban unemployment. In fact the most frequent response to unemployment is despair and eventually apathy, particularly if the period without work is prolonged. Nevertheless, insofar as these exceptions are a reaction to a sense of despair and injustice, they serve as warnings of the scale of the problem and of the need to give serious attention to the economic and social plight of the cities and their inner areas.

The plight of the cities

There can be little doubt that the urban core of Britain's cities and conurbations has become a focal point for many of the economic and social problems of the 1980s. Unemployment occupies a central role in the 'urban crisis' because it is both a symptom of the processes which have undermined the urban economies and an immediate cause of poverty, poor housing and other aspects of social deprivation.

Economic decline

The urban cores are at the centre of a nexus of three economic processes: de-industrialisation, the spatial reorganisation of production, and changes in the nature and conditions of employment (these processes are considered in more detail in Ch. 3). The first process refers to the apparently inexorable decline of Britain's manufacturing industries which, for historical reasons, have been concentrated in the conurbations and cities. This process has reduced the number of jobs in urban areas on a vast scale; between 1951 and 1981 there was a net loss of 1 million manufacturing jobs in the inner cities and a further 1 million job losses in the outer areas of the conurbations and the free-standing cities (Hausner and Robson 1986).

The decline in employment in cities has actually been greater than can be explained by de-industrialisation alone. The effects of industrial change have been reinforced by the spatial re-organisation of production involving the suburbanisation and decentralisation of employment and the gradual drift of economic activity to the south of England. In the conurbations (excepting London) and the large cities in the north of Britain these two aspects of change have compounded one another. However, spatial reorganisation is only one aspect of change. Changes in the nature of employment and labour requirements have also been important. Temporary and part-time work represents an increasing proportion of employment; many traditional production skills have become obsolete, and there has been an increased demand for administrative, supervisory, technical and managerial talent. These requirements for a cheaper, more flexible and compliant workforce have mainly been met by female labour and can often be most easily obtained by spatial reorganisation of the type discussed above. Cities, with their traditionally skilled, manual and often highly unionised workforce and low reserves of female labour because of their tradition of working women, are adversely affected by these changes.

This combination of processes has resulted in the virtual collapse of some urban economies and a rapid, and historically unprecedented, rise in urban unemployment. The extent and spatial pattern of this unemployment is outlined later in this chapter and examined in greater detail in Chapter 4.

Urban deprivation

Accompanying the economic decline of the urban economies has been an equally dramatic and related increase in social deprivation. As unemployment rises, not only does poverty and individual misery increase, but the capacity of the local community to maintain the physical and social infrastructure is reduced. In particular, the local authorities of many urban cores face a fiscal crisis brought about by a sharply reduced local tax base on the one hand and rapidly rising local need on the other. The near insolvency of Liverpool City Council in 1985 may have been an atypical case but many local authorities have found themselves in a similar and paradoxical situation of receiving central government financial aid for their inner-city areas while at the same time having the real value of their financial resources cut through inadequate rate support grants or penalties for overspending.

The cumulative results of urban decay can be gauged from evidence submitted to the National Economic Development Council (NEDC) in 1985 on the state of public sector built infrastructure (NEDC 1985). These submissions by government departments show clearly that Britain's public sector housing, roads, hospitals and schools, and other infrastructure were in a state of dilapidation although the full extent of this could not be ascertained because of a lack of central information. Nearly a quarter of urban principal roads, for instance, had an expected life of less than five years, while the backlog of repairs and maintenance of 'critical' sewers alone was estimated to require the expenditure of £1.5 billion. Housing in urban areas is just as bad; the Department of the Environment (1985) estimated that the local authority housing stock was in such a state of disrepair and decay that £18.8 billion would be required to restore it to good condition while the Association of Metropolitan Authorities (1983) placed the estimate even higher at £25 billion.

The concentration of unemployment, poverty, poor housing, a deteriorating environment and declining public services in the

core areas of the conurbations and cities has meant that these areas
are among the most deprived in the country. As Hausner and
Robson (1986) observe, 'social conditions worsen in an almost
straight line as one gets closer to urban cores'. Table 1.1 shows the
twenty most socially deprived areas in Britain based upon indices
which take account of a number of aspects of deprivation.
Although the ranking is dominated by the Inner City Partnerships

Table 1.1 Ranking of most deprived areas
(lowest ranking is most deprived)

Rank		Population change, 1971–81
1	Glasgow Old Core	–22.0
2	Glasgow Peripheral	–22.0
3	*Birmingham Old Core*	–19.3
4	Hull Core	–35.8
5	Derby Core	–20.1
6	*Manchester/Salford Old Core*	–25.5
7	*Liverpool Old Core*	–23.1
8	Nottingham Core	–31.3
9	Teesside Core	–15.6
10	Other West Midland Cores	– 8.2
11	Other Strathclyde Cores	–22.0
12	Other Greater Manchester Cores	–11.5
13	Leicester Core	– 7.1
14	Merseyside Peripherals	–15.3
15	West Yorkshire cores	–14.4
16	London Docklands	–16.9
17	Plymouth Core	–13.1
18	Other Tyne and Wear Cores	–17.0
19	Sheffield Core	–16.0
20	*Newcastle/Gateshead Old Core*	–13-9

Inner city Partnerships are shown in *italics*
Source: Hausner and Robson 1986:10

(see Ch. 5), the list contains many peripheral metropolitan areas. A
similar conclusion was reached by Bentham (1985) who found
serious deprivation in many non-designated urban areas, especially
in some London boroughs.

Not surprisingly, faced with environmental decay and social
deprivation, many households have abandoned the urban centres.
Table 1.1 reveals the strong association between deprivation and
population loss. The effect has been little short of disastrous; as
Seabrook (1985) puts it: 'What has been siphoned off from these
areas, long before the term inner city was ever heard, has been not
merely money, but the powers and the skills of the people; while

the people themselves, all who could sucessfully buy their way out, have gone.'

Unemployment: the national context

Unemployment in urban areas has to be viewed against the background of growing national unemployment. Unemployment has risen steadily throughout the post-war period, virtually doubling every decade since the 1950s, but the most rapid and sustained increase took place in the 1980s. From the last quarter of 1979 to the first quarter of 1983, the official count of the total number of people unemployed increased by around 1.8 million to over 3 million and subsequently continued to increase, reaching a peak in 1985 of nearly 3.3 million. It is likely that the number of people without jobs was even greater than these figures suggest. The 1984 Labour Force Survey estimated that 870,000 people were seeking work but were not claiming benefit and hence were not included in the official figures. In addition to these unregistered unemployed, a large number of people (495,000 by the end of 1985) were removed from the jobless count by such schemes as the Community Programme. When this hidden unemployment is taken into account the 'true' level of unemployment is likely to exceed 4 million people.

These high and sustained levels of unemployment are arguably the worst in Britain's economic history, even including the 1930s. In the latter period unemployment rose very sharply but, after four years, declined equally rapidly whereas in the 1980s unemployment has risen continuously for six years and shows little sign of declining. The two periods are contrasted in Fig. 1.1. In 1985 the level of unemployment stabilised and even declined slightly in the final quarter of the year. This may mark a turning point, but even if this were so, the rate at which unemployment was falling at the end of 1985 would not allow unemployment to fall below 3 million until the year 1992 and it would take a further 14 years to attain pre-1979 levels. Although economic forecasting is prone to a very considerable degree of uncertainty there are few forecasters who predict that unemployment will fall below 3 million before the end of the decade (future prospects for unemployment are discussed in Ch. 7).

The immediate reason, although not the ultimate cause, of the increase in unemployment was the collapse of employment

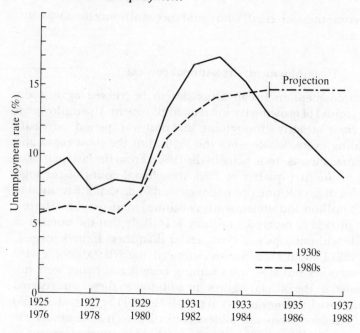

Fig. 1.1 Unemployment in Great Britain; the 1930s and the 1980s
Source: 'Charter for jobs', Economic Report No 1, Sept. 1985

between 1979 and 1983. As Fig. 1.2 shows, employment declined sharply by nearly 2 million jobs over this relatively short period. But even when employment began to increase again in mid-1983, it was insufficient to offset the increasing size of the working population which increased rapidly after falling slightly during the worst of the 1979–83 recession. Despite nearly 700,000 additional jobs (nearly one-third of the number lost during 1979–83) unemployment continued to increase slowly until the end of 1985.

Part of the reason for employment growth having little impact on unemployment lies in the nature of the new jobs and the labour required to fill them. The jobs created since 1983 have been very unlike the jobs that were lost during the recession; most have been in the service industries, most have been in areas of traditionally 'female work' of which much is on a part-time basis, while self-employment, which declined throughout most of the post-war years, has also increased. Job losses in the recession were dominated by the decline of male, full-time jobs in manufacturing

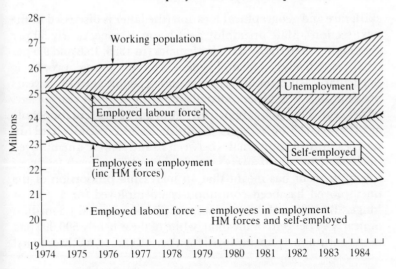

Fig. 1.2 Working population an employed labour force (UK)
(seasonally adjusted – quarterly figures)
Source: National Economic Development Council, 'New jobs
progress report', Memorandum by the Director General, NEDC
(85), 57, June 1985, Annex 1.

and this pattern has continued since then in a less dramatic
manner. It has been estimated (Prowse 1985) that the average
quarterly rise in employment since March 1983 amounts to around
88,000 jobs. This total has comprised a 58,000 increase in female
employment (of which 50,000 were part-time jobs), a 50,000
increase in the number of self-employed, and a decrease of 20,000 in
male employment. It would seem that the growth of employment
in the 1980s has not matched the available labour force and has
largely been accommodated by new workers, mainly women,
entering the labour market.

The burden of unemployment is not carried equally by all
sections of the workforce. This is partly the result of the imbalance
between the pattern of new jobs and that of previous job losses (as
discussed above), but it is also the case that for various reasons
(discussed in Ch. 4) some groups are more vulnerable or prone to
experience above average unemployment because of more frequent
spells of unemployment or because they have to endure longer
periods without work. There are substantial differences in the
measured unemployment rates of groups differentiated by age, sex,

skill, race and geographical location (the latter is discussed in the next section). Male unemployment is, on average, nearly 50 per cent higher than the average for females (in 1985, 15.8 and 9.5 per cent respectively). Unemployment among young people is particularly acute: the average rate among people aged 18–19 years of age in 1985 was 26 per cent and among those 20–24 years of age, 20 per cent. This compares with a rate of only 9 per cent for people aged between 35 and 55 years. Young males are especially hard hit; nearly a third of young males between 18 and 19 were unemployed in 1985. Not surprisingly, the high and sustained levels of unemployment has meant that an increasing proportion of the unemployed has been continuously unemployed for a year or longer. By 1985 such long-term unemployed exceeded 1.3 million or nearly 40 per cent of the total, while of these nearly 500,000 had been continuously unemployed for a period exceeding three years!

Spatial patterns of unemployment

The incidence of unemployment varies between the regions of Britain, between cities and towns of differing size and function, between the inner and outer areas of cities and between the urban areas in general and the rural remainder. These different dimensions interact with one another to produce a pattern of considerable complexity.

Intra-urban variation

The inner-city area has come to epitomise urban unemployment. In most cities and towns there is a concentration of high unemployment rates in districts in and around the inner area. The stark difference between the inner cities and other areas is revealed

Table 1.2 Unemployment by place of residence

	1951	1961	1971	1981
Inner cities	133	136	144	151
Outer cities	81	82	88	101
Free-standing cities	95	107	112	115
Towns and rural areas	95	93	90	90

Indices: Great Britain = 100
Source: Hausner and Robson 1986: 8.

in Table 1.2 which shows that Britain's inner city areas experienced relatively higher unemployment rates throughout the post-war period and that by 1981 the rate of unemployment among inner-city residents was more than 50 per cent greater than the national average and more than 66 per cent greater than the rate in towns and rural areas. The unemployment rates in the main conurbations and their central cities are compared in Table 1.3 and, while confirming the general pattern, the results suggest that there have been important differences between urban economies and between the male and female labour forces.

Table 1.3 Unemployment in the conurbations; the percentage of economically active residents out of employment, 1971 and 1981

	1971		1981	
	Male	Female	Male	Female
Greater London	4.4	2.8	9.3	4.6
Inner London	6.0	3.5	12.8	6.3
Outer London	3.2	2.3	7.3	3.6
Greater Manchester	5.7	3.0	12.6	5.9
Manchester	9.8	6.2	18.1	7.5
Merseyside	8.4	3.8	17.8	7.2
Liverpool	11.5	7.6	21.6	8.9
South Yorkshire	5.4	2.2	12.0	4.9
Sheffield	5.2	3.9	12.6	4.5
Tyne and Wear	8.6	3.0	16.5	5.8
Newcastle	9.8	5.5	16.2	5.6
West Midlands	5.0	2.7	15.7	6.3
Birmingham	6.5	5.3	16.7	6.9
West Yorkshire	5.3	2.4	11.3	4.9
Leeds	6.2	4.1	11.2	4.9
Central Clydeside	11.1	6.7	17.3	7.7
Great Britain	5.0	2.6	10.5	4.7

Source: derived from the Census of Population, 1971 and 1981.

At a more detailed level Fig. 1.3 shows the variation in unemployment rates within two metropolitan areas: the West Midlands and Greater London. In the former case, the wards with the highest unemployment rates can be seen to be clustered around the urban core of Birmingham, West Bromwich, Dudley,

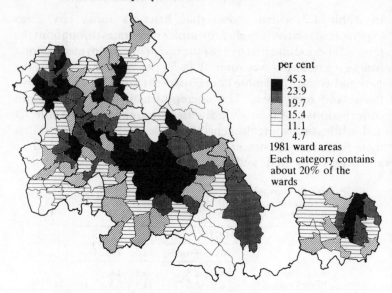

per cent
45.3
23.9
19.7
15.4
11.1
4.7
1981 ward areas
Each category contains
about 20% of the
wards

Fig. 1.3(a) Unemployment rates by Wards, West Midlands
Metropolitan County, Oct. 1983
Source: West Midlands County Council, 'Statistics '83', County
Planning Department, 1983: 67

Wolverhampton and Walsall. In many of these areas the
unemployment rate is more than five times the rate in suburban
locations (three wards had rates in excess of 40 per cent while the
rate exceeded 30 per cent in a further nine cases.) Unemployment
is, on average, much lower in Greater London but the same pattern
of unemployment can be discerned with the highest rates of
unemployment occurring in inner-city constituencies.

Although unemployment is generally higher in inner rather
than suburban locations, there are exceptions and within many
cities high unemployment can be found in isolated suburban
locations (often associated with public sector housing estates)
while high inner-city unemployment may be confined to distinct
sectors. In fact the inner–outer dichotomy is rather too crude a
generalisation; unemployment rates tend to lie on a gradient
which is positively related to proximity to inner areas. This
gradient varies from city to city and may be different for males and
females. Hall and Metcalf (1979) and Richardson (1980) observed
relatively low rates of unemployment for women in inner city

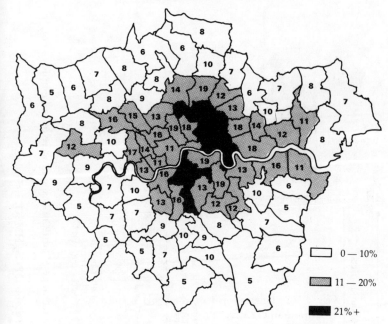

Fig. 1.3(b) Unemployment rates by Parliamentary Constituency, Greater London, Jan. 1985
Source: Greater London Council, 'The London industrial strategy', 1985: 5.

areas, and female unemployment (particularly for married women) may be more prevalent in the suburbs.

Differences between urban areas

In addition to differences within a locality there are also marked differences between one urban economy and another and Fig. 1.4 shows very clearly that the level of unemployment in an urban area, relative to the national average, is related to its functional type and its position in the urban hierarchy with well above average rates being found in the principal cities and other districts of the metropolitan areas.

Comparisons of change in the incidence of unemployment is complicated by the differences in the size and base rates of unemployment between areas. Comparisons can be made on the basis of the increase in the number of unemployed, or the

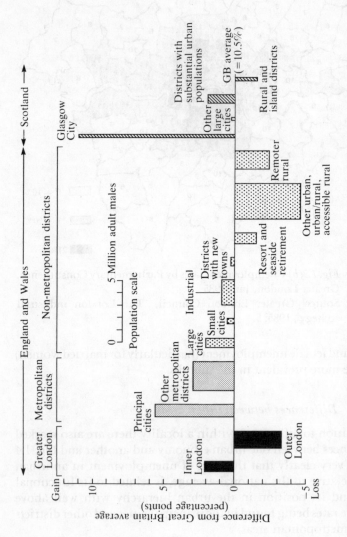

Fig. 1.4 Differences from the average for Great Britain in the percentage of adult males who were out of employment, by category of district, 1981

Source: *Census 1981: Key statistics for local authorities, Great Britain*. OPCS, HMSO, 1984: 146.

proportionate increase in the unemployment rate, or the percentage point change in unemployment rates. These alternative methods can produce conflicting rankings and this has led to some controversy as to which is the best measure of unemployment change (see Gillespie and Owen 1982, and Crouch 1982). Whatever the outcome of this debate, it can be observed that the number of unemployed is highest, and has increased by the largest number, in the conurbations simply because of their size; there are, for instance, more unemployed persons in Greater London than in the whole of Scotland. This concentration of unemployment (accounting for 43 per cent of all unemployment in 1985) has been reinforced by above average increases in unemployment rates.

The impact of rising national unemployment on the metropolitan labour markets can be seen from Table 1.4. In most cases the proportionate growth of unemployment between 1971 and 1981 was faster than the national average. When the percentage point change is considered it is clear that all conurbations other than Greater London have had a greater increase than the national average. As the percentage point change measures the proportion of the local labour force who have joined the ranks of the unemployed, it may be regarded as the more significant measure of the changing economic fortunes of a locality. As the greatest growth of unemployment was in areas of previously low

Table 1.4 The growth of urban unemployment: unemployment change in the conurbations, 1971–81 and 1981–85

	1971–81		1981–85	
	Percentage change	Percentage point change	Percentage change	Percentage point change
Greater London	111.4	4.9	52.2	3.5
Greater Manchester	121.0	6.9	38.4	4.3
Merseyside	112.0	9.4	35.0	5.5
South Yorkshire	122.0	6.6	50.9	5.8
Tyne and Wear	92.0	7.9	42.4	5.9
West Midlands	214.0	10.7	33.3	4.2
West Yorkshire	113.0	6.0	34.3	3.6
Great Britain	110.0	5.5	36.0	3.6

Source: Employment Gazette (various).

unemployment, such as the West Midlands, some convergence of metropolitan unemployment rates has taken place but it has been around a faster than average trend. This upward trend of unemployment has continued into the 1980s at much the same rate.

The regional dimension

Unemployment has increased in other urban areas outside the conurbations and the national pattern is illustrated by Fig. 1.5. This shows that between 1971 and 1981, both male and female unemployment increased in virtually every local labour market, but there were exceptionally large increases in the metropolitan areas of the north of Britain, most notably in the north-west and north-east of England, the Midlands, Central Scotland and South Wales. Keeble (1980) and Fothergill and Gudgin (1982) have claimed that most of the variation in economic performance between regions can be explained by the decline of metropolitan and large urban areas, but a regional dimension also appears to be important. This regional dimension does not conform to traditional notions of the regional problem. On the contrary it would appear to take the form of a simple north–south dichotomy, particularly for female unemployment. South of a line drawn between the Severn and the Wash, the increase in unemployment has been relatively small with the exception of the extreme south-west and, for males, metropolitan London. North of the north-south divide, unemployment has increased substantially and for males the increase has been most acute in the industrial heartland of metropolitan England. Thus the pattern of unemployment among urban areas is one of considerable variety and complexity.

Long-term unemployment

The crude percentage rate is actually a poor indicator of the incidence of unemployment which is best revealed by a combination of information on the frequency and duration of periods without work. Unfortunately little is known of the frequency of unemployment, but rather more is known of duration. Just as the rate of unemployment is related to the urban hierarchy so too is the incidence of long-term unemployment (defined as a continuous period of unemployment in excess of twelve months). Green (1985)

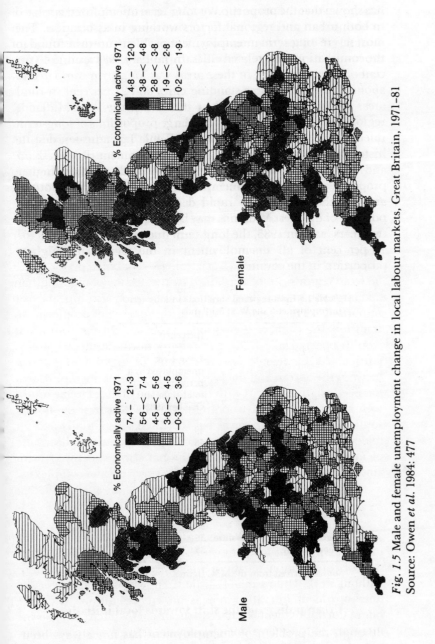

Fig. 1.5 Male and female unemployment change in local labour markets, Great Britain, 1971–81
Source: Owen et al. 1984: 477

has shown that the proportion of long-term unemployed is related to both urban and regional factors working in association. The most severe long-term unemployment problems are to be found in the conurbations and related cities. In January 1983 around 40 per cent of unemployment in these areas was long term compared to about 32 per cent in free-standing cities and 27 per cent in rural areas. This can be illustrated by the case of the West Midlands region which has experienced very large proportions of long-term unemployment in its urban core, as Table 1.5 indicates, despite historically being a region of low unemployment. Birmingham and the other inner-urban areas have had a much higher proportion of long-term unemployed than the non-metropolitan areas of the region. The rapid deterioration in the economic position of the West Midlands may be gauged by the fact that only two years later, in 1985, the long-term unemployed accounted for 49 per cent of all unemployment in the region, the highest proportion in the country.

Table 1.5 Intra-regional variations in long-term unemployment: the West Midlands

Area	(percents) Long-term unemployed as a percentage of total claimants October 1983
Birmingham	49
Sandwell	48
Wolverhampton	47
Walsall	46
Dudley	43
Coventry	45
Solihull	42
Staffordshire	39
Shropshire	38
Hereford and Worcestershire	36
Warwickshire	35

Source: derived from the MSC figures.

Urban policy and the shift towards local initiatives

Although the problem of unemployment has not always been recognised as an urban one, and in the immediate post-war period it was regarded as an almost purely macroeconomic issue since the 1977 White Paper on Policy for Inner Cities and the subsequent Inner Urban Areas of 1978, there has been a discernable shift of policy towards initiatives which are essentially urban in character. This trend has been particularly marked in the 1980s with local government developing its own forms of economic initiatives mainly as an act of desperation in the face of acute levels of urban unemployment and the apparent inability, or unwillingness, of central government to have any impact on the problem.

These local initiatives represent an immediate but pragmatic response to the problems of the cities. The growth and evolution of these schemes are examined in Chapters 5 and 6. There is considerable variation in the way in which local authorities perceive their role in the fight against unemployment. These differences reflect alternative perspectives on the way in which urban labour markets operate and the scope for state intervention. Some have been content to use their traditional powers to try to create an improved business environment within which local enterprise can flourish. Others see the problem as requiring more radical initiatives which involve direct intervention in the job creation process and which stretch their legal and financial powers to the limit. Despite these substantial and well-intentioned efforts, a large question mark continues to hang over such local economic policy. Initiatives sometimes seem to have impossible goals. In other cases inconsistent objectives appear to be pursued by different parts of the same authority or by different agencies. The inadequacy of local authority powers has often meant that local employment initiatives have been deflected from their real targets, while it is sometimes alleged that such policies represents 'old wine in new bottles' or, even worse, are merely cosmetic in nature.

In part, the problem of developing appropriate local economic strategies arises from the lack of an adequately developed theoretical framework within which to analyse the operation of local labour markets and the consequences of local employment initiatives. The development of such a framework is hampered by incomplete knowledge of urban labour markets processes, and by the fact that existing analysis is often the product of different disciplines using dissimilar research methods. There is a need to review existing knowledge and empirical evidence on urban labour markers and to utilise this knowledge to gain an understanding of the cause of unemployment in metropolitan areas. In the light of such an examination, it may be possible to begin to identify the most appropriate forms of local initiatives and to evaluate existing local labour market policy. This book represents a modest attempt to achieve this objective. In a text of this kind it is clearly not possible to fill all the gaps in existing knowledge, but at least their systematic identification may prove useful to researchers and policy-makers alike, both as a timely caveat and as a spur to further investigations.

Further reading

The spatial effects of Britain's deteriorating economic performance are well described by Townsend (1983) in *The Impact of the Recession: on industry, employment, and the regions, 1976–1981*, while Hausner and Robson (1986) provide a summary of research into five urban areas in 'Changing Cities', an introduction to the ESRC Inner Cities Research Programme. A rather different approach but one which lays bare the gravity of urban problems is provided by *Faith in the City*, the report of the Archbishop of Canterbury's commission on urban deprivation (CoE 1985). To obtain a vivid impression of life in the inner city when unemployed, see: Harrison (1983) *Inside the Inner city: life under the cutting edge*; Seabrook (1983) *Unemployment*; or Sinfield (1981) *What Unemployment Means*.

2
Workers and jobs in the city

The fact that unemployment is concentrated in major urban and metropolitan areas and the so-called inner-city areas is not coincidental. Some economic or social process, or combination of processes, has produced this unequal spatial distribution of the jobless. The purpose of this chapter is to examine the processes which affect labour most directly, namely, the urban labour market.

In the discussion which follows, the term 'labour market' is used as a general label to describe any set of processes and institutions through which employers and workers interact. While there may be agreement that some form of market exists, there are considerable differences of opinion as to how this market works. These differences reflect more than any simple disagreement about empirical evidence; they reflect fundamental differences in the way that the economic and social system are conceived. Not surprisingly, differences in theoretical explanations frequently lead to differences in policy recommendations. This chapter provides a foundation upon which to build the analysis of employment decline, urban unemployment and local policy initiatives found in later chapters.

Labour markets

In very general terms a labour market is a mechanism through which labour services are bought and sold and is the means by which the separate decisions of workers and employers are coordinated. Through transactions in the market, labour is allocated in accordance with demand to different occupations, industries and geographical locations, and in this process of allocation the market sets a price for labour, the wage, which in turn influences the allocative mechanism.

The essential element of a labour market is that buyers and sellers of labour must be at least potentially in contact with one another. Only a proportion of employers and workers will be active in the market (i.e. looking for new workers or new jobs) on any particular day, but all will enter the market from time to time and when they do they will seek out other market participants, exchange information on wages and employment, and, ultimately, make contracts of employment. The precise way in which market activity takes place varies from one market to another. In some cases it is very formal and subject to strictly observed rules and conventions while in others the process is much more casual. When the process of coordination is formalised within an organisation then an internal labour market is said to exist.

In reality employers and labour interact in a limited and partial manner. As the result, the labour market consists of a complex set of separate but interdependent submarkets within which buyers and sellers interact to a high degree although they have little contact with other workers or employers elsewhere. The boundaries between labour markets (in the limited sense of the term) are marked out by significant breaks in the interaction of workers or employers brought about by poor information or some form of barrier which prevents participants in one labour market from freely entering other markets. A fundamental division within the labour market is that of skill or occupation. Occupational markets develop because workers possess different skills, training or abilities while employers have requirements for different types of labour. The separation of such markets occurs because of the difficulty or cost of acquiring new skills or simply because of the extra cost of more extensive job-hunting. Other limitations on the interaction of buyers and sellers may result from the operation of internal labour markets, legislation, discrimination and other social practices and customs. Occupational markets will thus be subject to further divisions based upon industry, age, sex or ethnic group.

Local labour markets

One important source of labour market fragmentation is the friction of space. Geographical mobility involves costs which probably increase with distance. Most people travel some distance to work because few live at their place of employment but the extent of such travel is limited by the cost of transportation while more extensive mobility requires an even more costly change of residence. The effect of costly mobility will be to limit the geographical employment horizons of workers. In the short term only jobs within commuting distance will be considered. In the long term, employment opportunities outside the local area may be considered, but only if the costs of residential movement can be recovered in improved pay or conditions. Cheshire (1979) has described these two aspects of labour mobility as, respectively, continuous and discontinuous mobility.

Reinforcing the pecuniary and psychological costs of extensive daily travel and residential mobility are the costs and difficulties of acquiring information. Without information markets cannot function. Information about potential employers and workers can be obtained in many ways, but it is often the case that the most effective and cheapest methods are also the most geographically limited. Local information networks frequently consist of informal contacts between friends, relatives or employees (Reid 1972) but even formal methods such as newspaper advertising or Job Centres tend to be local in their focus. However, a limited geographical job horizon is more true of some occupational groups than others. Professional, managerial and skilled occupations often use national and sometimes international information networks and for them the labour market is much more extensive than the immediate locality.

With limited information and costly mobility there will be some spatial limit to the interaction of employers and workers. From the workers' perspective, the labour market consists of all known potential employers within an acceptable travelling distance from home. Similarly, from the employers' point of view, its potential labour force consists of all suitable workers within travelling distance of their plant. Employers therefore have some geographical catchment area from which they would expect to draw their labour. It is within this catchment area that market interaction between employer and labour will take place. In the case of a single employer the catchment area and the local labour market are one and the same, but when there are several employers then individual labour catchment areas will be linked by virtue of the competition between employers for workers and the competition between workers for jobs.

These ideas are illustrated in a simplified form in Fig. 2.1. Each

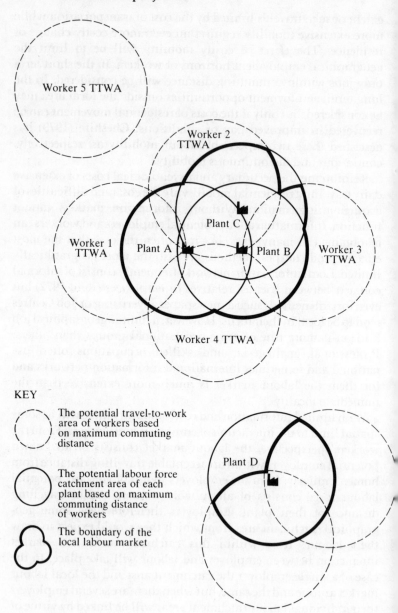

KEY

The potential travel-to-work area of workers based on maximum commuting distance

The potential labour force catchment area of each plant based on maximum commuting distance of workers

The boundary of the local labour market

Fig. 2.1 The local labour market

worker has a travel-to-work area (TTWA) (assumed the same for all workers) and these determine the catchment areas of each plant in the local economy. The local labour market embraces all those catchment areas which are linked together and within which, therefore, employers and workers are potentially in contact with one another. The boundary of the local labour market will be where there is a break in the chain of linkages such that local employers and local workers cease to interact with those located elsewhere. For instance, in Fig. 2.1 worker 5 lives too far away to be able to accept jobs in local plants and is not a participant in the local labour market. Equally, Plant D draws its labour force from elsewhere and does not form part of the local labour market. Even though this model is very simple it highlights the important conclusion that the size, extent and shape of the local labour market depends upon spatial patterns of residence, employment and the costs and other limitations to continuous mobility. A change in any of these factors will affect the local labour market, perhaps increasing its size, fragmenting it, or linking it to neighbouring labour markets. Local labour markets are not static entities but are dynamic and constantly changing.

In practice, the identification of a local labour market is not easy because workers differ in their spatial horizons. For some workers 'the local area' may mean little more than a few miles from home whereas others may be prepared to travel much more extensively and for them the local dimension will have only limited significance. These differences in the geographical size of individual TTWAs are related to household circumstances and to occupation. The local labour market really consists of several 'layers' of varying geographical scale (differentiated by skill, sex, marital status, etc.) superimposed on one another. In these circumstances it is unlikely that any local labour market will be entirely self-contained and have finite boundaries. Despite this, it is probably reasonable to conclude that 'there is, in most communities, a well-developed set of communications which provide the basis for a local labour market in which the bulk of workers in the area, and all employers for the major part of their labour force, will be actively concerned' (Hunter and Mulvey 1981: 137).

Urban labour markets

Local labour markets are often centred on towns or cities and it is therefore tempting to equate urban with local labour markets.

Hunter and Reid (1968) examined urban worker mobility within 'a geographical area surrounding a city (or cities a few miles apart) in which there is a concentration of labour demand and in which workers can change jobs without changing residence'. Similarly, empirical studies seeking to define and identify urban economies have often used local labour market criteria relating to employment levels and density, commuting patterns and some arbitrarily determined level of 'self containment'. The concepts of the Standard Metropolitan Labour Area (SMLA) and the Metropolitan Economic Labour Area (MELA) are examples of this approach (Hall *et al.* 1973: Drewitt 1974).

Local and urban labour markets are not necessarily congruent. By virtue of the way in which they are defined, local labour markets often contain areas that are suburban or even rural and which depend upon urban centres for employment. Equally important, many urban areas consist of several local labour markets. Urban labour markets are not just local but are those local labour markets which are quintessentially urban in character. Probably the best empirical approximation to such markets is the 'central urban zone' of the 280 British local labour markets identified by Coombes *et al.* (1982).

The quintessential features of urban labour markets can be illustrated by a set of stylised facts. These represent the features commonly found in such areas but, of course, are not an accurate description of any particular locality. They suggest certain general tendencies which can be seen in large towns, cities and inner areas. A typical metropolitan labour market is likely to possess the following features:

1. A large number of spatially concentrated jobs and workers.
2. Higher than average labour force participation rates, especially among women.
3. A resident workforce which tends to be relatively unskilled and in the lower occupational classes.
4. A large proportion of the population are members of ethnic minorities.
5. A relatively diversified industrial structure: manufacturing industries tend to dominate urban areas but in specific areas, such as the central business district, service activity dominates.
6. Employment is located in a limited number of large

individual employers and a great many small firms: the public sector is a major employer.

7. Internal mobility within the local market is easy and cheap and there are well-developed information networks (local newspapers, friends, relatives, etc.).

8. Large inward commuting flows occur and many jobs are filled by non-residents.

9. A bi-modal population distribution with above average population of young persons and the elderly (this is probably true only of the inner cities rather than all areas).

While there are very obvious variations between cities and indeed within them, nevertheless these stylised facts do provide a guide to the general characteristics of urban labour markets. Table 2.1 presents some evidence supporting this general picture. There appear to be, for example, marked differences between rural and urban areas in respect of married women's participation, social class structure (The Registrar General's Socio-economic classes II and V being used as proxies for this), skills as measured by higher educational attainment, and industrial structure. Not only is there a difference but the variations are related to position in the urban hierarchy; married women's participation is highest in the 'million plus' cities and lowest in very small towns, whereas the reverse is the case for the proportion of the population who are in unskilled occupations. Table 2.1 also confirms the concentration of unemployment in the major urban labour markets, as noted in the previous chapter.

Competing theoretical perspectives

The analysis of urban labour markets cannot proceed very far by description alone. Explanation requires some means of 'making sense' of observed patterns of behaviour and other empirical 'facts'. Theories of the labour market achieve this objective by providing a simplified but unified framework by means of which facts can be interpreted. Such theories enable particular occurrences or processes to be explained and their consequences speculated upon.

Following the typology of Corina (1972) it is possible to distinguish between four broad approaches which represent the labour market as, alternatively:

(a) a straightforward example of more general markets;

Table 2.1 Urban labour markets; some illustrative statistics

	Married women economically active as a percentage of the total population	Percentage of the resident population in social class		Percentage of males possessing a higher education qualification	Percentage of employed residents working in Manufacturing	Services	Percentage of resident population where head of household was born in New Commonwealth	Males out of work as a percentage of the economically active
		II	V					
Great Britain								
All rural areas (England & Wales)	56.9	18.8	4.1	13.7	27.0	34.0	NA	11.6
All urban areas (England & Wales)	49.2	29.1	2.4	16.1	19.9	32.3	0.8	7.2
(England & Wales)	57.8	17.9	4.1	13.5	28.2	34.2	4.9	11.8
Population size (England & Wales)								
1,000,000 and over	59.9	18.6	4.3	14.2	26.5	36.9	10.7	12.1
500,000–999,999	58.8	13.8	5.2	11.3	30.5	32.9	2.5	16.4
200,000–499,999	57.1	16.0	4.4	12.1	29.8	33.1	3.8	13.3
100,000–199,999	59.2	16.4	4.4	12.5	30.6	30.9	3.9	11.3
50,000–99,999	57.4	17.2	4.2	13.1	29.6	32.6	2.3	11.8
20,000–49,999	56.7	18.5	3.9	13.6	29.2	32.6	1.5	10.9
10,000–19,999	55.7	19.6	3.6	14.5	27.8	33.0	1.0	9.3
5,000–9,999	55.2	19.9	3.2	14.0	27.0	33.3	0.8	8.7
2,000–4,999	54.3	22.8	2.8	16.4	25.3	34.5	0.8	7.8

Source: derived from the Census of Population, 1981.

(b)   a special subcase, subject to distinctive processes and conditions but still, in principle, explicable in terms of market processes;

(c)   an atypical market form, the explanation of which requires special and, in particular, social factors to be taken into account; and

(d)   models of the labour process under capitalism; these models consider the labour market within the context of broad social and economic relationships.

It might be supposed that it would be possible to choose the correct approach from these four by means of an appeal to their explanatory power - that is, their ability to explain observed behaviour in labour markets. In practice this competition between explanations has proved inconclusive. There are many reasons for this including the difficulties of empirical testing, the differing definitions of the nature of the questions to be resolved and, perhaps most important, because value judgements interpose themselves between theory and evidence with the result that the same evidence is interpreted in different ways by alternative perspectives.

Ideological issues

An alternative name for value judgements is 'ideology' which may be defined as a set of ideas, concepts and propositions which represent a particular view of the way in which society works. Ideologies are often a reflection of the position and interests of groups in society and may be used to make existing social relationships legitimate and to justify particular policies. Ideologies tend to present 'a world view', an overall explanation of the processes within society of which the labour market is small but very important part. The ideological issues which impinge upon labour market analysis are concerned with the roles to be played by the structures of society and by state intervention in the economy. Three broad perspectives may be discerned: the competitive market perspective, the structuralist perspective and the radical perspective. The differences between these perspectives reflect different views about the extent to which individuals in the labour market are constrained by social processes and the extent to which state intervention can improve upon the market outcome.

Competing perspectives

The essential feature of the competitive market perspective is the emphasis placed on the market exchange relationship between labour and capital and the very limited role allowed for economic policy. Labour demand and supply interact within the market through some common influence (usually wages) to produce an 'equilibrium', a situation in which the individual decisions of employers and workers are coordinated. Although this perspective frequently draws upon the concepts and techniques of neoclassical economics, there is no simple correspondence (indeed much recent neoclassical labour economics has been set within the structuralist perspective – see later). There is, however, a close association between the competitive perspective and the ideology of *laissez-faire* capitalism. An emphasis on individual choice and the harmonious coordination of economic activity suggest that labour market processes will produce socially optimal results unless the market mechanism is interfered with by the state, monopolists or trade unions. The role of the state, according to this view, is simply to maintain a business environment that will encourage enterprise and productive activity while curbing the worst excesses of the free market through appropriate legislation.

While the market perspective abstracts almost wholly from historical and institutional factors in society, in contrast these features of the labour market are an integral part of the structuralist perspective. The common element in this viewpoint is that it attributes a role to economic and social structures, although the label can be applied to a very wide range of approaches. The labour market is not portrayed as being composed of individuals able to exercise free choice but instead there is an emphasis on the constraints on individual action and the inherent imperfections of the market mechanism. In recent years neoclassical analysis has tended to incorporate structural aspects into its analysis of labour markets through its treatment of imperfect information, uncertainty and costly adjustment. Other analyses have given a greater weight to the organisational and institutional aspects of labour market behaviour, particularly those of internal labour markets and trade unions. The imperfections of markets, combined with the notion that the private and social consequences of market activity do not always correspond, lead structuralists to the conclusion that labour markets are often in disequilibrium and that market outcomes may not always (if ever) be best.

Whatever the precise form of analysis, the structuralist perspective perceives the labour market as characterised by inefficiencies, inequalities and conflicting interests and as such may be improved upon by implementing appropriate labour market policies. On this point, however, there is an important ideological division between those who advocate policy designed to bolster and support the market mechanism and those who see policy as providing an alternative mechanism to the market. The former might be labelled 'right structuralists' while the latter are 'left' or 'radical structuralists', although these labels greatly understate the shades of opinion that can be encountered. Right structuralists recognise the imperfections of the labour market but regard the alternatives as being even worse. They prefer to strengthen competitive processes where possible rather than replace them with complex legislation or state bureaucracy; this is very much the view of the so-called 'new right' (Bosanquet 1983). In contrast, radical structuralists see reform of labour markets as being a desirable end in itself, and one which is necessary to enable individuals to overcome the broad social processes which constrain them.

Finally, there is the radical and Marxist perspective. This viewpoint tends to provide 'overarching' explanations which relegate institutional detail to a minor position. Central to this perspective is the notion that economic opportunities are determined by fundamental economic and social relationships within society (the capitalist mode of production) and that individuals have little, if any, power to affect matters. This being so, the behaviour of urban labour markets is to be understood more by reference to the quest for profit, capital accumulation and class conflict than by particular economic events or local factors. Ironically this perspective often stresses the role of markets which are seen as the means by which the economic system is propelled, but labour markets are a far from harmonious place according to this view as they are the arena within which the class struggle is fought out, with capital usually having the upper hand. As far as policy is concerned, radical perspectives emphasise the need for fundamental social change (in the long term) or, failing that, short-term measures which pave the way for social change such as the extension of state ownership of production.

The analysis of urban labour markets

The importance of competing theoretical perspectives is two-fold: first, they explain why disagreements exist and persist concerning the nature and causes of urban unemployment while, second, the competition between perspectives and the changing dominance of one perspective over another may explain shifts in labour market and urban policy. But before considering these issues, it is necessary to examine the theory of urban labour markets in a little more detail.

The market framework

According to the traditional, or neoclassical, analysis of urban labour markets, the level and pattern of employment and wages in an urban economy are the product of the interaction of the market forces of labour demand and labour supply operating through the market mechanism. In any urban economy, individual households will determine how much labour to supply, and local firms will establish the amount of labour they wish to hire. In this limited sense it will always be the case that labour demand and supply are important underlying determinants of local labour market conditions whether these separate decisions are coordinated through the market or not. An examination of the determinants of local labour demand and supply is an essential starting point to any analysis of the urban labour market.

Households and labour supply

The supply of labour can be defined as the amount of labour services available for hire in a particular set of economic circumstances. Labour is supplied by households for whom, if successful in selling their labour, the resulting wage is the main source of income. This dependence upon wage income means that most households participate in the urban labour market.

The main resource owned by households is its labour. It must decide whether to use this labour time in the home or whether to sell it on the labour market. Household time is intrinsically useful, either as leisure or for domestic production, so that the sale of labour services (i.e. work) can be seen as a necessary evil required in order that the household obtains income from which to buy goods and services it cannot produce itself. Decisions about how much time to sell will depend upon the particular circumstances of each household and the opportunities available to it. The latter include the level of wage rates and local job prospects, while the former include aspects of the household – such as its size and composition and its unearned income – which affect the need for income, its attitude to work and the amount of time available for sale.

Wages Economic analysis suggests that the effect of an increase in unearned income is a reduction in the amount of labour supplied as households will generally prefer more leisure time. The effects of an increase in wage rates is less clear. Although higher wages increase the return from the sale of labour, the household might wish to take part or all of the resulting increase in income in the form of extra leisure. These two conflicting aspects (known as the substitution and the income effects) mean that the overall change in labour supply in response to a change in wages is indeterminate. Most empirical studies suggest that the effect on the labour supply of adult males is very small and possibly negative. In contrast, the effect on the female labour supply is almost certainly positive and probably quite large (Creedy and Thomas 1982).

Household labour supply decisions are likely to be extremely complex, mainly because households often contain more than one person and because labour supply has several dimensions. Thus decisions must be made about who, if anyone, is to work, how many hours of labour to sell and the kind of labour to provide. These decisions will reflect the comparative advantages of household members in generating wage income or domestic production. Changes in the wage or job opportunities of one household member will therefore have consequences for the labour supply of other members, resulting in a complex pattern of responses to changing relative earnings and household income.

Participation As most households are dependent on wage income, they have little choice but to participate in the local labour market, but they have to make decisions as to which member participates. One of the most important trends in the post-war period has been the increased participation of married women (see Ch. 3). Participation decisions will be influenced by the need for income and the relative earning power of household members. In addition, the importance placed upon domestic production (especially child-rearing), the stock of household consumer durables, and the possibility of substituting paid labour services for domestic production will all affect the availability of household members for market work.

In principle, households can choose the hours of labour to be supplied, but in practice this is likely to be difficult because of institutionally fixed hours. Any individual seeking work is therefore constrained to a choice between non-participation, part-time work or full-time work and variations in household labour supply will take the form of discrete steps from non-, to part-time, to full-time participation. One result of this is that there is probably a level above which wages must rise (a reservation wage) in order to induce any individual to consider making the jump from not working to working.

Welfare benefits Another factor associated with the creation of a reservation wage is the welfare or social security system. Such a system allows households a choice between participation and the receipt of wage income or, alternatively, non-participation and the receipt of state benefits (although because of the rules of the benefit system it may be necessary to masquerade as a market participant). Such non-participation is most likely in households with poor wage or employment opportunities for whom the difference between wage and benefit income is small. The empirical evidence on the labour supply effects of benefits is rather mixed, not so much concerning the existence of such effects but as regards their magnitude and importance. Nickell (1979a, 1979b) found the effect to be quite small but others have argued that the effect of benefits is to create a floor to real wages below which no labour will be supplied (Minford 1983).

Skills and training Labour supply has a qualitative dimension when account is taken of the kinds of skills which households possess. As this involves the attainment of educational qualifications and the acquisition of skills by training and experience, then this aspect of supply is clearly a long-term one and one that can be considered as a form of household investment in 'human capital' (Becker 1975). Such household decisions may be expected to take place only infrequently and only at certain times during its member's life-cycle. In the short term the skills available to the local economy can be regarded as fixed, although the option always exists for skilled workers to seek unskilled work.

Local labour supply The amount of labour available to the urban economy, and its occupational composition, will depend upon the labour supply decisions of individual households and the socio-demographic characteristics of the local population.

For a given demographic structure, variations in labour supply will take the form of fluctuations in participation rates and hours of work. Local labour supply may be expected to be positively related to wages and job opportunities, particularly because of their effect on participation (Greenhalgh 1977, 1979). Labour supply may also exhibit a cyclical pattern. When unemployment is high, some households may be forced to increase their participation because of the loss of income caused by the unemployment of one of its members (the added worker effect). Conversely, high unemployment and reduced job prospects may lead some members of households to withdraw from the labour force, either as a temporary measure or permanently (the discouraged worker effect). Although both effects occur, the evidence suggests that the discouraged worker effect tends to dominate and participation falls in recessions (McNabb 1977; Greenhalgh 1977).

The number of workers in the local labour market is also affected by the mobility of labour, in the short term by net commuting and in the longer term by the migration of households. Both are likely to be influenced by labour market conditions. Geographical wage or employment differentials may lead to increased commuting if the higher wage compensates for the increased travel costs and may similarly affect residential movement in the longer term. Several studies have provided evidence that employment growth and relatively high wages do exert an attraction for households to move into an area (Gordon and Lamont 1982; Vickerman 1984a); however, it has to be acknowledged that such job-related movements represent only a very small fraction of movements (Gordon *et al.* 1983) and involve a very small proportion of households (Berthoud 1980). Within an urban area changes in labour supply through commuting may be much more substantial and rapid. Gudgin et al. (1982) and Hausner and Robson (1986) have shown that commuters accounted for as much as 40 per cent of employment in inner city areas, while Gillespie (1983) has provided evidence of the rapid changes which can occur in patterns of travel to work in urban economies.

The demand for labour

The demand for labour can be thought of as the number and pattern of jobs available in an urban area in any given set of circumstances. The level and structure of demand depends upon a number of factors. In the first place, each employer will decide on the number of employees, hours of work and the occupational mix of his or her labour force. In addition, since local employment is equal to the sum of employment in each firm, the aggregate level of local labour demand and its composition will depend upon the number, industrial mix and labour intensity of local firms.

The urban firm If production occurs under private enterprise then profit-seeking firms will seek to combine the services of labour, capital and other factors of production in some optimal manner to produce a saleable product. In this endeavour the firms will be constrained by three sets of forces:

1.   The demand for the product.
2.   The technological relationships which exist between inputs and outputs.
3.   The availability and price of inputs.

If the firm were free to choose, then with a given product demand and production function and a known set of factor prices the firm would select some combination of labour and capital so that profits are maximised. The quantity of labour employed will therefore depend upon wages relative to other input prices, the product price, and the prevailing state of technology.

In reality, historical decisions and inertia may constrain firms so that some aspects of their decisions can be regarded as fixed. Firms are probably best viewed as short-term, sequential decision-makers who will seek to maximise profits by selecting the most appropriate level of employment to combine with fixed plant and equipment. Labour will be hired as long as the additional revenue raised from production exceeds the cost of hiring the extra worker. More formally, labour will be hired as long as the marginal revenue product is greater than the wage and employment will be expanded to the point where the two are equal. Since the marginal revenue product is expected to decline as employment increases, then wages and employment will be inversely related (higher wages reduce employment) with the precise relationship depending upon the nature of the product being made and the technological conditions of production.

Employment location In the long run firms will be able to vary all of their factor inputs including land, labour and equipment. Firms are no longer constrained by past locational decisions and may seek some 'best' location. The current pattern of land use and the spatial distribution of employment in metropolitan areas is largely the result of past decisions of this type.

A firm's profitability may be affected by its location in the city if its revenues or its costs of production vary from place to place. If there are differences in rents or wages throughout the urban economy then firms will try to move to least cost locations, while production techniques at any location will be adapted to minimise the input of the relatively expensive factor of production. Plants using flow-line production might be expected to gravitate to locations where land costs are relatively cheap (usually suburban sites) while those activities which must locate in the city centre will economise on expensive land by substituting capital in the form of multi-storey office blocks. Revenues as well as costs may depend upon location, although this largely depends upon the scale of the market within which the firm is selling its products. This will be particularly true of certain types of retailing and service activities which are primarily concerned with accessibility to local customers, whereas firms selling in a national market may not experience any such variation in revenue.

The effect of these intra-urban variations in costs and revenues is to create a spatial pattern of labour demand within the urban economy with particular types of job being located in specific areas. Quite distinct zones of economic activity can be observed in most metropolitan economies, although historical factors, the effects of planning regulations and other unique aspects of local geography ensure that these zones are seldom as neat or as regular as those found in textbooks. Nevertheless it seems plausible to suggest that any economic or social change which affects the spatial pattern of costs or revenues within the urban economy may be expected to produce a change in the location of labour demand and employment.

The competitive market

A central tenet of the competitive market perspective is the proposition that the coordination of the separate decisions of firms and households will be achieved by means of competitive processes operating through the market mechanism. This view emphasises the common influence of wages and employment opportunities on local labour demand and supply, and suggests that any imbalance between the two will be eliminated by a combination of wage adjustment and worker mobility.

The competitive market is illustrated diagrammatically by Fig. 2.2 which represents an urban labour market. Changes in the wage rate have a negative effect on labour demand (D–D) but a positive effect on labour supply (S–S). At the wage rate W_e the plans of employers to employ E number of workers are consistent with the plans of households to supply a similar amount of labour. This situation is described as an equilibrium because competitive processes will counter any tendency to deviate from it. If firms attempt to cut wages below the equilibrium wage then shortages of labour will be experienced (because some workers look elsewhere for jobs while others withdraw from the labour force) and firms will have unfilled vacancies. Competition among firms in their attempts to fill these vacancies will lead to the bidding up of wages until the equilibrium is restored. Similarly, if wages rise above W_e then a surplus of labour (unemployment) will result which, ultimately, will be eliminated by competition between workers, resulting in a reduction of wages.

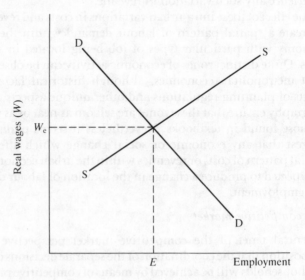

Fig. 2.2

As has already been commented upon, the local labour market will actually consist of a number of overlapping occupational markets. Consequently there will be a structure of wages and employment reflecting the different levels of demand and supply within each occupational submarket. The competitive perspective suggests that in the long term, when workers are able to change occupation, the wage structure will reflect differences in the costs of acquiring skills and the structure of employment will reflect the patterns of demand for labour.

From the spatial point of view, the competitive model suggests that any geographical mismatch between the demand and supply of a particular occupation will tend to be evened out between localities and between social groups and will eventually be eliminated altogether. Excess demand in one part of the city will raise wages and leave vacancies unfilled, and this will attract labour (by commuting or migration) from elsewhere in the city where wages and job opportunities are not as good. If sufficient time elapses then equilibrium will be achieved and wage levels and job opportunities will be same in all parts of the urban area. Thus the competitive perspective suggests that localised concentrations of unemployment are either a problem of short-term dis-equilibrium which will eventually be eliminated by market forces or they are evidence that the market has been prevented in some way from adjusting to equilibrium.

Aspects of labour market structure

Empirical studies of local labour markets have cast doubt on the simple conclusions of the competitive model. The evidence of persistent differences in the incidence of unemployment, between areas and between social groups was commented upon in Chapter 1. Other studies have found substantial variation in wages even among apparently similar workers in different plants in the same local labour market (Mackay *et al.* 1971; Robinson 1970). Similar evidence concerning the failure of the market mechanism to eliminate such differences led Robinson (1967) to conclude that 'the labour market does not work in the way generally supposed. It is far more chaotic than even the sceptics have believed'.

Critics of the competitive perspective have drawn attention to the inherent inefficiencies and the structural features of the labour market. In some instances, especially concerning questions of information and decision-making under uncertainty, the analysis has drawn upon the concepts and techniques of neoclassical economics. In other cases, alternative analytical frameworks are used which draw upon the ideas of the institutionalist school of labour economics and industrial relations, the Keynesian paradigm, or even radical and Marxist analysis. The structuralist perspective therefore embraces a broad spectrum of explanations about the way in which local labour markets work.

Information and labour market search

The need for information-gathering arises from the fact that there are differences among jobs and workers. There is an incentive, therefore, for workers to try to ascertain which jobs are good and which are poor. Similarly, workers vary in their productivity and suitability for a given job and it will pay employers to select the best workers from the possible applicants.

The process of information-gathering can take a number of forms; there are both different kinds of information and different sources from which information can be obtained. Rees (1966) distinguishes between search at the extensive margin and at the intensive margin. The former involves gathering more information while the latter involves increasing the quality of information about a particular worker or job offer. A similar type of distinction is drawn by Joll *et al.* (1983) between inspection and experience characteristics. The former involve easily observable information about workers or jobs such as wage rates or employment record, while the latter concern aspects such as a worker's reliability, or promotion prospects which can only be ascertained by experience.

Ideally workers and employers would obtain complete knowledge of each other before any transaction occurs, but because additional information is costly and is likely to bring only a decreasing return then information-gathering and search will stop short of perfection. How far short clearly depends on the costs and the benefits involved, search being terminated when the additional benefits no longer compensate for the marginal costs involved (Stigler 1962). The most typical process in labour markets is that of sequential searching in which an employer successively samples job applicants until an acceptable recruit is found and, in a similar fashion, workers search for jobs until some acceptable wage or job offer is revealed. Employers will have some minimum hiring standard which must be exceeded before a worker is hired, while workers will only accept a job offer if the pay is better than their reservation wage. These hiring standards and reservation wages will differ between employers and among workers depending upon their 'need for labour' and their 'need for work', respectively. It can also be expected that hiring standards and reservation wages will vary according to local economic conditions, with recruitment standards being raised and reservation wages being lowered in times of high or rising unemployment.

The importance of imperfect information and searching is that it explains how vacancies and unemployment can exist at the same time. A worker may be prepared to remain unemployed in order to continue looking for an acceptable job rather than accept the last (unacceptable) offer received (Reder 1969). Vacancies will remain unfilled if the employer would prefer to continue searching for a suitable recruit rather than hire a person who falls short of the minimum hiring standard. These points are taken up in greater detail in Chapter 4.

Wage and employment adjustment

A further deficiency of the competitive model is that it presumes that the labour market can adjust to shifts in demand or supply without cost and that households and firms know the appropriate responses to make to such changes in market conditions. This is unlikely.

The adjustment of employment levels is achieved by variation in the relative size of recruitment and hiring and by variation in labour turnover and redundancies; both involve costs. Hiring workers requires recruitment, selection and training costs to be incurred, while lay-offs result in severance and redundancy payments. These adjustment costs can be avoided if firms alter their hours of work rather than employment level, and this is made the more likely by the existence of fixed costs of employment. The latter are costs which are incurred on the basis of the number employed and not the number of hours worked. Taken together, fixed costs and adjustment costs have the effect of making labour, in the short term at any rate, a 'quasi-fixed factor of production' (Oi 1962). Short-term variations in labour requirements will be met by overtime or short-time working, or by part-time and casual workers if their hiring and firing costs are cheaper than paying overtime premia to existing employees.

When adjustment is costly, employment is likely to be changed only when a firm cannot make adequate adjustments in any other way. This short-term stability of employment is likely to be reinforced by the effects of uncertainty about the future. A firm which experiences fluctuations in its sales may have difficulty in determining whether such changes are merely temporary or whether they mark the beginning of a long-term decline in sales. A prudent strategy, given the costs of responding to such changes, might be to wait and see what happens and only adjust employment when market trends have become clear or when the firm can no longer afford to wait. The behaviour of employment in such circumstances can be quite complex, involving periods of employment stability with variations in hours of work followed by periods of rapid labour shedding or recruitment, depending upon the direction of market trends (Nickell 1978).

Wage adjustment will also be affected by imperfect information, uncertainty and adjustment costs. On the supply side, reservation wages will be reduced if searching repeatedly fails to reveal an acceptable job offer, but as the worker has no way of knowing whether the initial unacceptable job offers are just poor offers or whether they are typical of job offers in general the process of downward adjustment of the reservation wage will take some time. Similarly, an employer may be unwilling to reduce wages because to do so would mean increased labour turnover with the associated costs of attempting to recruit acceptable replacements at the lower wage. Instead employers may attempt to hoard their expensively trained labour force and reduce turnover by maintaining stable wages. They may even enter into implicit contracts (Azariadis 1975) with employees which guarantee wage levels.

Once these dynamic aspects of the labour market are taken into account, it seems unlikely that wage competition will be effective as a means of achieving market equilibrium. The labour market is unlikely to be in a state of equilibrium except in the long term, and even this seems unlikely if there is continuous change in the economy.

Dominated labour markets

The process of competition relies upon the interaction of many buyers and sellers. In contrast, a small number of buyers or sellers or a group acting together may be able to exert some influence on the market and non-competitive outcomes may result. The extreme form of dominance, a single employer known as a monopsonist, is rarely (if ever) encountered. The most likely situation is where one or a small number of firms employ a disproportionately large share of the local workforce. Although most firms are small relative to the size of the urban labour market, there may be situations in which some firms are large enough to affect, at least potentially, local market conditions.

The actual extent of employer dominance of urban economies has been largely neglected and there are few studies either of its extent or its consequences. This is perhaps a reflection of the slippery nature of the concept which is difficult to define together with the problems of obtaining sufficient information. In a study of employer concentration Lever (1979) used the arbitary criterion that a market was dominated when the largest non-service sector firm employed more than 12.5 per cent of total employment. On this basis it was concluded that approximately one-third (95) of urban labour markets in Britain exhibited employer dominance although there was considerable variation in the degree of such dominance (ranging from 12.5 to 66.6 per cent). Dominating firms were generally from an industry with significant economies of scale – for example, ship-building, vehicle manufacture, iron and steel production and domestic electrical goods. In a later study Lever (1981) reached similar conclusions concerning employer dominance of a number of Scottish and English local labour markets. It seems that while dominance may exist in some local labour markets, it does not in others, which may not be entirely unexpected if, as seems likely, there is a negative relationship between the size of an urban economy and the extent of employer concentration. Lever found that areas with the highest employer concentration ratios were small towns such as Stafford or Rugby, whereas larger urban labour markets, Leeds and Birmingham, had low concentration ratios.

There is little agreement on the likely consequences of employer dominance even when it exists. The simple monopsony model, based upon a single profit-maximising employer, suggests that firms will operate at lower levels of employment and pay lower wages than would be the case under competitive conditions. This standard conclusion is less easily demonstrated when the market consists of a small number of employers rather than just one. In this case employment outcomes will depend on whether the firms collaborate and collude and what employment strategies they adopt. Rees (1979) has argued that successful collusion is unlikely since in slack market conditions there is no need for an agreement and when labour is in short supply the temptation to raise wages in order to attract labour will prove irresistible. Thus where the local economy is dominated by a small number of firms the market structure is really oligopolistic rather than monopsonistic and the behaviour of firms will be affected more by strategic considerations (such as the likely reactions of their competitors) than by any simple short-run profit-maximising calculation. The fear that other local employers will match wage increases leads to strategies whereby employment and wages are kept stable as long as variations in the demand for labour keep within acceptable bounds set by considerations of profit. Should demand move outside these bounds then employment or wages will be changed whatever the consequences. If other firms respond then periods of rapid change may occur. Thus oligopsonistic market structures may reinforce the erratic behaviour of employment brought about by the quasi-fixity of labour.

Corporate structure and control

Modern business corporations are large organisations which have grown through internal expansion and by mergers. This has had the paradoxical effect of simultaneously diversifying and concentrating economic enterprise. In the first place, production activities are often geographically dispersed because, despite the existence of large plants, it is usual for production to take place in many medium- or even small-sized plants. In contrast, corporate organisation has become more hierarchical with strategic decision-making being concentrated in head offices leaving only routine administration in what are otherwise production-only establishments. Corporate headquarters have tended to be regionally based, often in major provincial cities, where economies of scale in interpersonal and intercorporate communications could be fully reaped. Recent developments in telecommunications and transportation have enabled further concentration to occur at the expense of office activity in the provinces. By 1977 over 56 per cent of the headquarters of the leading 1,000 UK firms were located in London (Goddard and Smith 1978).

One consequence of these developments is that even in the largest urban areas an increasing proportion of employment is in branch plants controlled from outside the area. Decisions affecting employment in the local area are made outside the local community, in all probability in London or even overseas. In Bristol, for instance, the eighteen largest externally controlled firms employed more than half of all employees in manufacturing (Bassett 1984). There can be substantial differences between localities in the extent of external control and this may be reflected in differing patterns of corporate behaviour. In a comparative study of Greater Manchester and Merseyside, Lloyd and Dicken (1983) demonstrated that the manufacturing sector in Manchester exhibited a much higher level of local control than that of Merseyside (Table 2.2). It is also notable that there was a marked decline in the extent of local control in each locality between 1966 and 1975 and by the end of the period local control in outer Merseyside was almost negligible.

The effect of branch plants on the operation of the urban labour market may be surmised from the fact that local and multi-locational firms operate in different corporate contexts. Issues of central concern to the local firm such as the state of the local labour market may be of little more than marginal interest to a multi-national corporation. Branch plants are said to be more 'open' – that is, they are likely to be more affected by external events than locally controlled firms – and may be forced to play their part in implementing a corporate strategy which bears no relation to the conditions in the local economy, although this could be to the advantage of an area just as much as to its detriment. External control of local plants may also affect the structure of employment since jobs will be largely production orientated and mainly manual and low-level supervisory occupations. Senior management, scientific and technical occupations tend to be located elsewhere, either in company headquarters or in specialised research and development units. Employment in branch plants may also be less stable than in local firms because adjustment during recessions usually falls upon the production sector rather than the white collar or managerial group, and the former are concentrated in branch plants.

In the long term, the survival of a branch plant will be determined not by its local economic performance but by apparently distant factors such as corporate investment policy and responses to technological change. Because of its generally marginal status a branch plant is vulnerable to complete closure rather than *in-situ* reductions in its labour force. A corporation

Table 2.2 Ownership composition of manufacturing employment, Greater Manchester and Merseyside, 1966-75

	Percentage of total manufacturing employment											
	Single Plant Firms		Multi-plant firms						Local control		External control	
			Local HQ		UK HQ		Foreign HQ					
	1966	1975	1966	1975	1966	1975	1966	1975	1966	1975	1966	1975
Greater Manchester												
Conurbation	26.0	19.6	31.4	28.5	38.7	42.8	3.9	9.1	57.4	48.1	42.6	51.9
Inner Manchester	43.9	34.5	30.1	26.3	24.3	33.5	1.7	5.7	74.0	60.8	26.0	39.2
Outer Manchester	21.6	16.9	31.7	28.9	42.3	44.5	4.4	9.7	53.3	45.8	46.7	54.2
Merseyside												
Conurbation	14.5	9.2	7.9	4.9	62.3	60.5	15.3	25.4	22.4	14.2	77.6	85.8
Inner Merseyside	23.4	18.0	13.1	10.3	62.6	65.6	0.9	6.1	36.5	28.3	63.5	71.7
Outer Merseyside	7.3	4.9	3.7	2.2	62.0	59.9	27.0	35.0	11.0	7.1	89.0	92.9

Source: Lloyd and Dicken: Ch. 3 of Goddard and Champion 1983: 63.

faced with the need to cut output can make marginal adjustments by closing whole branch plants thereby rationalising production into its remaining plants and maintaining full capacity working. The presence of externally controlled branch plants will materially effect labour market conditions; an urban area with a low level of local control will have an employment structure which is disproportionately unskilled and is subject to sudden changes due to plant closures or openings.

Labour market segmentation

Important though employer concentration and corporate control may be, they can both be seen as different facets of a more general process of labour market segmentation and stratification. The most simple version of this approach is the 'dual labour market' model which was introduced into the British context by Bosanquet and Doeringer (1973). In the dual market jobs are divided between a 'primary' and a 'secondary' sector. The former comprise jobs which offer good conditions, high wages, job security, promotion prospects, on-the-job training and a well-ordered internal labour market. Secondary jobs are poor jobs having low pay, poor conditions, insecurity, no prospects or training and such jobs will tend to be filled by hiring on the external labour market. Although the dual market model is simplistic, it can easily be developed to take account of the variety of experience found in reality. Loveridge and Mok (1979), for instance, use the primary-secondary distinction in conjunction with an internal–external market dimension to produce a four-sector model of the labour market while Dawson (1982) distinguishes between three strata, upper and lower primary, and secondary sectors, each of which is segmented internally on the basis of industry or corporation.

Segmented labour market models all suggest that access to good jobs will be limited for many workers. In primary sectors entry into jobs will be on the basis of skills, and educational or professional attainment and access to high-level primary jobs is achieved by progression up an internal career structure. External mobility is low except at the highest occupational levels. Workers not qualified to gain entry to primary jobs are limited to the secondary market in which there is a high level of mobility between jobs and occupations, but only at the same relatively unskilled level. It is to be expected that workers who are disadvantaged by a lack of educational attainment or social position will tend to gravitate towards secondary jobs. Important feedback mechanisms help to perpetuate the process, for example when high turnover rates are taken as a sign of employee unreliability by primary sector employers.

The origins of labour market segmentation are to be found in recent developments of corporate capitalism. Production has become concentrated in a core of large national and multinational corporations who are able to exert considerable economic power by virtue of their size. These corporations are highly capital intensive and engage in mass production, characteristics which require stability of product demand, production levels and of their labour force. If production deviates to any great extent from full capacity levels then costs rise and profits are squeezed. The stability needs of core firms are secured by the development of highly structured internal labour markets within which wages and employment are largely outside the influence of market forces. However, no firm can be completely insulated from external market forces and unanticipated shocks and in order to meet this eventuality corporate capitalism has developed the additional strategy of fostering the growth of a periphery of firms and a reserve of labour which can be drawn upon and dispensed with as needed. This periphery consists of small, competitive and labour-intensive firms often operating on a subcontracting basis. Peripheral workers in these firms and secondary workers who are hired directly by core employers for marginal jobs will together comprise the secondary labour market.

Primary labour markets serve the needs of corporate capital by providing control and stability over its labour force. In core firms labour may possess a degree of countervailing power especially where employers have invested in specific training. Employers may respond to this by segmenting the primary market as much as possible and seeking other ways to weaken the position of labour – for example, by reducing skill requirements through technological change. Berger and Piore (1980) and Cooke (1983) have emphasised the strength of labour's countervailing power and suggested that segmentation (or in their terms, labour market discontinuity) takes place because powerful, organised labour can exclude some groups from jobs and secure better pay and conditions as a consequence. Stratification and segmentation of labour markets is, in this view, best seen as the outcome of a complex struggle between corporate capital on the one hand and organised labour on the other.

Although the segmented labour market is not a specifically spatial concept it does have clear spatial implications. The character of the local labour market will be a reflection of the status of the firms and workers who participate in it. If secondary jobs cluster in one locality while primary jobs are located in another then a spatial dimension is superimposed upon the overall pattern of segmentation. Differences in the locational requirements of primary and secondary firms and the operation of the housing market make such spatial division of labour quite likely. Cooke (1983) provides a taxonomy of spatially segmented labour market types as shown in Table 2.3. The complexity of these spatial patterns is evident. Major urban and metropolitan labour markets are likely to contain a number of different segments and the precise pattern of segmentation will depend upon their historical development and industrial structure. However, it is quite possible for a specific locality within the city to display an employment structure dominated by one type of labour market sector or another.

The macroeconomics or urban employment

The analysis so far has concentrated on the microeconomics of urban labour markets. This partial analysis regards individual local firms and households as responding independently to market signals (in the form of wage changes and employment opportunities). The assumption of independent decision-making is likely to be inappropriate in the context of the urban economy, whose very existence is usually explained in terms of economic interdependence, and a more macroeconomic approach is required which will enable the labour market to be considered as a constituent part of a wider urban economic system. Within the local economy, interdependencies or 'feedbacks' arise either directly through the organisation of production activity or indirectly through the links between local employment, local incomes and the demand for locally produced goods and services. Despite the importance of such local interdependence it must be recognised that the local economy, even in the large metropolitan areas, will remain heavily influenced by external forces and events in the rest of the economy.

Table 2.3 Labour market segmentation and the spatial division of labour

PRIMARY

Independent functionaries
Higher-order state/private
administrative, managerial and
professional.
Primate cities or specialized
centres of government, finance
or production

Subordinate functionaries
Middle-order state/private
administrative, managerial and
professional.
Primate, regional-metropolitan
and local administrative/
commercial centres

Self-employed
Small/medium, independent
businesses. Subcontractors,
suppliers, primary producers.
Periphery of industrial
conurbations, rural areas,
specialist inner-city 'quarters'

Crafts (revaluing)
Male, skilled, manual workers
in specialized manufacturing
and service occupations, not
necessarily large firms.
Periphery of industrial
conurbations, semirural (e.g. air-
ports, power stations). Primate
cities

Crafts (devaluing)
Male, skilled, manual workers
in large manufacturing firms
undergoing technological or
labour restructuring. 'Traditional'
industrial concentrations. Assisted
Areas

'Normal' resistant
Semiskilled male employees in
large manufacturing firms.
Industrial conurbations,
Assisted Areas

SECONDARY

'Normal' compliant
Small-firm male/female employees
non-skilled and subcontracting,
supplying. Periphery of industrial
conurbations, specialist inner-city
'quarters'. Market and administrative
towns

Feminised
Fulltime lower-order manufacturing
and service workers.
Industrial conurbations, assisted
areas (branch plants).
Administrative/commercial
centres

Selective
Temporary and periodic workers.
Regional-metropolitan and
primate cities. Female
secretarial, commercial. Male/
Female, educational, legal, clerical,
entertainment

Precarious
Guestworkers, seasonal, limited
contract, parttime workers.
Agricultural and construction
workers. All urban centres
employing 'casual' labour. Rural
areas, tourism, leisure 'reserves'

Underclass
Unemployed, redundant, deskilled
or unskilled males. State-assisted
regions, metropolitant 'industrial
communities, ethnic enclaves

Marginalised
Illegal immigrants, criminalized
workers. 'Sweatshops', informal
or black economy. Inner-city,
regional-metropolitan, primate cities

Source: Cooke 1983: 557

Local employment linkages

Economic activity and employment are concentrated in urban areas because these localities offer economic advantages over others. These advantages arise from the economies of scale and agglomeration economies which are associated with production in towns and cities. Although internal economies of scale may be important, the external economies which come from the clustering of an industry and from the size and proximity of a range of economic activities constitute the real benefit of urbanisation (Richardson 1978).

The urban economy is characterised by both specialisation and diversity of production. The scale of activity results in the division of production into separate stages carried out in vertically linked establishments. At the same time, the size and range of activities allows firms to emerge (as critical demand thresholds are exceeded) who provide specialist products and services for a wide variety of industries. The advantages offered by urban areas are likely to be cumulative and, as time passes, both the concentration and range of activities in an area will increase. Thus metropolitan economies exhibit a considerable range of activities and depend less on particular industries than many smaller cities or towns. Nevertheless there will still be very strong interdependence between local firms because of their vertical and horizontal linkages in the production of intermediate goods and services. Such links may be reinforced by the dual nature of the organisation of production in which large numbers of peripheral firms supply specialist services or other inputs, undertake subcontract production, or provide market outlets for large primary sector corporations. Enterprises in the urban economy enjoy a kind of symbiotic relationship, which means they are dependent on one another.

Input–output analysis

The dependence of output and employment in one plant upon the level of production in other plants later in the chain of production or in other industries suggests that employment in the former plant is, in effect, supported by the output and employment of the others. A crude representation of this aspect of employment dependence is the economic base model. This suggests that local employment consists of an employment base supported by demand from outside the local economy and a dependent sector which is created through the industrial linkages in local production. Although highlighting the importance of local industrial linkages, the approach is far too crude and places undue emphasis on the role of 'export' production (Richardson 1978).

A more detailed description of the interrelationships in local production is provided by input–output accounts. These accounts describe the flow of goods and services between sectors in the local economy and relate these flows to the final demand for output. In practice, input–output analysis quickly becomes complex but the underlying principles are simple enough; the value of output sold by each sector in the local economy must equal the value of all inputs purchased. A generalised accounts framework for a local economy is illustrated in Fig. 2.3. These accounts show that each sector buys inputs from other local firms, imports inputs from outside the area, and hires labour and capital services. The output produced by each sector supplies other local firms, local final demand and demand from outside the locality. The local interindustry linkages are described by the matrix of sales and purchases of intermediate goods and services and, if employment in each industry is related to output levels, a similar matrix of interdependent jobs can be derived.

Input–output accounts can be used to trace out the overall employment effects of a change in final demand for the products of local industry. If there is a fall in demand there will be a corresponding fall in production and employment in the industry concerned. Subsequent reductions in the purchase of locally produced inputs will create further cutbacks in output and employment in other local firms, and so on, with the initial reduction in production and employment being multiplied up into a greater overall fall in economic activity. The greater the interdependence of local production the larger the overall employment effect will be. To quantify these effects on local employment, information is required on the input needs of local firms (their so-called technical coefficients) and on the amount of employment associated with the output of each firm (a model of employment interdependency is provided in the appendix at the end of this chapter: but this may be ignored by those unhappy about the mathematics involved). Because much of the information required for input–output accounts is unavailable for local or urban economies there have been few applications of the technique

Sales \ Purchases		Industries 1	Industries j	Industries n	Local final demand: Consumption	Local final demand: Investment	Local final demand: Government expenditure	Exports to other localities	Gross local output
Industries	1	Q_{11}	Q_{ij}	Q_{In}	C_1	I_1	G_1	X_1	Q_1
	•	•	•	•	•	•	•	•	•
	•	•	•	•	•	•	•	•	•
	•	•	•	•	•	•	•	•	•
	i	Q_{il}	Q_{ij}	Q_{In}	C_i	I_i	G_i	X_i	Q_i
	•	•	•	•	•	•	•	•	•
	•	•	•	•	•	•	•	•	•
	•	•	•	•	•	•	•	•	•
	n	Q_{nl}	Q_{nj}	Q_{nn}	C_n	I_n	G_n	X_n	Q_n
Labour input		E_1	E_j	E_n	E_c	E_x	E_G	E_x	E
Value added		V_1	V_j	V_n	V_c	V_x	V_G	V_x	V
Imports		M_1	M_j	M_n	M_c	M_x	M_G	—	M
Gross expenditure		Q_1	Q_j	Q_n	C	I	G	X	Q

Local income = E + V = C + I + G + X − M = Local aggregate expenditure

Fig. 2.3 A generalised input–output accounting framework for a local economy

(see Morrison 1973) and where it has been used it is usually in a greatly scaled-down version. Nevertheless it remains a useful way of illustrating the linkages through which employment in one sector of the local economy will be affected by change in another.

Local employment multipliers

Although local links in production are important, the ultimate determinant of employment in the urban economy is the level of final demand for locally produced goods and services. A change in final demand will create an initial change in employment but the eventual change will be greater still because of the effects of changing economic activity on local incomes; change in the profits of local firms and the incomes of local households will lead to further changes in the level of local final demand. This essentially Keynesian view of the labour market is encapsulated in the concept of the local employment multiplier which measures the relation-ship between an initial change in employment and the level of employment which eventually results after the subsequent induced expenditure effects have taken place.

The components of local final demand consist of the expenditure of local households, local businesses and government (less their purchases from outside the local economy) plus the expenditure on locally produced goods by customers elsewhere in the economy. The latter includes the expenditure of non-residents and the intermediate and final purchases of firms located outside the urban economy. Increases in local incomes are expected to increase household consumption spending with the precise relationship being determined by the propensity of local households to save and the marginal tax rate. These will vary from one locality to another as the result of differences in the demographic structure and the spatial distribution of incomes (Madden and Batey 1983). of any increase in household expenditure, only a proportion will be spent on the products of local firms, depending on such factors as the local industrial structure and the level and distribution of incomes. Business final demand consists of investment in capital. This is usually thought to be determined by long-term considerations but variations in local production and incomes may exert some influence through their effect on business expectations or the financing of investment from retained profits; this link may be strongest in the case of locally owned firms. However, even if local economic activity does affect investment spending it is likely that the local component of such spending is low.

A change in any of the components of local final demand will produce an initial change in local output and employment, both directly and as the result of industrial linkages in production. After a period of time there will be further changes in the level of economic activity and employment as the effects of changing output and incomes feed back into local final demand. After several rounds of change a new stable level of local output, income and employment will be established which will be some multiple of the initial change. The size of the local multiplier depends on the proportion of additional income which passed on as local demand in each round of spending and this will depend on the marginal propensity to spend and the propensity to spend locally.

Where employment multipliers have been estimated their magnitudes have been small. Brown (1967) suggested a value of no more than 1.24 while Greig (1971) estimated that the value of the local multiplier might fall within the range 1.44 to 1.55. This low value is not unexpected because of the extreme 'openness' of urban economies; consumer and business expenditure more frequently leaks out of the area than remains within it. Estimates for more self-contained areas, such as regions, are generally larger than for smaller urban areas. The local multiplier could even be negative if locally produced goods and services were 'inferior' so that an increase in income led to expenditure being switched to suppliers outside the area, although this is unlikely. There is some evidence (Lever 1974) that multipliers vary in respect to time and the direction of change; employment multipliers will be smaller in the short run than in the long term because of lags in adjustment, while the effects of recession may differ from those of expansion. Other possibilities relate to the life-cycle of firms. As small local firms expand they may shift to external suppliers if local firms cannot meet their growing needs. This would tend to lower the value of the multiplier. On the other hand, newly established branch plants may depend upon their parent companies at first and use local suppliers later; as their reliance on local suppliers increases, so too will the local employment multiplier.

Government and local employment

The government clearly has a central role to play in the income and employment generation process but its influence upon a particular urban economy is more difficult to ascertain because of the spatially asymmetric pattern of financial flows involved, the complexities of public finance and the different levels of government involved. Central government expenditure in an urban area represents a component of local final demand and will support employment both directly and indirectly through the multiplier process. National taxation, on the other hand, will withdraw spending from the local economy and reduce employment. The overall effect of central government on local employment will depend on the relative size of these financial flows into and out of the urban economy. It is unlikely that these flows will balance because public spending is determined by national objectives and its spatial distribution is a reflection of the location of government activity and that of its suppliers, while the spatial pattern of taxation is the product of the geographical distribution of incomes and there is no reason to suppose that these correspond. Local economic conditions will exert some influence on the pattern of government spending through the payment of unemployment and other welfare benefits while some spending may be targeted on specific localities as part of the government's regional and urban policy. Changes in national fiscal policy will have spatial ramifications because they will alter the local balance of central government spending and taxation, while the urban and regional balance of government spending may change because of shifting emphases in its spatial policies.

Local authorities also levy taxes and spend, and if they were entirely independent of central government then their position would be similar except that revenue would be raised from local taxation and expenditure would be determined by local needs and preferences. In practice, the fiscal position of local authorities is complicated by the fact that central government requires them to provide certain services while providing a major proportion of their finance. Thus, although local government is less likely to run a deficit in its budget, there will be a considerable imbalance between local public expenditure and local taxation because of the receipt of central government grants. Insofar as these grants are not offset by national taxation, then their effect will be expansionary even when there is an overall balance in the local authority budget (in addition to the slightly expansionary effect of any balanced budget). Conversely, reductions in grants from central government will reduce local employment either directly through a reduction in local authority services or because of the increase in local taxation required to make up the lost revenue. Thus the share of local government finance raised by rates will be an important influence upon the effects of their fiscal policy.

Empirical studies of the employment effects of local authority fiscal policy are relatively few despite the considerable importance of the subject for the debate on economic policy and local economic initiatives. Cuthbertson *et al.* (1979) found that the fiscal policy of London boroughs had a considerable effect on the level and pattern of local economic activity and they concluded that the overall effect was negative. A more comprehensive study of local authority fiscal policy in England and Wales (overcoming many of the deficiencies of the previous study) confirmed an impact on employment but suggested that the effect was positive although its size depended on the extent to which expenditure was financed by local taxation (Gripaios 1982). Local government fiscal policy is not, however, neutral in its effects and appears to create service sector jobs at the expense of those in manufacturing especially when expenditure is financed from rate revenue.

The radical and Marxist perspective

The broadest of all explanations of the nature and operation of urban economies is that of the radical perspective. According to this viewpoint, the characteristics of urban labour markets can 'only be understood in terms of the interaction between economic, political and social phenomena and that attempting to study economic phenomena in isolation can lead only to a misleading or superficial analysis' (Smith in Aaronovitch *et al.* 1981).

Although there is considerable variety in the form taken by radical analysis, a number of generalisations define the perspective. Most fundamentally, economic organisation is seen to be socially determined and, ultimately, reflects the social relations of production. The economic organisation of capitalist societies such as Britain will reflect the fundamental features of capitalism, the central element of which is the ownership and control of the means of production by the capitalist class. It is this characteristic of capitalism which creates a labour market in the first place since the working class is dependent solely on the sale of its labour. The central driving force of the economic system is the constant quest for profitable production opportunities.

One particularly important aspect of the radical perspective is that it provides insights into the dynamics of economic change. The tensions and conflicts which exist within capitalism, both between capital and labour and between capitalists, lead to the evolution of new institutions, new economic structures and create situations of instability and change. This means that there is an important historical element in many radical accounts of events although this is not to suggest any inevitability in the course of events. Particular emphasis has been placed on the historical trends of concentration into monopoly capitalism (Baron and Sweezy 1966), the de-skilling of labour (Braverman 1974) and the harnessing of technological change to gain greater control over production and to create increased opportunities for profitable activity.

Because of their emphasis on the interaction of economic, social and political processes, radical theories often show little direct concern with the details of economic institutions or events and operate at a high level of abstraction. One result of this is that, until relatively recently, radical analysis virtually ignored spatial and urban issues preferring to concentrate on developments in national and international capitalism. However, while it is undoubtedly incorrect to see local events as determined solely by specifically local events, it is wrong to argue that broad social and political trends are simply reproduced in each and every locality. Local economic, social and political factors together with 'layers' of historical experiences will affect the way in which the broad processes of industrial capitalism operate within particular urban areas. As Massey (1984) observes, 'while an abstract model of capitalism is an aid to analysis, it cannot substitute for the analysis itself'. Massey and others have been successful in providing this radical version of spatial analysis. Such analysis is probably best seen not as a specific body of urban theories but as a particular way of interpreting the structures in the urban labour market and the behaviour of employers and workers within it.

Summary and conclusion

Labour markets possess a local dimension because of the frictions of space, the costs of mobility and imperfect information, which limit the interaction of firms and households. Urban labour markets are local labour markets which are quintessentially urban in character. Although this is really a matter of emphasis rather than of kind, the labour markets of the metropolitan areas and inner cities are quite distinct from those of other localities.

The importance of the local dimension of labour markets, and the interpretation placed upon labour market behaviour in general, depends crucially upon the theoretical perspective which is adopted. According to the competitive market perspective the local labour market will coordinate the individual demand and supply decisions of local firms and households and will link the local area to the rest of the economy. Competitive wage adjustments and labour mobility will equate labour demand and supply and bring about a spatial equalisation of wages and job opportunities across all local labour markets. Unemployment may exist in the local economy but in equilibrium this will be limited to that which arises from inadequate information and other frictions. Any unemployment above this level can be eliminated if local firms and households adjust their wage levels and if labour is prepared to be mobile.

An alternative perspective, that of the structuralists, argues that such competitive adjustments are unlikely or will be very slow. The main reasons for this are the inherent imperfections of the labour market, the impact of social and institutional factors, and the fact that the local economy is a small economic system. If wages in urban labour markets are relatively inflexible and slow to adjust then the level of employment will be determined by the level of local aggregate demand which in turn is the product of cumulative processes in the local economy and external influences. Conditions in the local labour market are determined by factors which are largely beyond the control of individuals. Local employment is determined by structural forces in the local economy and any imbalance between labour demand and supply is likely to persist since no adjustment processes exist whereby local labour demand can be increased.

Radical explanations of urban labour markets also stress the importance of structural forces but raise the level of analysis to that of the nature of production under capitalism. The behavior of the local labour market is explicable only in terms of broad economic, social and political processes. Local factors are important in so far as they influence the manner in which these broad processes operate in particular localities, but it remains the case that there is very little scope for individual agents to exert any influence over levels of employment and unemployment in urban economies. This can only be achieved by state intervention.

These alternative perspectives are important because they influence the interpretation of evidence relating to the decline of employment and the increase in unemployment in metropolitan areas, and so influence the strategies adopted to tackle urban unemployment. It is to these issues that subsequent chapters are addressed.

Further reading

The basic theory of labour markets can be found in Sapsford (1981) *Labour Market Economics* and in Creedy and Thomas (1982) *The Economics of Labour*. For a more advanced treatment see Joll *et al.* (1983) *Developments in Labour Market Analysis. Modern Western Society: a geographical perspective on work, home and well-being* by Lloyd and Dicken (1981) and Vickerman (1984b) *Urban Economics: analysis and policy*, both contain much material relating to urban labour markets. An interesting set of discussions of methods and ideological issues is to be found in *Politics and Method: contrasting studies in industrial geography* edited by Massey and Meegan (1985). For those readers who wish to explore Marxist analysis a little further, *The Political Economy of British Capitalism: a Marxist analysis* by Aaronovitch *et al.* (1981) will serve as a very clear introduction.

Appendix

A model of local employment interdependence

Employment in an urban economy is the sum of two components: employment generated by the sale of intermediate goods to local firms, and employment generated by sales to local final demand (including exports to firms and households elsewhere in the economy). Hence

$$E_i = E_{ij} + E_{ik}$$

where E_i is local employment in industry i (with j and k denoting intermediate and final demands, respectively). This identity can, in turn, be broken down into its constituent components and written in matrix form:

$$E = LQ = LRQ + LD$$

where E = a vector of local employment in each industry (i.e. E_i)

L = a diagonal matrix of local employment per unit of gross output

Q = a vector of local gross output

D = a vector of local final demands

R = a matrix showing the intermediate input requirements for a unit of gross output.

Employment in the local area is equal to the product of gross output and local employment per unit of gross output (LQ), which in turn is equal to the sum of employment supported by intermediate demand (LRQ) and employment supported directly by final output demand (LD).

By some simple matrix algebra it is possible to compute another matrix Z which consists of employment coefficients. These coefficients show the employment in each industry which is required in order to support a unit level of output for final demand. Since

$$LQ = LRQ + LD$$

then rearranging the equation gives

$$LD = L(I - R)Q$$

where $(I - R)$ is the Leontief matrix (I is the unit matrix). Rearrangement of the equation gives

$$LQ = L(I - R)^{-1}D.$$

Since $LQ = E$ and by denoting $L(I - R)^{-1}$ by Z, then it follows that

$$E = ZD.$$

The matrix Z gives the local employment requirements per unit of local final demand. Multiplying Z by D, the level of local final demand, gives the structure of employment required to support any given pattern of final demand.

3

The economics of urban decline

The pattern of economic and social activity in towns and cities is subject to almost continuous change. Although imperceptible at times, there are periods when such change is rapid, even traumatic. The decade which straddles the late 1970s and early 1980s was just such a period, when a number of long-term and fundamental changes combined with an unusually acute period of recession to precipitate change in urban areas on a scale hitherto not experienced since the beginnings of the Industrial Revolution. One consequence of these changes has been a rapid increase in urban unemployment as described in the first chapter.

Recent changes in unemployment are the product of a number of different economic and demographic factors working in conjunction and any explanation of these changes must look to the relative or differential shifts in labour demand and supply rather than to any one specific structural change. Indeed, because of what economists refer to as 'the identification problem', attributing change to supply side or demand side factors is quite difficult because outcomes in the labour market are jointly determined by demand and supply. Despite this technical difficulty it is quite useful to preserve the distinction between demand and supply side change and the discussion of recent structural change in urban labour markets has been organised in this way.

The examination of recent structural change is limited by the lack of data for local economies. With the exception of unemployment, most other information is available only after a considerable delay and is often inaccurate. Therefore it is only possible to examine changes up to the early 1980s.

Levels of change

Changes in a local economy will be the outcome of many different processes interacting with one another in the locality. These processes of change can be viewed as operating at different levels: there are broad economic and social trends, there are spatial tendencies and there are localised events. Change will be a reflection of these three sets of forces and the particular way in which they interact in the locality.

National trends

It is beyond the scope of this book to review all major post-war economic and social trends, but the most important as far as labour markets are concerned are outlined briefly below. The processes are not mutually exclusive but are closely related and tend to be reinforcing.

The UK economy has been stagnating or has been in serious recession since the end of the 1960s. Labour demand, measured by employment, was relatively constant between 1971 and 1979 but since that time it has decreased sharply. Between December 1979 and June 1983 employment fell by nearly 2.5 million although subsequent growth of employment reduced this fall to 1.5 million by mid-1984. There has been a marked shift in employment away from manufacturing towards the service industries in a process often referred to as de-industrialisation. This trend can be seen in relative terms over a long period but absolute decline in manufacturing employment began around 1966 and has been acute in the 1980s. Between 1966 and 1984 the share of employment in manufacturing fell from over 38 to 26 per cent, a total loss of 3 million jobs. Over 1.2 million manufacturing jobs were lost in the first two years of the 1980s. Accompanying de-industrialisation there has been a substantial growth in public sector employment with the most rapid increases occurring in local authorities. This employment growth has now been reversed.

The size of the labour force has increased steadily during the 1970s as the result of demographic factors which have increased the size of the population of working age. Higher participation rates have compounded these increases and raised the size of the working population by a substantial number. The total increase in the workforce between 1973 and 1984 was of the order of 2 million extra potential workers. Not only did the workforce increase but its composition has also changed. The participation rate of women (particularly married women) has increased while there has been a small fall in male activity rates. Associated with these changes in participation has been a movement away from full-time to part-time work and (to a lesser extent) shift working. These changes are related to the growth of the service sector where employment grew by 225,000 between 1978 and 1981, of which 83 per cent (177,000) were part-time jobs (*Employment Gazette*, Dec. 1982). Equally important changes have taken place in the occupational and social composition of the workforce as the result of changing production technologies and the changing mix of industries in the economy. There has been a shift towards non-manual work of a managerial, technical or clerical nature and a corresponding decline in manual work, both skilled and unskilled.

While none of these processes is specifically spatial in character, spatial effects will arise as these trends are reflected in urban economies to a greater or lesser extent depending upon each area's economic and social structure. Thus broad national trends will produce spatial outcomes as they differentially effect local labour trends.

Spatial trends

In addition to general processes there are also tendencies which are more fundamentally spatial in character. The first such trend relates to the differential economic performance of regional economies. Some regions, such as Scotland, Wales and the northern regions of England, have traditionally been poor while others, such as the West Midlands and the South East, have been relatively prosperous. During the past decade or so there have been some marked shifts in the relative performance of these regions with previously prosperous areas such as the West Midlands declining rapidly while the prosperous South East and southern England have, if anything, enhanced their favourable position in the national economy. As Hall (1981) observed, the really booming places in contemporary Britain lie on a diagonal across southern England, from Exeter via Taunton and Bristol and Swindon to Oxford, Milton Keynes, Northampton, Bedford and Cambridge to Norwich.

To some extent the changing relative fortunes of regions is a reflection of the second spatial trend which is the suburbanisation and decentralisation of population and employment. This process refers to the tendency for suburban and outer areas of cities to grow at a faster rate than their inner areas. The process has been observed

for some time in relative terms and finally as absolute decentralisation when the population and employment of inner areas actually
decreased. Figure 3.1 shows the relative growth rates of population
and employment by urban zone and by region. While there are
differences in experience between regions, in general it can be seen
that the growth of population was higher in the inner rings than in
the metropolitan core areas during both decades. The differential
growth increased in the second decade, 1961–71, with many core
areas experiencing absolute declines in population. A similar
pattern can be seen for employment although the changes occurred
rather later than was the case for population.

Local factors

In any town or city there are changes which are unique to the
locality. Such idiosyncratic change may not be typical of the
nation or society as a whole but will be a reflection of the impact of
local history, local personalities and even random events. The
importance of local culture and the inherited characteristics of an
area has been pointed out by Massey (1983 and 1984) who sees the
structure of the local economy as consisting of multiple 'layers'
built up as the product of successive rounds of structural change.
Each new wave of change interacts with the existing structures of
the locality and in the process is metamorphosed. Local economies
do not simply reflect broad national trends, but exhibit a unique
local version of them. Urban areas are not simply the passive
recipients of changes emanating from the national economy; each
area has a unique local character which will determine the manner
in which these broad processes operate.

Structural change in urban labour markets

It was argued in the previous chapter that urban labour markets are
distinctive in a number of respects. It appears from the gravity of
the problems discussed in Chapter 1 that these areas have also
experienced the effects of economic and social change on a scale
not matched by any other localities. The following sections will
consider the changes which have lead to the growth of unemployment in the metropolitan labour markets.

Fig. 3.1 Relative population and relative employment change for
the constituent zones of MELAs averaged for Economic
Planning Regions, 1951–61, 1961–71. Source: Spence 1982: 22
(see over)

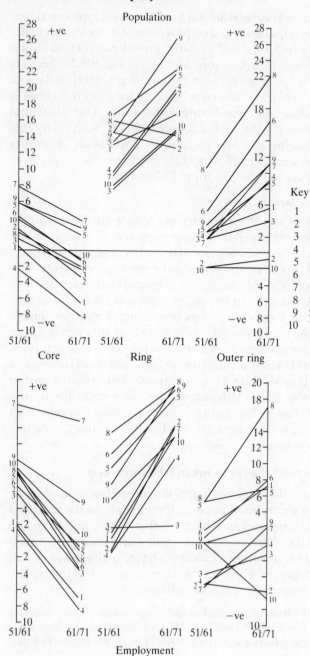

Population

Key

1 Scotland
2 North
3 Yorks & H.
4 North West
5 East Midlands
6 West Midlands
7 East Anglia
8 South East
9 South West
10 Wales

Core   Ring   Outer ring

Employment

Changes in labour supply

Between 1971 and 1981 the labour force in Britain grew by nearly 3 per cent. In sharp contrast the resident labour force in metropolitan labour markets declined markedly with the largest reductions taking place in the principal city areas (Table 3.1). The immediate reason for these declines was a reduction in the population of working age or 'potential labour supply'. This reduction was not a reflection of national demographic trends because these were tending to increase the number of people of working age. The primary cause of the reduction in potential labour supply was outward migration from the major urban centres to the suburbs and beyond. There is a clear positive relationship between the size of an urban area and its proportionate change in population over the period, as can be seen from Fig. 3.2.

Table 3.1 Change in the number of economically active residents in the main metropolitan areas, 1971–1981

	% change in economically active population	
	Metropolitan area	Urban core*
Greater London	−32.4	n.a.
West Midlands	−7.9	−12.5
Greater Manchester	−5.8	−20.9
Merseyside	−7.1	−17.0
West Yorkshire	−2.0	−4.8
South Yorkshire	−0.1	−7.0
Tyne and Wear	−2.6	−7.6
Great Britain	+2.9	+2.9

Source: derived from the Census of Population, 1971 and 1981.
*The urban cores are defined as Inner London, Birmingham MB, Manchester MB, Liverpool MB, Leeds, Sheffield and Newcastle upon Tyne.

Labour force migration

The reasons for the movement of population away from large urban centres are complex and only indirectly associated with the process of employment decentralisation. Although there is a link between the two processes they occur largely for different reasons and at different rates, with the former almost certainly commencing before the latter. Most movements between labour markets are for non-job-related reasons and the movement of population towards

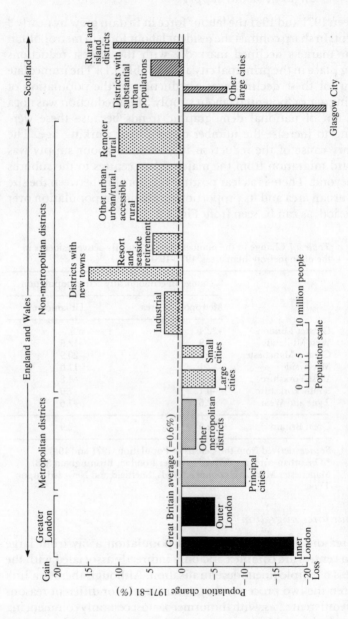

Fig. 3.2 Percentage population change, 1971–81 by category of district

Source: *Census 1981: Key statistics for local authorities, Great Britain.* OPCS, HMSO, 1984: 146

the suburbs relates mainly to housing and environmental factors. Rising real incomes and the perceived higher status of suburban locations have led many households to leave old, decaying and overcrowded inner city areas in favour of newly built and largely owner-occupied housing in the suburbs. Even the public sector has acknowledged the superiority of such suburban locations by its housing programmes and the allocation of tenancies. These residential movements, together with later job losses, industrial dereliction and the decline of public sector services hastened the decay of the urban environment and accelerated the process of population out-migration. Evidence from London (Gordon *et al.* 1983) showed that over 40 per cent of households declared 'better housing' or a 'better area' as the objective of moves from Inner to Outer London, whereas job-related reasons were mentioned by only 3 per cent of households. One result of this migration has been a growing divergence between the patterns of residence and work which produces more complex and longer journeys to work.

One important feature of population decentralisation is that it has proceeded at a rate which is faster than the loss of jobs in the urban core. Gillespie (1983) estimated that between 1966 and 1971 the employed population of the metropolitan cores declined by 7 per cent as compared to a 4 per cent loss of jobs. In contrast the outer-city areas experienced an average population growth of 5.4 per cent which exceeded the average 3.8 per cent increase of employment. Gudgin *et al.* (1982) found a similar divergence in a number of inner areas between 1951 and 1976; for instance, the working population of Liverpool fell by 30 per cent while employment declined by 25 per cent and the corresponding figures for Birmingham were 19 and 16 per cent, respectively. This loss of workforce relative to employment has led to an increased volume of commuting from suburban areas into the urban cores at the same time as internal movements within inner areas has declined because of the fall in employment. It is a paradox that while the economic importance of core areas is diminishing, the suburban areas are increasingly dependent upon them for their employment.

There are signs that the population movements of the 1960s and the 1970s are not being repeated in the 1980s. While it is the case that net metropolitan out-migration is still occurring, there is evidence (Champion 1983) that its rate has decreased. Although counter-urbanism may not yet be regarded as a spent force, it has probably been blunted by a combination of factors including the saturation of suburban and outer areas, the resulting shortage of new housing, the improvement and refurbishment of inner areas and the effects of the economic recession, which all tend to reduce the propensity to migrate.

Activity rates

The pattern of demographic change in the metropolitan areas in the case of males has been reinforced by the long-term trend of declining participation rates. This trend has accelerated since the mid-1970s as increasing proportions of older men retire (frequently before the age of 65) in response to improved pension provision and government measures such as the Job Release Scheme. The expansion of further and higher education has likewise reduced activity rates in the younger age groups (there was a 37 per cent increase in the proportion of full-time students among men aged 16–64 in the metropolitan counties). Although activity rates among prime age males have not fallen appreciably, within the core of metropolitan labour markets activity rates are less than the national average and have decreased at an above average rate. Compared to the reduction in male employment in urban areas this fall in the male workforce, which probably reflects a 'discouraged worker' effect, is modest and the result has been a sharp increase in male unemployment.

In contrast, changes in women's participation over the post-war period have been dramatic. Between 1971 and 1981 the female activity rate in Great Britain rose from 55 to 61 per cent with an even more pronounced increase for married women whose rate increased from 49 to 57 per cent. These broad trends have been reflected in the urban labour markets but have been superimposed on a falling population with the result that the increase in female labour supply has been smaller than that experienced nationally. In the case of Greater London and many principal cities (e.g. Birmingham, Manchester and Liverpool) the increase in activity rates was insufficient to offset the fall in numbers of women of working age, and in those areas the female labour force has declined.

The reason for the increased participation of women, especially married women, is likely to be a mixture of economic and social factors. Increased participation may result from higher earnings for women or from other changes in household income. Average female earnings as a proportion of (non-agricultural) male earnings rose from around 60 per cent in 1969 to approximately 70 per by 1977 while studies at a regional level have identified earnings as a significant factor in explaining regional differences in participation rates (Molho 1983). Household income may also be important and Manley and Sawbridge (1980) have associated increased participation by women with the growth of low-income and single-parent households. High unemployment, especially among males, could also be a factor leading to lower household income and therefore to higher activity rates. On the other hand, social changes relating to the size and timing of families together with improvements in domestic technology and the provision of childcare and nursery education have been significant in freeing women from domestic roles and facilitating re-entry into the labour force (Martin and Roberts 1984). Social attitudes have also changed, not least among women themselves, often as the result of the spread of further and higher education.

Important though the above may be, it must be noted that the rapid growth of female participation has coincided with a massive sectoral shift in the pattern of employment. Most of the new jobs created during the 1970s have been in activities and occupations mainly associated with the employment of women and with the service sector in particular. Many of these jobs were part time, and this has been an added attraction to married women who have family responsibilities. These new jobs have often been of relatively low status and pay and it could be argued that women were being drawn into the labour market in order to form a pool of secondary labour from which fluctuations in economic activity could be met (Dex and Perry 1984).

These factors in combination have produced high levels of female participation in urban labour markets. High wages, substantial job opportunities and supportive urban infrastructure have produced increases in the participation rotas of married women which were up to 50 per cent greater than the national average. However, it is generally the case that areas with the lowest historical levels of female participation have experienced the greatest increases. The result has been a convergence of activity rates and a narrowing of the differences between areas. Table 3.2 shows that by 1981 differences in activity rates among the metropolitan areas had largely disappeared although the rates remain above the national average. This narrowing of differences

Table 3.2 Index of married womens activity
rates, 1961–81, in metropolitan areas

	1961*	1971*	1981
Greater London	147	114	105
Merseyside	112	101	100
Greater Manchester	156	115	109
West Midlands	139	111	103
West Yorkshire	148	113	106
Tyne and Wear	97	97	100
Great Britain	100	100	100

Source: derived from the Census of Population.
*Based upon activity rates in conurbations.
Strictly these areas are not comparable with the
metropolitan counties because of boundary
difference. They serve as an approximation.

in participation rates may be largely the result of a convergence in
unemployment and wage rates between areas.

The collapse of urban employment

The decline of employment in urban centres is a long-run
phenomenon and has persisted throughout recent cycles of
economic activity. In the immediate post-war period this decline
was relative with employment in urban areas growing at a slower
rate than the rest of Britain. From about 1966 onwards, this relative
decline became absolute, as Table 3.3 shows, with job losses
occurring at an accelerating rate.

Table 3.3 Employment change 1951–81

	Conurbations		Metropolitan county areas
	1951–61	1961–71	1971–81
Greater London	+4.7	-9.0	-24.5
Merseyside	+2.0	-7.6	-13.5
Greater Manchester	-1.0	-8.3	-4.2
Tyne and Wear	+5.2	-2.1	-4.7
West Midlands	+9.0	-2.0	-10.8
West Yorkshire	+1.8	-5.4	+0.4
Great Britain	+7.0	+1.3	-2.7

Source: derived from the Census of Population

Although the secular trend of employment is downwards, the rate at which urban employment declines is influenced by the state of the national economy, being more rapid during recessions such as 1968-72 and stabilising during periods of increasing national economic activity. It is therefore not surprising that the most dramatic instances of employment decline in metropolitan areas should have occurred during the 1979-82 recession. During this period the level of national employment fell by over 2 million jobs, a rate of net job loss estimated to be more than 2,000 per day (Martin 1982). Most of this employment decline was focused on the major urban centres. For instance, employment in the West Midlands Metropolitan County declined by over 153,000 (a decline of nearly 12 per cent) between 1978 and 1981 while it has been estimated that more than 250,000 jobs were lost in manufacturing alone between 1978 and 1983 (West Midlands County Council 1984). Townsend (1983) estimated that net job losses in Greater London over the 1978-81 period were of the order of 182,000 of which 108,000 were in manufacturing (a 14 per cent decline over three years). Similar reductions in employment have taken place in other metropolitan labour markets.

Huge though they were, the employment reductions of the early 1980s were no more than rather dramatic variations around the long-run trend of employment decline in cities. Continued high levels of redundancies and unemployment in these areas suggest that there is little prospect that these urban labour markets have departed from this secular decline.

The suburbanisation of employment

The greatest net job losses have occurred in the core or inner city areas of urban labour markets while suburban and fringe areas have experienced, at worst, only small employment declines or even slight increases in the numbers employed. Just as the overall decline in urban employment is a process of long standing, so too is the spatial relocation of jobs.

Table 3.4 summarises the spatial and industrial variation in employment decline. It clearly shows that the most rapid decline of employment has been in the inner-city areas. The outer-city areas experienced a reduction in employment only during the decade 1971-81, and even then the rate of decline was less than half that of the inner areas. The result of these differential rates of change is that throughout the period there was a marked relative shift of

Table 3.4 Changes in employment 1951–81
(Employment changes are shown in thousands; percentage changes are given in *italics*)

	Inner cities	Outer cities	Free-standing cities	Small towns and rural areas	Great Britain
Manufacturing					
1951–61	–143 *–8.0*	+84 *+5.0*	–21 *–2.0*	+453 *+14.0*	+374 *+5.0*
1961–71	–428 *–26.1*	–217 *–10.3*	–93 *–6.2*	+489 *+12.5*	–255 *–3.9*
1971–81	–447 *–36.8*	–480 *–32.6*	–311 *–28.6*	–717 *–17.2*	–1929 *–24.5*
Private services					
1951–61	+192 *+11.0*	+110 *+11.0*	+128 *+17.0*	+514 *+16.0*	+944 *+14.0*
1961–71	–297 *–15.3*	+92 *+8.1*	–7 *–0.8*	+535 *+14.5*	+318 *+4.2*
1971–81	–105 *–6.4*	+170 *+17.3*	+91 *+10.9*	+805 *+24.8*	+958 *+14.4*
Public services					
1951–61	+13 *+1.0*	+54 *+7.0*	+38 *+6.0*	+200 *+8.0*	+302 *+6.0*
1961–71	+25 *+2.0*	+170 *+21.6*	+110 *+17.7*	+502 *+17.3*	+807 *+14.5*
1971–81	–78 *–7.4*	+102 *+8.8*	+53 *+6.5*	+456 *+14.1*	+488 *+7.7*
Total employment					
1951–61	+43 *+1.0*	+231	+140 *+6.0*	+1060 *+10.0*	+1490 *+7.0*
1961–71	–643 *–14.8*	+19 *+0.6*	+54 *+2.4*	+1022 *+8.5*	+320 *+1.3*
1971–81	–538 *–14.6*	–236 *–7.1*	–150 *–5.4*	+404 *+3.5*	–590 *–2.7*

Source: Hausner and Robson 1986: 9.

employment to suburban areas in the outer city. A similar but less dramatic reduction in employment has taken place in free-standing cities, but the most remarkable trend is the continuous growth of employment in small towns and rural areas. Despite the stagnation of demand in the 1970s and the post-1979 recession, employment in these areas continued to increase and there was a net increase of nearly 2.5 million jobs between 1951 and 1981.

These differential rates of employment change have produced a structural shift in labour demand away from the main urban centres towards suburban, small town and rural locations, and both the proportion and the number of jobs located in the inner cities has declined substantially as the result. This decline actually understates the true reduction in the demand for the labour services of inner-area residents because an increasing proportion of inner-city jobs are filled by non-resident commuters. In Birmingham 92 per cent of inner-city jobs were taken by residents in 1951 but this figure had declined to 68 per cent by 1981. On average, inner-city residents obtained only slightly over 60 per cent of inner city jobs in 1981. Although this inner-area decline matches the popular image of urban problems it still seems strange that employment has declined so much in an area which contains the central business district, major shopping centres and other relatively buoyant parts of the economy. This apparent paradox highlights the gross oversimplification which results from the dichotomous, inner and outer, treatment of urban structure. Most models of urban structure have identified a number of zones, whether segments or rings, and expect some clustering of activities within areas of common land use. Thus, the rather broad 'inner city' zone will contain within it a variety of different economic activities, land uses and socio-economic groups of residents. It might be more accurate to say that the inner area contains two subareas: the central business district and an 'inner ring' which is sometimes called 'the zone of transition' to indicate the mixed land use, ageing structures and general instability of the area. Where attempts have been made to distinguish between the central and inner area it has usually been apparent that the greatest job losses occur in the zone of transition and employment may even have grown in central areas. The rate of net employment decline for the whole 'inner city' may therefore understate the extent and severity of job losses in some subareas of the city (see Warnes 1980).

Industrial change

The changes in total employment are dramatic but they conceal the full extent of the changes which have occurred in labour markets, particularly changes in the composition of labour demand as the result of the changing pattern of industrial activity and the decline of manufacturing industry. This sectoral change is particularly important because it produces changes in the sex and skill composition of jobs and affects the mode of employment. These changes are crucially important because they raise the possibility that workers who become redundant in one sector may not possess the appropriate skills to fill any new jobs created elsewhere in the urban economy.

The changes in the industrial structure that have been observed in advanced industrial countries reveal a general tendency for primary and secondary (mainly manufacturing) employment to decline relative to the service sector. Such trends have led, over time, to what Fuchs (1968) has called the 'service economy' (i.e. one where the majority of the working population is employed in the service sector) and to considerable concern over 'de-industrialisation' (not easily defined but seen as a sustained decline in the share of manufacturing employment) as elaborated on in Blackaby *et al.* (1979). Many different processes have been suggested as explanations of this sectoral shift and these include:

(a)   the tendency of productivity to grow faster in manufacturing than in service industry leading, even with no change in the pattern of demand, to changes in the pattern of employment;

(b)   the possibility that the income elasticity of demand for services is greater than that of goods so that, as GDP rises, the composition of demand will change and a greater proportion of resources will be devoted to the service sector;

(c)   the pre-empting of resources by the expanding public sector which has squeezed manpower from manufacturing industry and prevented the expansion of the private sector in other activities;

(d)   the decline of manufacturing industry in Great Britain because of a loss of international competitiveness, as shown by the fall in the British share of world trade in manufactured goods and in increasing import penetration;

(e)   shifts that are occurring in the worldwide location of industry and the production decisions of multinational companies.

Whichever processes are at work, employment in the manufacturing industries has declined relatively from 1955 onwards with an absolute loss of manufacturing jobs from 1966, while the service sector increased steadily until the 1979–82 recession temporarily halted this growth. These changes have not been uniform across sectors with the textile, metal, leather, clothing and footwear industries all well to the forefront of manufacturing contraction. Engineering and motor vehicles also experienced severe cutbacks in employment. Similarly, experiences differed in the service sector with most growth being concentrated in the insurance, banking and the professional and scientific services while transport and distribution employment declined. The severe recession of 1979–82 brought about a more general decline in employment with job losses being experienced even in those industries which had previously been relatively unaffected (Townsend 1983).

The local impact of these broad industrial trends is influenced by the existing industrial structure and the relative performance of local industries and firms. In the past, large cities and the conurbations have had a strong reliance upon manufacturing activity and not surprisingly major job losses have occurred. However, the scale of manufacturing employment decline far exceeds what might otherwise have been expected while the performance of employment growth sectors such as services has not matched that of other areas. The pattern of change by sector and by location can be seen by referring back to Table 3.4. Employment decline in the inner areas is not restricted to manufacturing, although this has been by far the most rapid. Even during the 1960s employment growth in the inner cities was restricted to the public service sector and by the 1970s employment was declining in all sectors. In contrast, service sector employment growth (both private and public) has been significant in outer-city locations and free-standing cities, and very considerable in small towns and rural areas. The crudity of the inner–outer dichotomy needs to be kept in mind during these comparisons as it may be the case that employment growth in the central business district is being offset by reductions in the 'zone of transition'.

The general pattern of employment change is quite clear;

massive manufacturing job losses in all locations, but especially in the conurbations (both inner and outer areas) and large urban areas, accompanied by a small decline in service employment in the inner cities and substantial growth of service sector employment in all other areas. In outer city locations and in free-standing cities the growth of new service jobs has been insufficient to offset the impact of manufacturing job losses and employment levels have declined overall. Remarkably, manufacturing employment in small towns and rural areas did not even begin to decline until the 1970s and the rapid growth of new jobs in the service sector has easily outstripped manufacturing losses leading to a modest growth in employment overall despite the recession. Between 1951 and 1981 there was a net reduction over the period of around 1.1 million jobs in the inner areas of the conurbations of which 1 million were in manufacturing (a decline of 57 per cent over the period).

As the result of these changes, by 1981 manufacturing was no longer the most important source of jobs in the conurbations which had been the case (with the exception of Greater London) as recently as 1971 (Department of Employment 1977). In the conurbations as a whole manufacturing still represents a slightly higher than national average proportion of employment (with London markedly below and the West Midlands markedly above), but in the inner cities manufacturing is generally under-represented in employment structures, the exceptions being Sheffield and Birmingham. Such a pattern reflects the continued erosion of the manufacturing industries of these areas and the relative suburbanisation of such employment. Despite the crucial importance of manufacturing job losses, the rate of decline in the conurbations has been fairly uniform and it seems that differences in the economic performance of these areas can be largely accounted for by variations in the rate of service industry growth. This is consistent with the findings of Lloyd and Reeve (1982) who demonstrated that the relative prosperity of Greater Manchester was mainly due to the good performance of its service sector.

The sectoral shifts described above have brought with them associated changes in the nature of the jobs available. Jobs lost in manufacturing have tended to be full-time, manual jobs for men whereas job growth elsewhere in the service and public sectors have been non-manual, often part time, and frequently filled by women. The effects of these trends can be seen in Table 3.5.

Table 3.5 Percentage change in employment of residents in the Metropolitan Counties, 1971–1981; males aged 16–64 and females aged 16–59

	Males	Females Full time	Part time
Greater London	-17.2	-4.6	-11.2
Greater Manchester	-6.3	-4.0	+5.7
Merseyside	-19.8	-6.9	+5.5
South Yorkshire	-5.7	+0	+25.0
Tyne and Wear	-14.2	-5.0	-3.0
West Yorkshire	-1.8	-0	+12.11

Source: derived from the Census of Population, 1971 and 1981

Nationally, the changing pattern of employment has produced a general upward shift in the socio-economic structure. These trends have not been fully reflected in metropolitan areas where the greatest relative expansion of employment has been in the non-professional, non-manual groups together with personal service and semi-skilled manual workers. In Merseyside for instance, the share of non-professional, non-manual workers in the labour force increased from 12.8 per cent in 1971 to 27.8 per cent in 1981. The biggest decreases have been in the skilled manual groups; in the West Midlands they declined from 40.9 per cent of the labour force to under 23 per cent between 1971 and 1981. Unlike Britain as a whole there have also been reductions in the shares of managers and professional workers while the employment share of the unskilled has fallen rather less than has been the case nationally. This is more the result of differential migration than changes in the occupational structure of jobs in cities as these groups have been the most mobile. Thus, while the evidence does not support the proposition that urban labour markets are becoming dominated by unskilled manual workers, it is the case that such areas have missed out on the fast-expanding professional and managerial occupations. It also needs to be recalled that the changing composition relates to a greatly reduced labour force and therefore changing shares understate the severity of the absolute changes which have taken place in some socio-economic groups.

The processes of job loss

Change in net employment within urban labour markets is an indicator of the shifts which have occurred in labour demand.

From the point of view of trying to understand the way in which these net changes come about and their impact on different groups in the labour market, it is necessary to examine the processes by which employment change takes place.

Components of change

Labour markets are dynamic institutions in which change is always taking place. New jobs are continually being created either within existing or in new firms just as other jobs are being lost as firms decline and others close down. Net employment change can occur as the result of a number of events, namely:

(a)   a fall in the number of new plant openings;
(b)   an increase in the number of plant closures;
(c)   a net change in the employment of existing firms;
(d)   a net movement into or out of the area.

The relationship between these various components of change is shown in Fig. 3.3.

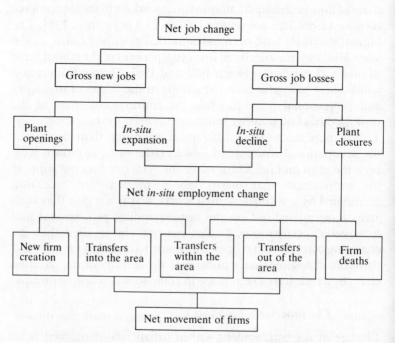

Fig. 3.3 The components of employment change

Different local economies can experience the same net employment change as the result of different processes. A given decline in employment may be the result of an excess of plant closures over openings, net *in-situ* decline among existing employers, net outmigration of firms, or some combination of all of these. In fact, studies of large urban markets (summarised in Table 3.6) suggest that fairly similar processes have been taking place. These studies suggest that an excess of plant closures over new openings is the most dominant feature of employment change with contraction of employment by surviving plants being an important secondary source of job loss. One exception is Coventry which has experienced massive in-situ job losses, mainly in motor vehicle plants. Industrial movement has not been important except in Greater London. Mason (1980) showed that half of all manufacturing plants in Greater Manchester in 1966 (accounting for a quarter of all employment) failed to survive until 1975. Dicken and Lloyd (1978) estimated that 86 per cent of the overall loss of manufacturing employment in the inner area of Manchester during 1966–75 resulted from an excess of closures over plant openings. In an earlier study of Glasgow, Firn and Hughes (1973) found that more than 60 per cent of manufacturing job losses within the city resulted from closures, with less than 5 per cent arising from the relocation of firms. Industrial relocation has been more important in Greater London where 34 and 42 per cent of job losses in Inner and Outer London have been attributed to this process (Dennis 1978). Even in this case, plant closure remains the most important process (Gripaios 1977). It seems that employment change and decentralisation have been brought about by differential rates of change in indigenous employment rather than through industrial relocation.

Redundancies

If net employment decline results from a process of labour turnover involving massive gross job losses then the issue arises as to how firms deal with the need to shed labour on this scale. One possibility is that they simply shed surplus labour by means of compulsory redundancies. Townsend (1983) has argued that such redundancies lie at the heart of the recession and it is true that the volume of recorded redundancies has increased markedly during the 1979–82 recession. However, firms need not respond to reductions in labour demand simply by sacking workers; hours of

Table 3.6 Components of manufacturing employment change for various areas in Great Britain

Area	Years	No. of years	Base year employment	Standardised rate of employment change*					
				Total change	Entries	Exits	Expansions in situ	Contractions in situ	Net change in situ
Coventry	1974-82	8	115,317	-5.74	+0.34	-1.51	+0.40	-4.96	-4.57
Inner Clydeside	1963-73	10	NA	-2.73	+0.50	-3.29	—	—	+0.60
Outer Clydeside				+1.08	+1.61	-2.26	—	—	+1.73
Greater London	1966-74	5	1,436,800	-3.39	+0.11	-2.51	—	—	-1.00
Merseyside†	1966-75	9	169,610	-1.00	+1.75	-1.98	—	—	+0.14
Inner Merseyside			76,087	-2.92	+0.91	-2.50	—	—	-1.34
Outer Merseyside			93,523	+2.20	+2.43	-1.57	—	—	+1.34
Greater Manchester†	1966-75	9	447,606	-2.76	+1.27	-3.56	—	—	-0.48
Inner Manchester			89,849	-4.84	+1.44	-5.67	—	—	-0.61
Outer Manchester			357,757	-2.24	+1.23	-3.02	—	—	-0.44
East Midlands†	1968-75	7							
Cities			285,000	-1.16	+1.14	-1.74	+1.70	-2.23	-0.43
Larger towns			77,400	-0.21	+1.59	-1.47	+1.64	-1.96	-0.31
Smaller towns			161,800	+0.71	+1.74	-1.89	+2.64	-1.77	+0.87
Rural areas			48,500	+2.40	+2.06	-1.34	+3.56	-1.81	+1.74
Cleveland	1965-78	13	114,485	-1.85	+0.95	-0.98	+0.34	-2.17	-1.83
Durham			66,373	+1.11	+2.25	-1.47	+1.78	-1.46	+0.32
Tyne and Wear			203,905	-1.24	+0.88	-1.18	+0.82	-1.75	-0.93

Source: Healey and Clark 1985: 1361.
*The standardised rates are calculated by dividing the employment changes (expressed as percentages of base year employment) by the number of years in the study.

work may be changed or employment may be reduced by means of natural wastage. Since compulsory redundancies can be costly both financially and in terms of good will and worker morale, firms will be expected to avoid this strategy if possible. Brown (1981) has suggested that enforced redundancy, early retirement and transfers within the organisation are likely in only 30 per cent of cases of job loss, whereas in 70 per cent of cases natural wastage would be used.

If this emphasis on non-redundancy methods of achieving employment reductions is correct then redundancy might be expected to account for only a fraction of all jobs lost. Meager (1984) estimated that non-redundancy methods accounted for at least 46 per cent of job losses in the Motherwell area in 1974–82. Martin (1984) draws a similar conclusion but notes that the ratio of redundancies to total discharges (or job losses) is highest in those areas with the highest rates of net employment decline. What these findings suggest is not that redundancy is unimportant, but that it is a far more complex labour market phenomenon than has previously been recognised. Variations in the extent to which job losses result in redundancies may have very important implications for the levels of unemployment that result from employment loss in a local labour market.

The cause of employment decline

A number of different explanations have been advanced to account for the decline of urban employment. These can be grouped together under two broad viewpoints. First, there are explanations which see urban structural change as arising from factors and processes that have their origin outside the urban area. This perspective embraces such diverse explanations as those that emphasise the effect of adverse industrial structure to radical perspectives that focus upon the nature of production processes under capitalism. The second perspective sees the changes as being rooted in the nature of urban areas themselves and explains the decline in terms of the increasingly uncompetitive nature of urban locations.

Industrial structure

One simple explanation of the decline in demand for labour is that urban areas, and inner cities particularly, have been unfortunate enough to possess adverse industrial structures. Largely as an historical legacy of the industrialisation process, urban areas are portrayed as possessing disproportionately large shares of nationally declining industries, mainly, but not exclusively, manufacturing industries. National trends in industrial change have little to do with urban areas *per se* as they relate to factors such as the general process of de-industrialisation, a lack of international competitiveness, sectoral differences in the response to recession and so forth. Shift-share analysis has been widely used to test the proposition that urban employment decline is a structural reflection of national changes in industrial structure. The method attempts to divide local changes in employment into three components:

1. *The National Component.* This measures the change that would have occurred if total employment in the area had changed at the same rate as the economy as a whole.

2. *The Structural Component.* This measures the change that would have occurred if each local industry had grown at the national rate for that industry less the national component. If the local economy has an industrial structure which is identical to the national economy then this component will equal zero. If positive, it suggests a positive contribution is being made to local employment growth by a higher than average proportion of fast-growing industries in the local economy.

3. *The Differential Shift.* This is measured as a residual by subtracting the expected change (1 plus 2) from the actual change. It represents the extent to which employment change is higher or lower than expected after account has been taken of national trends and industrial structure. A positive shift component signals a better than expected local performance. In some studies this component will be subdivided into other categories; for instance, to account for plant relocation.

Shift-share analysis has been subject to considerable criticism on the grounds that it is descriptive rather than analytical and on a number of technical grounds (see Brown 1972; Richardson 1978). Nevertheless, the technique has been extensively used.

Most shift-share analyses of urban markets have restricted themselves to an examination of manufacturing employment. Such analyses generally agree that industrial structure is not a major explanatory factor in urban manufacturing decline. The largest component is usually the differential shift or local performance component. Dennis (1978) showed that of the 390,000 manufacturing jobs lost in Greater London between 1966 and 1974, only 30,000, or 7.7 per cent could be attributed to industrial structure. Fothergill and Gudgin (1982), in a very detailed examination of urban and regional growth between 1959 and 1975, conducted a shift-share analysis for urban areas of varying size. Their results suggest that the conurbations did in fact suffer from adverse industrial structures but this could only account for 25 per cent of job losses. In contrast, London was shown to have a positive structural component although, again, the local component was the largest of the three components. A similar conclusion was reached by Danson *et al.* (1980) who applied their shift-share analysis to the inner and outer areas of the six main conurbations. They concluded that the industrial structures of inner areas were in general more favourable than those of corresponding outer areas, and yet the former had suffered more severe job losses. This was reflected in large negative local or differential shifts for the inner areas. The apparently favourable industrial structure of the inner areas could be due to a failure to disaggregate sufficiently in order to distinguish the central business district from the zone of transition. In a study of Leicester, Cook and Rendall (1984) used a three-way division of the city which distinguished between the inner city (as designated under the Inner Area Programme), the remaining outer part of the city, and the urban–rural fringe. Their results are unusual in that they find an adverse industrial structure in all parts of Leicester, while within the inner area the industrial structure is considerably less favourable than in either the outer or urban fringe areas.

The evidence on the role of industrial structure is therefore a little mixed. For some areas an adverse industrial structure has been a factor in job decline, but for most urban and inner-city areas the industrial structure has been favourable to employment growth; the job losses of recent years must be explained in some other way.

The restructuring of production

An alternative perspective emphasising economy-wide processes is that of economic restructuring. This radical explanation, which is probably most closely associated with Massey and Meegan (1978 and 1982), sees the pattern of employment change as being a spatial manifestation of the response by capital to the deepening 'profits crisis' of the post-war period. Profits in British industry fell dramatically during the late 1960s and 1970s as the result of a number of national and international factors, including the decline of international competitiveness of British exports, rapidly rising energy and commodity prices, wage inflation and falling domestic aggregate demand. Faced with the need to restore profitability, firms have been forced to seek ways of reducing costs. Corporate restructuring relates to the strategies adopted by firms to achieve these reductions in costs of production.

Restructuring can take a variety of forms depending upon the form that the crisis takes for a particular industry. In some industries the situation faced is that of falling product demand resulting in excess capacity and high production costs. In other sectors product demand may be stable or even expanding but firms are faced with the need to maintain a high and competitively priced output in the face of rapid technological competition. In the first situation the need is to cut output and costs. Small adjustments in production may be achieved through the intensification of production; if the productivity of the existing workforce can be raised then reduced output levels can be achieved with a more than proportionate reduction in employment, thus saving on labour costs. Where there is a need to reduce production by a large amount, or intensification of the work process is not feasible, then plant closures or rationalisation may be a more effective method of achieving substantial reductions in capacity while at the same time keeping down production costs. In the case of the industry faced with intense competition, increased efficiency may be sought through investment in product innovation and technological change in production. This may actually involve an expansion in the scale of operations during which there may be an increased division of labour within the corporation with production, administration, and research being concentrated in separate establishments. During such corporate reorganisation the opportunity may be taken to achieve a measure of rationalisation at the same time as production is switched from one plant to another. Although production capacity is expanded it does not automatically follow that employment will be increased as new technology and automation will raise labour productivity and reduce the need to increase employment (which might even fall) as well as reducing skill requirements. Such changes as these may be accompanied by other changes in the corporate structure of industries, with mergers occurring in order to facilitate investment in new technology and to bring about the rationalisation of production.

Reorganisation of production in response to economic crisis is not a fundamentally spatial process but it has spatial consequences. These effects vary according to the particular form of re-organisation that is taking place and the likely consequences for employment are summarised in Fig. 3.4. Intensification of production simply reduces employment at existing locations, whereas rationalisation may involve both *in-situ* job losses and plant closures. Some areas may experience an increase in employment during rationalisation as production is switched around between plants. The introduction of new production technology through investment brings with it the greatest range of possible effects and

Forms of production reorganisation	Product demand conditions		
	Falling	Stable	Rising
Intensification	(a) *In-situ* employment reduction		Indeterminate
Rationalisation	(a) *In-situ* employment reduction (b) Plant closures (c) Spatial redistribution of jobs brings some employment gains for remaining plants		Indeterminate
Technological change	(a) *In-situ* employment cuts (b) New locations and plant closures	Any combination of *in-situ* job losses, new locations and plant closures to meet capacity requirements	

Fig. 3.4 The spatial implications of production reorganisations
Source: adapted from Massey and Meegan 1982

can involve any combination of new plant and new locations, *in-situ* decline or closures. The structure of local industry within an urban economy and the nature of the reorganisation within it will determine the pattern of employment change found in the local labour market. In the conurbations and other older industrial cities a large proportion of jobs are located in branch plants and subsidiary firms; in Merseyside over 70 per cent of manual manufacturing workers were employed in plants employing over 500 workers, but only 14 per cent of plants were controlled by local corporations. Such economies are prone not only to high *in-situ* job losses arising from new production technologies, but also to losses through branch plant closures. Multiplant firms will rationalise production on the most favourably located plants which tend not to be in large urban areas. In addition, plants in the city may be starved of the new investment necessary to make them profitable because corporations would prefer to invest in labour markets with strong secondary characteristics.

The question remains as to why metropolitan and inner-city areas should fare so badly out of any reorganisation of production. The answer relates to the fact that the effect of changes in production processes has been to change the nature of the labour requirements of firms. There is less need for skilled labour because of automation but an increased need for unskilled and semi-skilled workers. There is also a greater need for flexibility of working practices and new forms of working, such as part-time working. Cheaper, flexible, semi-skilled and non-unionised labour often means female labour and firms will seek out areas with high reserves of potential female workers. Changes in the spatial pattern of production will occur as firms seek out those locations where these kinds of secondary labour market conditions prevail. As Chapter 2 suggested, the urban labour markets may not possess the kind of labour which industry now requires as these areas have low reserves of female labour, old skills and a tradition of trade union organisation.

The corporate restructuring explanation, like the industrial structure hypothesis, sees employment decline in urban areas as the product of national and international forces. Unlike the latter explanation, restructuring sees these forces interacting with the unique characteristics of the local economy to produce differing results in different locations (Massey, 1983, 1984). It is not so much the case that cities contain a concentration of declining industries but that decline in industries is focused upon these areas as the result of their particular economic and labour market characteristics. In terms of shift-share analysis, restructuring provides an explanation of the local growth component, even though the root cause of decline is not of local origin.

The competitiveness of urban economies

An alternative explanation of urban decline places its emphasis not on the struggle between capital and labour but on the declining competitiveness of urban areas as locations for economic activity. These explanations see above-average employment loss as the result of competitive market responses to rising costs and falling profits in urban locations; the fundamental cause of decline is located within urban areas. The idea of urban areas suffering a decline in competitiveness is often linked to the notion of an 'urban life-cycle' in which there are distinct phases of urban development. Initially, it is suggested, towns grow rapidly with increasing concentration of activity, but eventually this phase gives way to growth through suburbanisation as the high costs of central locations come to outweigh agglomeration economies. Ultimately the stagnation of inner areas leads to cumulative decline and the collapse of inner city economies as economic activity and population are lost to other areas. While this final phase has probably yet to arrive, it has been conceivable for some urban areas, especially London, to be described as approaching the status of a 'post-industrial city' (Young and Mills 1983).

Fothergill and Gudgin (1982) have argued that a combination of physical constraints on expansion and long-run competitive pressures to increase the capital intensity of production (which requires more floor space per worker) inevitably lead to urban decline. Hemmed in by existing urban development, firms are unable to expand other than by split site operation or by transferring production to other sites (in the case of multiplant firms). Even if large or adjoining sites could be found, their acquisition is very costly because of high land values and the cost of redevelopment. Compounding these difficulties is the fact that many city premises are obsolete, Victorian multistorey buildings of no use to manufacturing industries utilising flowline production processes which require single-storey buildings of large area. Physical obsolescence has even spread to the office sector because of the requirements of new office technologies

(Duffy 1980). Faced with these kinds of difficulties, firms can either cease trading or seek cheaper purpose-built and modern premises in suburban locations. There is certainly evidence to support this view from surveys of relocating firms in which the need to expand output, the inadequacy of existing premises and site congestion are the reasons most frequently cited by firms (Dennis 1978).

The decentralisation of population also has a part to play in explaining urban employment decline. The rapidly falling labour force has created labour shortages in some of the more skilled occupations (which are also the most mobile) while wages may have to be raised to induce labour back to jobs in the cities (e.g. the London weighting). Both labour shortages and higher wages place city firms at a cost disadvantage relative to those in suburban locations. However, this is a process more likely to affect manufacturing than the service industries which may be able to draw upon increased labour supply from women. Service industries are more likely to be affected by the reduction in the market for consumer services which population decline will bring about, while business services may be affected by the decline of manufacturing activity. Fothergill and Gudgin (1982) estimated a large negative local multiplier effect on service industry growth in London and the conurbations (−7.6 and −4.9 per cent, respectively) between 1959 and 1975. Only the national trend of high growth prevented service employment from declining in these areas.

Regional policy has frequently been cited as a cause of metropolitan decline, especially in respect of London and the West Midlands conurbation (Keeble 1978; Gripaios 1977). While there is evidence of such policy having attracted employment to the assisted areas, most evaluations suggest that the scale of such effects was small and virtually non-existent from the mid-1970s onwards (Keeble 1980; Fothergill and Gudgin 1982). Attention has therefore shifted to the impact of local government planning policies and local taxation. Planning restrictions may reinforce some of the difficulties faced by firms when seeking to expand in central city locations. Local taxation in the form of business rates has also attracted attention. A number of studies have attributed employment decline to high business rates; Cuthbertson *et al.* (1979) concluded that one-quarter of all job losses in London between 1966 and 1971 were due to the fiscal policies of local authorities. Business rates have increased more rapidly than other costs. Industrial rates increased by a national average of 76 per cent between 1979 and 1982 as compared with 4.5 per cent for fuel and materials and 48 per cent for earnings, while over the same period the price of manufactured goods rose by only 40 per cent with obvious consequences for profits (Birdseye and Webb 1984). Similar arguments can be found in Waine (1983) and Willis (1984). However, it is not altogether clear that rising industrial rates necessarily lead to higher rates of job loss. Rates constitute a very small proportion of total costs and Roper (1982) estimated that rates in Leicester amounted to an average of around 0.5 per cent of firms total costs. Furthermore, as a tax on property, rates may be shifted backwards to land and property owners resulting in lower property prices and lower commercial rents, thus leaving costs relatively unchanged. Lower rentals might affect future property development, but may not lead to uncompetitiveness among city firms. A number of studies have sought but failed to find any statistical relationship between rate poundages and job losses or unemployment (Straw 1981; Hughs 1981; and Othick 1983) and although these studies have been criticised as being too simplistic it remains the case that there are no studies to the contrary.

The most comprehensive study of the impact of local authority rates and industrial location is that of Crawford *et al.* (1985) who examined the factors affecting employment change in the boroughs and districts of England between 1974 and 1981. Their findings are important in two respects: first, because they found no evidence to support the view that rates (either their levels or rate of increase) had any effect upon the location of employment and, second, because of the factors revealed as affecting employment location. The most important influences on manufacturing employment in a local economy are the mix of industries, the size of plants and the extent of urbanisation in the area. In the case of the service sector, the overwhelming influence on employment change was the rate of change of local population which could be interpreted as being evidence of the importance of local markets and the operation of a local multiplier process (see Ch. 2). There was no evidence to suggest that rates affected the rate of employment change in general in either industrial sector. They did appear to be important as a factor in the change of office employment in metropolitan areas, but this appeared to be a reflection of the specific process of office relocation from London rather than a more general phenomenon.

Shortages of space, unsuitable premises, high land and labour costs, unsympathetic planning and high local authority rates all suggest an environment which is not particularly conducive to economic activity. Such an environment represents, it has been suggested, a break with the historical role of cities as 'seedbeds' or 'incubators' in which new firms and businesses are created. The incubator theory suggests that new firm formation will be high in central city areas because of the accessibility to customers and suppliers, availability of small, cheap premises and good transport links. If it ever was generally true of cities, the evidence suggests that inner cities do not perform this function now. Cameron (1980) found no evidence of an incubator process operating in Clydeside even though certain activities did find the inner area an attractive location. Similar conclusions were reached by Nicholson *et al.* (1981) as regards Inner London. The only strong evidence in favour of the incubation role is that of Fagg (1980). These negative findings may not be so surprising since they relate to relatively recent (i.e. post-war) periods when the advantages of inner area location had already been greatly eroded. In a rare study of new firm formation in inter-war Birmingham, Beesley (1955) concluded that the inner city area had offered significant advantages and enjoyed a high rate of new firm formation; in contrast, later studies of the area suggest that this was no longer the case (Firn and Swales 1978). In one of the very few direct tests of locational disadvantage, Bayldon *et al.* (1984) found no evidence of significant differences in profitability between an inner area, Islington, and rival new town locations of Peterborough, Northampton and Milton Keynes. Nevertheless, on balance, it seems unlikely that large urban centres offer the degree of economic advantage which was hitherto the case. Indeed, it is possible that these areas have been affected by a 'social-psychology of decline' in which a combination of real and subjective factors influence the behaviour of firms in a negative manner. Townsend (1983) observed that the scale and speed of redundancies in some areas exceeded that which a rational long-term business appraisal might suggest was necessary. Business decisions are often interdependent and when other firms are laying off workers this course of action does not seem quite so undesirable as it otherwise would. Fothergill and Gudgin (1982) talk of a synergism which either hampers or stimulates indigenous economic activity. Such a perspective – the most individualistic of the explanations examined here – emphasises rather intangible qualities of the local community: its cultural history and attitudes, the quality of local entrepreneurs and of labour and the political economy of the area.

The differing experience of change

A crude measure of labour market imbalance would be the difference between the change in the number of economically active residents of an area and the change in the number of jobs in the area. Corkindale (1980) demonstrated the substantial change in the economic fortunes of the conurbations over the post-war period using this approach. Whereas labour demand was increasing ahead of labour force growth in all but south-east Lancashire during the 1950s, only a decade later decline had replaced growth in all the conurbations, although employment was decreasing more slowly than the labour force. Evidence from the 1981 Census of Population confirms that these processes have continued but that decreases in demand have outstripped those of labour supply (Table 3.7). Most of this increase in demand deficiency has been concentrated in the market for male workers although the female labour market has also suffered, most notably in Liverpool where a growth in female labour supply was juxtaposed against falling demand.

What is evident even from these simple comparisons of employment and labour force change is that the pattern of change is complex and simple generalisations may be misleading. While all urban labour markets experienced falling male employment,

Table 3.7 Change in resident labour force and employment in metropolitan cities, 1971–81

	Totals		Males		Females	
	LF	Emp	LF	Emp	LF	Emp
Inner London	—	—	-21	-29	-16	-19
Birmingham	-13	-15	-14	-19	-8	-9
Manchester	-21	-12	-21	-14	-14	-9
Liverpool	-17	-20	-19	-24	+12	-14
Leeds	-5	-10	-7	-14	+1	-4
Sheffield	-7	-11	-11	-18	+2	+0
Newcastle	-8	-3	-11	-14	+0	+6

Source: derived from the Census of Population, 1971 and 1981.

the extent of the decline varies substantially relative to labour force change. The pattern of change among females is even more complex with some areas facing both labour force and employment declines while others experienced growing demand deficiency only because employment failed to keep pace with the growing female labour force. There is a need for some form of accounts which will allow these differing experiences to be measured. Such a framework is provided by the 'labour market accounts' methodology applied by Owen *et al.* (1984) to British local labour markets.

The method attempts to estimate a number of elements contributing to labour demand deficiency (referred to as job shortfalls). These elements are: employment change; the natural increase in the population of working age; the participation increase which measures the expected change in the number of economically active due to changes in the age structure of the population and activity rates; unemployment change; and finally net migration. The latter is measured as a residual, being the difference between the expected and actual number of economically active (see Owen *et al.* 1984, for a full description of the method). Job shortfalls are measured by subtracting the change in employment from the change in the expected number of economically active and consist of the change in unemployment plus net migration. Both are feasible responses to local demand deficiency.

Owen *et al.* estimated job shortfalls in 280 local labour markets in Great Britain in 1981. These labour markets were then grouped together into seven categories of broadly similar experience. The groups, ordered by size of job surplus/shortfall were:

1.   *Rapid growth.* Few in number, these areas exhibited rapid employment growth, job surpluses and in-migration, e.g. Peterborough and Milton Keynes.
2.   *Low supply growth.* Low population and activity rate increases leading to shortages of labour. Examples are mainly coastal or retirement areas.
3.   *Slow growth.* Low employment growth but largely offset by even slower labour force growth often as the result of out-migration. Examples are exclusively non-metropolitan in character, e.g. St Albans, Gloucester and Shrewsbury.
4.   *High supply.* Demographic factors induce increases in

labour supply which swamp an otherwise reasonably high employment growth and result in increased unemployment, e.g. Oxford, Swindon and some New Towns such as Harlow or Welwyn.

5. *Slow decline.* Sluggish employment decline and small increases in labour supply. Unemployment partly offset by reductions in activity rates. Main examples are in the traditional industrial areas of Lancashire, Yorkshire and the East Midlands.

6. *Marked decline.* Substantial job shortfalls due to a large reduction in demand for males and rapid increase in female labour supply (increased activity rates outstripped the large increase in female employment). High unemployment is the result in these localities which are mainly in south Wales and other traditional steel-making areas.

7. *Rapid decline.* The main focus of economic decline. Very rapid falls in labour demand combined with increases in supply have produced massive job shortfalls. Unemployment has risen rapidly as has net outward migration. The main areas in this cluster were the metropolitan labour markets of Merseyside, Greater Manchester, West Midlands and Clydeside together with the old industrial areas of north-east England, particularly Tyne and Wear.

It is notable that the large metropolitan labour markets are largely to be found in group 7 and Table 3.8 confirms that there is a

Table 3.8 Local labour market experience by size of urban area

Labour market experience in order of increasing job shortfall	Better than average		High supply and slow decline	Worse than average
	Rapid growth	Low supply and slow growth		Marked and Rapid decline
London dominant	—	—	1	
Conurbation dominant	—	—	—	5
Provincial dominant	—	2	3	—
Cities	—	16	26	19
Towns	9	75	44	28
Rural	3	33	13	3
Totals	12	126	87	55

Source: derived from Owen *et al.* 1984

relationship between position in the urban hierarchy and the size of the shortfall experienced.

Summary and conclusions

It seems very likely that the urban areas, and especially the conurbations, would have experienced employment decline and high unemployment even if there had been no recession in the late 1970s. The processes of sectoral change and de-industrialisation in post-war Britain would have inevitably resulted in major employment difficulties for these areas because of the historically high proportion of manufacturing activity in their industrial structures. However, industrial structure alone does not explain the scale of the decline. It is the relative movement of industrial activity and employment from the city core to the suburbs and the rural periphery which has added to the process of decline. The only mitigating factor is that population has also been decentralising so that the pressure of labour supply in urban labour markets has been correspondingly reduced (although not as much as might appear at first sight because of commuting).

On top of these long-term trends has been superimposed the impact of the 1979–82 recession and the subsequent low levels of economic activity. This has simply hastened the process of urban decline. Decentralisation of employment has continued with renewed vigour as a new spatial division of labour has been created. Massive job losses and large numbers of plant closures have been the dominant trends in urban labour markets. Views differ as to the cause of the decline. One view is that urban areas no longer provide the economic advantages that they did in the past; urban firms have been forced out by a combination of factors including high costs, shrinking markets and local taxation. An alternative view is that firms have changed their production requirements in response to the need to reorganise production and have abandoned the cities and the conurbations in a quest for different kinds of production environments, generally those displaying secondary labour market characteristics.

While the same general processes are at work in all urban areas, when combined with local features they lead to a considerable variety of experiences of economic and social change but it is most notable that the group of local labour markets which have experienced the greatest job shortfalls contain most of the older industrial cities and the conurbations. A look at these areas seems to provide a glimpse of post-industrial Britain.

Further reading

The pattern and processes of spatial change are comprehensively reviewed in the various chapters of *The Urban and Regional Transformation of Britain* edited by Goddard and Champion (1983). More detailed analysis can be found in Fothergill and Gudgin (1982) *Unequal Growth: urban and regional employment change in the UK*. From a different perspective, *The Anatomy of Job Loss: the how, why and where of employment decline* by Massey and Meegan (1982) and *Spatial Divisions of Labour: social structures and the geography of production* by Massey (1984) provide insights into the restructuring of employment and its spatial consequences.

4

Urban unemployment

Mass unemployment in Britain is largely an urban problem. Chapter 1 described the economic plight of the cities and the relationship between urbanisation and mass unemployment. In the inner areas of the conurbations and large cities unemployment is much higher than the national average and in some localities within these cities between one-third and one-half of the labour force are out of work. Yet, even in the depths of the recession, some local economies managed to retain their relative economic buoyancy, most notably small towns and rural areas and suburban areas in the south of England.

Such a pattern might seem self-evident given the evidence of massive employment decline in the metropolitan economies which was examined in the previous chapter. However, job losses need not, and according to the competitive market perspective will not, necessarily lead to increased unemployment if the labour market can adjust to the changes in the level and pattern of labour demand. Such adjustments have evidently not yet taken place or have been of an insufficent order of magnitude. This chapter is concerned with the issue of why urban unemployment has increased to the extent that it has, and begins by considering the relationship between urban unemployment and labour market processes, structures and economic change. The subsequent focus of attention is the explanation of the severe unemployment problems of the metropolitan labour markets and the differences in unemployment rates which exist between and within urban labour markets.

The measurement of unemployment

In principle, unemployment relates to those people who are not at work, who want or seek a job, are capable of work, and are available for work. In practice it is not possible to be quite so precise because workers vary in their degree of attachment to the labour force. Equally, it is not always unambiguously clear when a person can be regarded as having a job (e.g. part-time and voluntary work). In reality an operational definition of unemployment is largely a matter of convention and the constraints of available data.

The main sources of information on unemployment are administrative records relating to the unemployment benefit and social security system and a variety of censuses and surveys. Although unemployment is measured in both the General Household Survey and the Labour Force Survey, it is the Census of Population which is most useful to the urban analyst and details of unemployment rates can be obtained for any spatial area from enumeration district upwards. Unfortunately the decennial nature of the census limits its use to cross-section and long-term trend analysis. In the UK the 'official' unemployment figures are compiled by the Department of Employment on a monthly basis as the by-product of its administration of National Insurance Unemployment Benefit. The monthly count consists of all claimants of benefit registered at unemployment benefit offices, although certain categories such as the temporarily stopped and students claiming benefit during vacations are not counted in the total. The computerised system of record-keeping (the Joint Unemployment and Vacancy Operating System, or JUVOS) enables monthly totals of registered unemployment to be calculated with more detailed cross-analysis of unemployment by sex, age and duration on a quarterly basis. Of particular interest to the urban economist is the fact that the JUVOS unemployment records are indexed by a number of codes relating to different spatial entities. By using the postcode in the address of claimants, it is possible to compute the numbers unemployed in any spatial grouping, such as local employment office areas, groups of interdependent areas known as travel-to-work areas (TTWAs), counties and local government districts and even parliamentary constituencies. As the source of the postcode is the claimant's home address, the measurement of unemployment is related systematically to the place of residence of the unemployed. Additional information on the last occupation of the unemployed is available from registrations at Job Centres but these relate only to a proportion of the unemployed and in any case do not correspond to the spatial areas for which unemployment totals are computed.

The official unemployment figures almost certainly under-estimate the true level of unemployment. Prior to October 1982 when the JUVOS system was introduced, the monthly count was based on the returns of local employment offices and career offices. Registrations at these offices consisted not only of those claiming benefit (for whom registration was compulsory) but also non-claimants who registered in order to make use of the employment service. The change to the JUVOS count at benefit offices excluded all such non-claimants from the official total of unemployment; a comparison between the two systems in October 1982 showed that 246,000 had been excluded from the count by the new system. In addition to the registered (at a Job Centre) uncounted unemployed, there is an additional amount of unemployment which is unregistered and this is often referred to as 'hidden unemployment'. This is likely to consist of workers who are not entitled to, or have exhausted their entitlement to, benefits as well as workers whose attachment to the labour force is weak. Married women provide examples of both categories as do young entrants and workers over retirement age. The unemployed who are briefly out of work between jobs will also not be included. It has been suggested (Wood 1972) that the short-term unemployed, who are briefly between jobs, should not be counted in the number unemployed and neither should other categories such as occupational pen-sioners, the 'unemployables' or fraudulent claimants. Details of this debate can be found in Miller and Wood (1982), Garside (1980), Thatcher (1976) or Hughes (1975).

Despite the shortcomings of the official unemployment statistics, it is probably the case that more is known about unemployment than any other aspect of urban labour markets. Many local authorities make extensive use of such information for monitoring local economic conditions (Hasluck 1982), partly because of the easy availability of these data but also because of the centrality of unemployment as a target for local economic policy.

Unemployment and labour market structure

In a perfectly competitive labour market, unemployment would exist only as a temporary phenomenon. In this idealised economic environment labour demand would always just equal labour supply, a situation brought about and maintained by a series of instantaneous adjustments. In the event of shifts in supply or demand, changes in the level and structure of wages and, in the longer term, a combination of occupational and geographical mobility would ensure that full employment was maintained.

In fact labour markets, as Chapter 2 showed, exhibit many deviations from the conditions necessary for perfect competition and these inevitably lead to the existence of some persistent unemployment. The main imperfections inhibiting the achievement of full employment are:

1. *A lack of knowledge by workers and employers.* Since neither workers nor jobs are identical, information is required in order to distinguish between them. This frequently involves a period of search during which jobs are left vacant and workers remain unemployed.

2. *Adjustment costs.* Accepting a job offer or filling a vacancy may involve costs such as training, recruitment and, most important, the opportunity cost of accepting a poor job offer or filling a vacancy with a less productive worker when this precludes better choices at a later date. The importance of adjustment costs is inversely related to the expected duration of the job and will be more important for temporary or seasonal work.

3. *Wage rigidity.* Labour market adjustments will not occur if wages are inflexible and do not fall in response to market pressures. Wage inflexibility may arise from money illusion, trade unions or a worker's concern with maintaining differentials. While this form of adjustment may, in principle, reduce unemployment in a single submarket it is not so obvious that it will have this effect when generalised over the whole labour market because of the importance of feedbacks between wages and the level of demand for labour (see Ch. 2).

4. *Rigidity in the wage structure.* In a competitive market some pattern of wage differentials will emerge at which the demand and supply of each type of labour is equal. If institutional processes maintain a structure of wages which is different from this competitive one, then there may be excess demand in some sectors and excess supply (unemployment) in others. Most attention has focused on occupational wage structures, but spatial wage structures

may also be important. If wages are determined by national processes involving trade unions or wages councils, then spatial imbalances in the wages structure may be a possibility.

5.   *Barriers to mobility.* Occupational or geographical mobility would produce the re-allocation of labour required to eliminate unemployment. Barriers to the entry of occupations or the costs of mobility will prevent adjustment from taking place on a scale sufficient to achieve this competitive result.

The existence of these imperfections will mean that adjustments are either slow or do not fully occur. Even if there is a long-run tendency for competitive forces to drive the labour market towards full employment the market will be in a continual state of change and some unemployment will exist at all times. Accepting that some unemployment is inevitable because of the existence of imperfect adjustment does not necessarily lead to a rejection of the competitive ideal. On the contrary, some economists and politicians have seen the strengthening of competitive processes as the most effective way of reducing unemployment. They would advocate policies designed to increase wage flexibility and to promote mobility. Trade unions and wages councils are often singled out as two important institutional impediments to competitive adjustment. On the other hand it may be argued that the imperfections of the labour market are so great that policies should be designed to replace the market altogether and substitute some other process or at least to intervene in the market to a very considerable extent. The alternative perspectives on policy are considered in the next chapter.

Types of unemployment

It may be useful to distinguish between types of unemployment. There are numerous taxonomies from which to choose, some based on an analysis of cause, others on policy prescriptions, and yet others concerned with empirically observable characteristics of the unemployed. There is probably no single best categorisation but it is difficult to improve on the conventional distinction between frictional, structural and demand-deficient unemployment, especially since each type can be associated with one or more of the market imperfections identified above.

Frictional unemployment

This type of unemployment arises because of a lack of instantaneous adjustment to the turnover of jobs and workers which takes place in all labour markets. Firms close or shed labour while others expand and new firms are created. Workers quit jobs or are fired; some retire while others enter the labour force for the first or second time. The requirements of firms change as they adopt new techniques of production or switch to new products. Workers' preferences for jobs and their skills also change. The result of these changes is that there are large gross flows into and out of employment. The main stocks and flows in the labour market are shown diagrammatically in Fig. 4.1.

Even during the worst of the 1980–82 recession the national average rate of job turnover in manufacturing was over 14 per cent per annum (although discharges were occurring at the rate of over 22 per cent, hence the massive and rapid reduction in employment during this period). As long as some finite time is taken to find a job during which the worker is without work, then unemployment will exist even if the number of jobs is equal to the number of workers.

The main reasons for delay in matching workers with jobs are imperfect knowledge of job opportunities and the cost of adjustment. Several types of informational unemployment can be distinguished. The first is search unemployment which arises where an individual chooses not to accept a job offer but searches for a better one. Reder (1969) represents the worker as making repeated searches among employers until a wage offer at least as good as some reservation wage is discovered. The amount of such search depends upon the distribution of wage offers and the reservation wage (which depends upon the costs of search). Much searching will be carried out while in employment but in some circumstances it may be more efficient to leave a current job in order to engage in full-time searching while unemployed. Over a long period it might be expected that workers would learn by experience and engage in less search activity, but permanently high levels of search activity can be expected where a large proportion of the labour force are new entrants or if the rate of job turnover is rapidly rendering previous experience obsolete.

Another form of frictional unemployment is waiting un-employment (Phelps 1972). In this instance the individual is faced

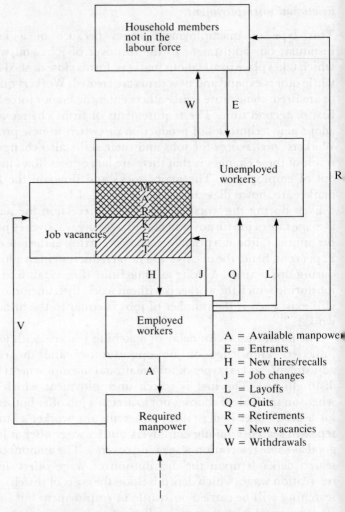

Fig. 4.1 Major stocks and flows in the labour market
Source: Hasluck 1982

with a choice between a job at the present time or a different job in the future. A job at the present time may be rejected if it significantly reduces the prospects of a better job at some future date. Examples are mainly drawn from fields where there are substantial variations in the demand for labour such as seasonal work, professional services, or indeed any situation where an individual will feel obligated to their employer or wishes to avoid being labelled as unreliable. A similar type, referred to as queue unemployment, relates to situations where wages are institutionally determined and differ between two markets. The high-wage sector will attract an excess supply of labour who will queue for the better paid jobs. Workers will contrast the present value of their expected income streams from the two markets, one with some possibility of unemployment but high prospective wages, the other with low wages but a certainty of employment. As long as there is a wage differential between the markets, a queue of unemployed workers will exist especially if individuals differ in their attitudes to risk.

Frictional unemployment is likely to be affected by the level of aggregate economic activity. As demand rises so too will the distribution of wage offers and the frequency of intermittent job offers; search activity and waiting will therefore be of shorter duration. Offsetting this, there may be an increase in the number of new or re-entrants into the labour force and an increase in the volume of voluntary quits. Changes in institutional, social or technological factors will also affect the level of frictional unemployment through their effect upon labour market turnover and the efficiency of search. Localities with a high turnover, perhaps because of a concentration of seasonal work or secondary labour markets, will have a relatively high level of frictional unemployment as compared to some other area with a more stable workforce.

Structural unemployment

Structural unemployment is in many respects a more serious and longer lasting version of frictional unemployment. Whereas the latter arises from a temporal mismatch between demand and supply within a labour market, the former relates to more serious mismatch of the structure of demand and supply between labour markets.

Shifts in the structure of labour demand across submarkets arise for a variety of reasons including changes in the composition of final demand, technological change or changes in the spatial location of economic activity. They result in a new pattern of labour demands relative to the existing pattern of labour supply. There will be extra demand for some types of labour and in some locations, but for others demand will decline creating excess supply and unemployment. Such change is taking place all the time (albeit at a differing pace) and there will always be some level of unemployment during the period of intervening adjustment. Although this sounds much like frictional unemployment the adjustments required to accommodate the changing pattern of relative labour demands go far beyond the mere acquisition of information. There is a need for change in wage structures and the movement of labour from one submarket to another. These adjustments are substantially more difficult to achieve and structural unemployment is a more serious and long-term problem.

One reason why adjustment may not take place is the relative rigidity of the wage structure. Lower wages in markets where unemployment is high might lead to the substitution of unemployed workers for more expensive ones or the location of new enterprises in low-wage localities while increasing the demand for labour through product market adjustments induced by price changes. The scale of the wage changes required to achieve these results is unclear as it would depend upon a host of factors such as the elasticity of substitution between labour and capital and between types of occupation and skills, the price elasticity of demand for products, the proportion of costs accounted for by labour while the inflexibility of relative money wages is well known. While there appears to be little relationship between the level of unemployment and the level of earnings in a locality, some association has been found between changes in the unemployment manual workers and changes in their earnings. Counties with rapid unemployment growth experienced a relative decline in earnings (Bentham 1985). Although this appears to lend support to the competitive view of the labour market, it must be noted that the relative earnings decline has been insufficient to prevent unemployment from rising rapidly in metropolitan areas and the extent of the reduction in earnings required to do so may be socially and politically unattainable.

An alternative form of adjustment to wage change is mobility of labour. If skills are readily transferable between occupations then the unemployed, after a period of search, will switch from declining occupations to expanding ones. Such mobility will be limited when it requires the acquisition of additional skills through investment in training and further education. Geographical mobility may be required if the spatial structure of the labour market is changing. Both geographical mobility and retraining involve more substantial costs and information than is the case for search within a single occupation and local labour market. At the very least this will mean a greater delay in adjustment and for older workers these investments may not be economically viable. Compounding this situation are the barriers to occupational change which arise from internal labour markets. Firms erect barriers to mobility in the form of seniority rules and limited ports of entry in an attempt to reduce the risk of losing their investments in trained labour. These barriers may prevent or severely limit labour market adjustment.

The access to jobs of some workers is limited because their personal characteristics place them at the end of the job queue. Although in most cases capable of work, this hard-core may remain unemployed because from the employers perspective they are not qualified for jobs. Such workers may be permanently sick or disabled, or have work records suggesting unreliability. Groups against whom employers discriminate may also be placed in this category, e.g. ethnic minorities or older workers. In each case the individual has a much reduced probability of finding work and a considerably reduced range of job opportunities.

The scale of structural unemployment is likely to be influenced by the level of aggregate economic activity. At low levels of demand the lack of jobs in general rather than their structure is most crucial but as demand increases structural unemployment will become more important as bottlenecks emerge in production and shortages of labour exist alongside unemployment. Sustained high levels of demand may reduce structural unemployment in the long term if employers lower hiring standards in an attempt to fill vacancies, or if relative wage changes can be achieved by changes in the general level of money wages.

Demand-deficient unemployment

Most economists would accept that a fall in the aggregate level of spending on goods and services will lead to more unemployment in the short term. Rather more controversy surrounds the question of whether such unemployment can persist and, if so, for what reasons. The issues are complex and this discussion provides no more than a brief outline of the competing perspectives (for a more detailed discussion see Hughes and Perlman 1984; Greenhalgh *et al.* 1983).

Demand-deficient unemployment is fundamentally a Keynesian notion. The central proposition is that deficient expenditure on goods and services will lead, through the derived demand for labour, to levels of employment which are insufficient to fully employ the current labour force and that there is no market adjustment to generate a return to full employment. This situation is illustrated in Fig. 4.2.

If labour demand depends on the real wage and on expected output and sales, then a fall in expenditure, sales, and output will reduce labour requirements from N_f to N_i. At the prevailing wage of W_1 unemployment will be equal to the difference between the new, lower employment level and the previous full employment level (distance A–B which equals N_f-N_i). Such unemployment is often termed involuntary unemployment since the unemployed would be prepared to work at the prevailing wage rate but are unable to do so because of a general lack of employment opportunities. Firms in this situation are in disequilibrium in the sense that the marginal productivity of their workforce exceeds the

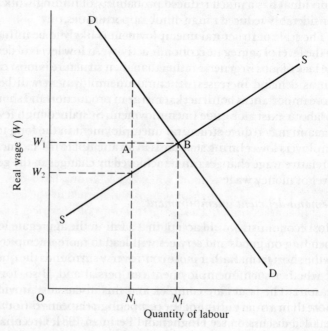

Fig. 4.2

current wage, but any firm attempting to expand will find its inventories increasing and will be forced to cut production again as long as the aggregate level of expenditure remains unchanged.

On the face of it, this explanation of unemployment appears to depend upon wage rigidity to explain its persistence. The neoclassical perspective argues that with high levels of unemployment, competition will drive down real wages to W_2 at which level demand-deficient unemployment is eliminated (although it is important to note that this result is achieved by driving marginal workers out of the labour force). According to this view, if such unemployment persists it must be because money wage rates are not flexible enough. Conventionally such wage rigidity has been explained in terms of institutional factors such as the activities of trade unions and governments who, through collective bargaining or wages councils, create minimum money wage levels which prevent real wages from falling. More modern versions of the neoclassical perspective see short-term real wage inflexibility as the result of incorrect or inappropriate wage expectations (Phelps *et al.* 1972). Individual workers will be unaware of any reductions in demand and will maintain reservation wages at too high a level, rejecting jobs more frequently, and search and wait employment will increase (Lucas 1981). After some period of time has elapsed, wage expectations will be revised downwards and, as this happens, unemployment will fall. The most significant aspect of this version of the neoclassical perspective is that it denies the existence of demand-deficient unemployment in the long term. A reduction in demand will increase unemployment only as long as erroneous wage expectations prevail. The more rapidly expectations are adjusted, the more rapid the elimination of demand-deficient unemployment. All that will remain when expectations have been fully adjusted is a level of unemployment determined by the prevailing level of market imperfections, the frictions of imperfect information and adjustment costs and the effects of random change. This basic irreducible core of unemployment has been termed the 'natural rate' of unemployment (Friedman 1968).

Even if wage flexibility were possible in the long term it is not clear that this will inevitably reduce demand-deficient unemployment. If firms cut prices and money wages at the same time then the real wage change may be small or even non-existent. Keynesians would argue that there is no positive link between wage reductions and aggregate demand. On the contrary, a fall in wages can lead to further reductions in aggregate demand (as was argued in Ch. 2). In Fig. 4.2, a reduction in the real wage to W_2 will not increase employment, it merely reduces labour supply. Employment only increases if aggregate demand increases, and this does not require a reduction in the wage level.

The real significance of the debate about the cause of unemployment arises in respect of policy; Keynesians would argue that the expansion of demand is a prerequisite for reducing unemployment, whereas neoclassical inspired policy-makers would see this as unnecessary and seek instead to reduce the underlying natural rate of unemployment by policies designed to reduce labour market imperfections and promote wage flexibility.

Disaggregating unemployment

It may be useful for local policy-makers to be able to identify the size and relative importance of different types of unemployment in their local labour market. An analytical construction which provides the basis for this is the unemployment–vacancy relationship (the *UV* curve). The derivation of the *UV* curve can be seen by considering the labour market illustrated diagrammatically by Fig. 4.3. Because of frictions and imperfections of the labour market, some jobs remain unfilled and employment is less than demand by an amount equal to the number of unfilled vacancies. For similar reasons, part of labour supply will fail to obtain employment and remain frictionally unemployed. In equilibrium, at wage rate W_e, demand equals supply but employment is only equal to W_eB with vacancies and unemployment both equal to distance BA. At a higher wage, W_1, unfilled vacancies are GE but unemployment has increased substantially and is the difference between employment (W_1G) and labour supply, the distance GF. Similarly, at wage W_2, employment is equal to W_2H, frictional unemployment is HC and unfilled vacancies are equal to the difference between demand and employment, distance HD. The curve $\overline{EE}$ represents the locus of all feasible employment levels.

Consideration of Fig. 4.3 suggests that in periods of excess demand a low level of frictional unemployment will coexist with a high level of unfilled vacancies. When there is deficient demand in the labour market there will be high unemployment and a small number of unfilled vacancies. Clearly, the levels of unemployment

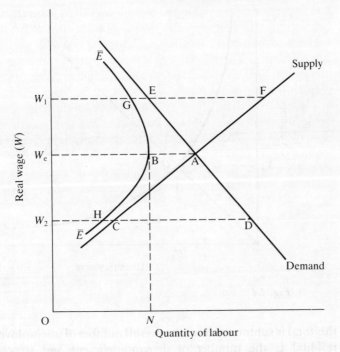

Fig. 4.3

and vacancies are inversely related to one another in the manner mapped out by the *UV* curve in Fig. 4.4. When demand equals supply, unemployment equals vacancies and therefore point Q on the *UV* curve and the corresponding levels of unemployment and vacancies (U_1 and V_1 respectively) represent a situation of market equilibrium. Unemployment above the level of U_1 is the result of deficient demand.

The UV curve can be used to identify different types of unemployment by considering the relationship between local unemployment and unfilled vacancies for different occupations. Frictional unemployment exists where a local unemployed worker is matched by, and qualified to fill, a local vacancy. If vacancies exceed the number of unemployed in an occupation then all unemployment is frictional, otherwise the number of frictionally unemployed equals the number of vacancies. Adding together the frictional unemployment in each occupation gives the total number of frictionally unemployed in the local economy and if

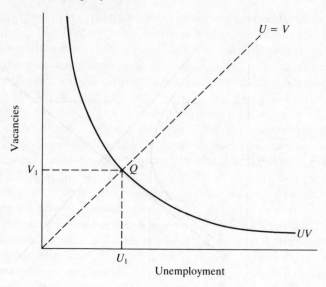

Fig. 4.4

this total is subtracted from the overall number of unemployed, the residual is the number of demand-deficient and structurally unemployed.

To identify the structural component, occupations are considered where vacancies exceeds the number of unemployed. These are known as structurally overemployed counterparts (or SOCs) and it is the existence of these SOCs that signal the presence of structural unemployment. A structural imbalance can be said to exist if local unemployed workers in one occupation are matched by local vacancies (net of frictional unemployment) in another. There is as much structural unemployment as there are local net vacancies and this component of unemployment can be estimated by adding together the 'surplus' vacancies in all local *SOCs*.

Having estimated the frictional and structural components, any remaining unemployment must be local demand-deficient unemployment. This could have been calculated directly by subtracting the total number of vacancies from the total number of unemployed, provided that *U* is greater than *V*. Such local demand-deficient unemployment represents the number of local workers who are not matched by local vacancies and thus the net local deficiency of jobs. From a national perspective some of this unemployment will be structural because vacancies exist in other parts of the country for which the local unemployed are wrongly located but qualified (geographical structural unemployment) or unqualified (mixed geographical and occupational structural unemployment) but from the local perspective the reason for such unemployment is simply a lack of jobs.

In practice any attempts to identify the components of local unemployment using *UV* analysis face the difficulty of obtaining accurate vacancy data for local labour markets as well as technical problems relating to the definition of occupations. The technique also produces results which are extremely sensitive to the level of national economic activity, claiming that structural unemployment is zero when unemployment exceeds vacancies in every occupation. An alternative approach involves estimating the relationship between local and national unemployment and the sensitivity of the former to the latter. The local demand-deficient rate of unemployment is equal to the difference between the current national rate and an estimated national equilibrium rate of unemployment, multiplied by a factor representing the sensitivity of local unemployment to national unemployment. This technique does not disaggregate unemployment to the same degree as the *UV* method and it is an interesting question as to how the equilibrium rate should be calculated (Taylor and Bradley 1983).

Spatial variations in unemployment

Variations in unemployment rates between localities may arise because of:

(a)   spatial variations in the level of labour demand;

(b)   spatial variations in labour supply;

(c)   structural and institutional factors which determine the extent and speed of adjustment, the degree of mismatch and the amount of search.

The level of local labour demand may decline (relative to other areas) because of a cyclical reduction in national aggregate demand, structural change in the economy or as the result of some more localised set of circumstances. Although a decline in demand will raise unemployment in the short run, differences in unemployment rates between areas will only persist in the absence of adjustment. These adjustments initially involve wage and participation changes, but in the long run they will take the form of mobility between labour markets. If adjustment is slow, differences in unemployment will persist. Similarly, changes in labour supply can also raise unemployment. Local population growth, increased activity rates, or net migration may raise labour supply relative to demand. Again, the resulting unemployment differences will persist only if adjustments are slow.

The interrelationships of demand, supply, migration and unemployment may be illustrated by the following simple model. The change in the unemployment rate of an area (ΔU_i) will depend upon the local rates of change of the economically active population (ΔL_i), employment (ΔE_i) and net migration (m_i), (for simplicity, commuting is ignored). The rates of change of the local labour force and employment can each be expressed as the sum of a national rate of change plus a local deviation from the national average:

$$\Delta L_i = \Delta L_n + l_i \quad \text{and} \quad \Delta E_i = \Delta E_n + e_i$$

where the subscript n denotes nation change and l and e are local deviations from the national trend. This can be written as the identity:

$$\Delta U_i = (\Delta L_n + l_i) - (\Delta E_n + e_i) + m_i.$$

National unemployment will change at a rate determined by the difference between the change in the labour force and employment (if net migration is zero), hence:

$$\Delta U_n = \Delta L_n - \Delta E_n$$

and differential unemployment growth in the local economy is therefore

$$\Delta(U_i - U_n) = l_i - e_i - m_i.$$

This identity suggests that an urban area may experience above-average unemployment growth because of a higher than average growth in the labour force, an employment growth rate below the national rate, or positive net migration. Adjustments may occur if m_i and l_i are related to $\Delta(U_i - U_n)$; that is, above-average unemployment growth may lead to discouraged worker effects or net out-migration.

In addition to differences in the level of demand deficiency there may also be differing degrees of labour market mismatch from one urban area to another. In part these differences may simply be another aspect of changes in demand since some groups of workers may be more vulnerable to reductions in demand than others; unskilled workers may be less likely to be hoarded by employers (Oi 1962) or subject to intensified competition by unemployed skilled workers who displace them from jobs at the bottom of the job hierarchy (Reder 1955). Spatial processes can also result in labour market mismatch and differences in structural unemployment between urban areas. Unbalanced industrial decline or technological change in production may cause the demand for some occupations and skills to decline more than others. In particular, the decline of manufacturing and the growth of the service sector together with the gradual de-skilling of the labour force and the increased demand for female and part-time workers have produced differential shifts in labour demand. On the supply side, differential patterns of migration and labour force growth have also been responsible for creating a mismatch between the spatial pattern of labour demand and supply. Again it must be noted that unemployment differences between areas will only persist as long as adjustments are not forthcoming. Studies of occupational mobility have drawn attention to such factors as age and obsolete qualifications as being factors inhibiting occupational change (Metcalf and Nickell 1981) and the extent to which a local mismatch continues may be a reflection of the personal characteristics of the labour force insofar as these characteristics are associated with a lack of geographical or occupational mobility.

Two other factors may also affect the level of frictional unemployment in a local labour market. The characteristics of the labour force may affect search behaviour as the scale and duration of search varies markedly between groups as do the processes of search and their efficiency. Institutional factors can also affect the amount of search – for instance, the distribution of wage offers may be influenced by the size and industrial structure of local firms – while search costs may vary with the geography of the locality.

Unemployment and urban size

The size of an urban labour market and its density of jobs may affect the efficiency at matching workers to jobs. As city size increases the number of vacant jobs is larger and this may raise the probability of receiving acceptable job offers and thus reduce search-related unemployment. Alternatively, the increased range of job vacancies may make search more profitable and the spatial frictions of a large city may reduce the likelihood of finding an acceptable job offer. The relationship between city size and unemployment can only be established empirically.

Chapter 1 suggested, on the basis of Fig. 1.4, that there is a very marked positive relationship between city size and unemployment. The ranking of urban areas by size and the ranking of male unemployment rates is more similar than can be explained by random chance. More systematic investigations have confirmed the existence of a positive relationship between size and unemployment for males although the reverse situation appears to hold for females. Vipond (1974) studied 155 cities and found that a ten-fold increase in population raised male unemployment by about 0.73 per cent and reduced female unemployment by 0.46 per cent. Similar results were found by Sirmans (1977), but Evans and Richardson (1980), while finding city size and unemployment to be positively related in a cross-sectional study of 123 British urban areas, were unable to detect such a relationship when the sample was restricted to 78 self-contained urban labour markets. They attributed the difference in results to distortions introduced into the sample by treating the inner-urban areas as labour markets separate from their associated suburbs.

Much stronger statistical support for the positive relationship between male unemployment and urban size is provided by Burridge and Gordon (1981). They found that population size and density were significantly related to an urban areas unemployment rates; a ten-fold increase in the population of an urban labour market was estimated to increase the unemployment rate by an extra 1 per cent. Burridge and Gordon link job search to migration by suggesting that the gains to search are, or at least are perceived to be, greatest in large urban areas. Such areas will attract migrant workers, a phenomenon which they describe as the Dick Whittington Syndrome. This high inward migration coupled with above-average search activity raises the level of frictional unemployment. This explanation is supported by Taylor and Bradley (1983) who found that the size of locality was positively related to variations in non-cyclical unemployment in the 28 TTWAs of the North West region.

Differences between cities

Although urban size and frictional unemployment appear to be positively related, it is unlikely that such unemployment represents more than a fraction of the total difference between localities. Additional variation may arise because of differences in local demand deficiency or occupational and spatial mismatch.

The demand for labour

It has been argued that the most important single source of differences between urban labour markets is differences in the level of excess demand for labour (Cheshire 1979). Owen *et al.* (1984) found that the pattern of job shortfalls (or surpluses) was almost the opposite of the pattern of employment growth, which suggests an association between unemployment and demand deficiency. In addition there is also evidence of a relationship between labour market size and demand deficiency. London, the conurbations and the urban areas dominated by conurbations all suffer from the worst employment performances in their respective regions, while small towns and rural areas have experienced employment growth and job surpluses.

Although there is clearly a very strong relationship between employment decline and local demand deficiency, the relationship between employment decline and unemployment growth is weaker. This is because local economies may adjust to demand deficiency by changes in migration or economic activity rates. This suggests that the main urban areas would have experienced even greater unemployment had it not been for these adjustments. Unemployment in an urban economy will be positively related to local demand deficiency (which is equivalent to employment decline if the local labour force does not change) and negatively related to factors which affect the accessibility of the market and the mobility of the local labour force.

These determinants of urban unemployment have been examined by Burridge and Gordon (1981). In their model, urban unemployment depends on the difference between labour demand growth and the natural growth of labour supply, levels of unemployment in other areas, and factors which effect the attractiveness of the area to migrants. The frictions of space and accessibility are taken into account by defining some variables in terms of their 'potential' – that is, weighting their values in other areas inversely by their distance. Thus local unemployment would be expected to be positively related to its 'unemployment rate potential' (the spatial average of unemployment in other areas) because demand deficiency in other areas will spill over into the local economy via migration and commuting. Local unemployment will reflect the difference between local demand and supply to an extent which depends upon the accessibility of the locality. The accessibility of a labour market will depend upon a number of factors including distance, the characteristics of its labour force and area characteristics such as size, environment and so on.

Applying the model to an analysis of male unemployment in British metropolitan labour markets, Burridge and Gordon found strong empirical support for their hypotheses. A significant statistical relationship was found between the unemployment rate and measures of demand deficiency, labour force characteristics, and area characteristics. The skill and age structures of an area affected unemployment and these variables were interpreted as measuring the potential mobility of the resident labour force. Earnings differentials between labour markets appeared to be weakly related to unemployment in a small but positive manner. Although migrants were attracted by earnings differences they appeared to be much more responsive to unemployment differentials and employment opportunities. The most striking conclusion of the study is the very open nature of local labour markets. It was estimated that to secure a continuing reduction in local unemployment of one person requires the generation of five additional jobs per year in the average labour market. In more accessible labour markets even greater employment growth would be required to achieve the same outcome.

It can be concluded from the evidence that much of the high unemployment of metropolitan labour markets is to be explained by local demand deficiency with the spatial characteristics of the area and the composition of its labour force affecting the relationship between the two. The reason for the demand deficiency is the massive decline in employment which has occurred in these large urban areas. The previous chapter reviewed the explanations of this decline which is partly a reflection of national employment decline and the industrial structure of the metropolitan areas but primarily the result of processes which concentrate employment decline in the large urban areas. It is therefore no surprise to find that there is little association between unemployment in an area and its industrial structure (Owen and Gillespie 1980; Taylor and Bradley 1983). Townsend (1983) has argued, in contrast, that counties which experienced an above-average increase in unemployment between 1970 and 1981 were the areas with an above-average proportion of employment in manufacturing. This pointed to the 1979–81 recession being different in kind from previous reductions in economic activity. According to this view, recent unemployment growth in the metropolitan areas is a reflection of national recession operating spatially through the differences in industrial structure. Nevertheless, whether local demand deficiency has its origins in a decline in national economic activity or is the product of a spatial restructuring of labour demand, this does not change the conclusion that the primary reason for urban unemployment is a lack of demand for labour.

Labour force characteristics

An alternative approach to the analysis of unemployment has involved the examination of the characteristics of the unemployed or the labour force in an area. Although a study of the former may reveal important insights into the vulnerability of different groups in the economy, it does little to indicate the causes of unemployment because vulnerable groups will tend to be over-represented among the unemployed as economic conditions deteriorate (Cheshire 1973, 1979). However, the composition of the labour force may exert an influence upon local unemployment rates. If unemployment rates vary between workers, either because of differing degrees of vulnerability or because of different search behaviour, then areas with concentrations of unemployment-prone groups will tend to experience above-average unemployment rates. The characteristics likely to affect unemployment rates include skill and occupational class, age, sex, marital status, family size and race. A detailed discussion of the reasons for expecting an association between each of these characteristics and unemployment is deferred until a later section dealing with vulnerable groups.

Models of urban unemployment which emphasise the characteristics of the labour force are frequently represented as being supply side models. This interpretation is false; the models are really reduced-form models in which the simultaneous interaction of labour demand and supply establish differing rates of unemployment for the various groups in the labour force. This means that the interpretation of any association between unemployment and labour force characteristics requires considerable caution because the correlation may be consistent with either supply factors or demand deficiency. As an example of the problem, consider the study of urban unemployment by Metcalf (1975) who in a study of male unemployment in English county boroughs during 1971 found that the proportion of a town's labour force which was unskilled and semi-skilled was positively related to its unemployment rate. An increase in the proportion of unskilled by eight percentage points would raise the average unemployment rate by one percentage point. This led Metcalf to suggest that upgrading the quality of labour supply through training would be an appropriate policy as a means of reducing unemployment. This conclusion was reached despite earlier arguments that demand side factors such as differential hoarding and occupational bumping down might cause unemployment to be relatively high among the unskilled. If this were so it is difficult to see how the acquisition of skills through training would reduce unemployment in the absence of an increase in local labour demand.

In addition to the proportion of unskilled in the labour force, Metcalf also found that the proportion of elderly workers (over 54 years of age) was associated with higher unemployment while the reverse was true the proportion of married males and immigrants. Similar results have been found by Vipond (1974), Sirmans (1977) and others. Metcalf did attempt to allow for variations in demand between towns by considering the proportion of employment in manufacturing and a variable which measured regional demand deficiency. The latter was a substantial influence upon unemployment while employment in manufacturing exerted a small but significant effect (strangely this produced a negative effect but this was a reflection of the relatively good performance of manufacturing between 1966 and 1971). These two variables again underline the importance of the level of demand for labour.

Studies which link unemployment with labour force characteristics face the problem of inferring the direction of causation. It is possible that over a period of time the characteristics of the labour force are determined by the level of unemployment, and not the other way round. Possible sources of simultaneity are differential migration in which the most mobile, the skilled and the young leave high unemployment areas. This increases the proportion of unskilled and elderly workers in the labour force. Similarly, there may be a tendency to delay marriage when unemployment is high so that the proportion of single persons will increase. Simultaneity may explain the puzzle of the negative association noted by Metcalf between immigrants and unemployment; most studies of ethnic minorities suggest that they experience a high rate of unemployment. This paradox can be explained if immigrants tend to locate in towns offering the best employment opportunities (i.e. having the lowest unemployment) but once settled in a town they nevertheless experience relatively high unemployment.

On balance, the characteristics approach to the analysis of differences in unemployment between cities is not particularly helpful. As will be seen in the next section there is a stronger argument for considering the characteristics of the resident labour force when considering the pattern of unemployment within urban areas. Evans and Richardson (1980) have argued that Metcalf's results reflect a mixing together of inter- and intra-urban differences in unemployment because of his use of data relating to county boroughs. As boroughs are political units rather than economic entities they rarely correspond to a self-contained labour market. Evans and Richardson re-estimated Metcalf's equations using similar variables, first for a similar sample of urban areas and then for subsets of 'more' and 'most' self-contained labour markets. Similar results to those of Metcalf were obtained from the large sample, but the associations weakened when the more self-contained areas were examined while there was no relationship between personal characteristics and unemployment when the most self-contained markets were considered.

Local variations in unemployment

Explanations of local variations in unemployment rates tend to differ according to the role which they afford to competitive processes in the urban labour market. According to one view, local labour markets will be sufficiently competitive for job opportunities to be equalised over the area. If unemployment remains high in one district as compared to another it is the result of the patterns of residence among the labour force. Alternatively, it has been argued that the existence of frictions will prevent perfect adjustment from taking place even within a local labour market. In this case spatial factors relating to the structure of the urban area will be important influences on the distribution of unemployment within a town.

The competitive view maintains that a fall in labour demand in one part of the city will initially raise unemployment in the immediate vicinity, but will induce additional commuting and some residential relocations as workers seek jobs in neighbouring districts. Local demand deficiency will be dissipated and the unemployment rate will be equalised across the urban areas. In so far as workers cannot compete, the unemployment differences will remain, but these barriers to mobility are seen as relating mainly to occupation rather than space. Rates will vary between occupational groups but not for workers of a similar skill. The reason for unemployment differences is to be found in the operation of urban housing markets. Residential segregation, by class and by tenure, means that the composition of the workforce in different parts of the city is not uniform. In some districts there may be a concentration of residents who possess characteristics associated with relatively high unemployment. These areas will experience above-average unemployment rates but this reflects the nature of the resident labour force rather than labour market disequilibrium in the district. The interesting implication of this is that the provision of jobs specifically in the high unemployment district may have little effect upon unemployment while the unemployed may benefit from a general expansion of jobs wherever these occur within the city.

The empirical evidence lends some support to the competitive model. Evans (1980) has shown that the rate of unemployment among similar occupational groups was more or less equal in all Greater London boroughs (in 1971) even though unemployment rates were inversely related to skill. Metcalf and Richardson (1980), also examining London, showed that most of the variation in male unemployment between boroughs could be explained by differences in the composition of the labour force. Boroughs with a large resident unskilled male labour force or an above-average proportion of single males would experience relatively high unemployment rates. Family size was also positively related to unemployment (this apparently perverse result might be explained by the operation of the social security system). The proportion of immigrants was found to be negatively related to unemployment in a borough and this acts as a reminder that the problem of simultaneity discussed in the previous section may still be relevant in the intra-urban context. Broadly similar results have been generated by later studies; Simpson (1982) found that the proportion of unskilled and semi-skilled and personal service workers together with marital status were positively related to male and female unemployment in Greater London. Male unemployment was also positively related to the proportion of elderly workers (55–64 years of age) and family size.

Although there can be no doubt that the individual characteristics of workers and the spatial pattern of residence are important determinants of the distribution of unemployment within the city, the competitive model rests upon the premise that mobility is frictionless both in terms of travel and the acquisition of information. Although surprisingly high levels of mobility and commuting can take place in and between labour markets, the degree of mobility varies substantially between social groups and over the economic cycle. This raises the possibility, for some workers at any rate, that spatial structure may be an additional source of unemployment differences within the city.

Spatial frictions are central to the so-called 'trapped worker' explanation of inner city unemployment. According to this hypothesis the high rates of unemployment in the inner city are linked to the process of population and employment decentralisation and the inability of some groups to participate in it. As employment declines in inner areas the most mobile workers will move to suburban residential locations while the least mobile are trapped in areas of declining job opportunities. Unskilled and low-income groups are least likely to be mobile because of the high relative costs of commuting or moving house. Housing tenure may also affect mobility, particularly for rented accommodation (both private and public). The 'trapped' hypothesis has come to be exemplified by the Inner Area Studies (Department of the Environment 1977) which emphasised the importance of these kinds of barriers to mobility in their explanations of high unemployment in Lambeth and Liverpool. The trapped hypothesis has been criticised both on theoretical grounds (Cheshire 1979) and on empirical grounds (Evans 1980). The explanation does seem to be too heavily dependent upon the specific processes of decentralisation and suburbanisation.

A more general approach suggests that the probability of

employment varies between locations depending the number of job opportunities available to residents. These in turn depend not just on the number of jobs in the locality but also on the number of accessible jobs elsewhere. The latter will vary from location to location and from one worker to another because of differences in the physical accessibility of jobs, the costs of commuting and the range of the information networks utilized. Physical accessibility will be affected by local transport networks and the differing propensities to use public or private transport for travel to work. The probability of unemployment in a locality will vary positively with its distance (as a proxy for spatial frictions) from the location of jobs. Since jobs are scattered all over urban areas, the density of jobs per worker might act as an approximation of the spatial pattern of job opportunities. Simpson (1982) found that the spatial pattern of job opportunities in Greater London did affect the unemployment rate of both men and women; the higher the number of jobs per resident the lower the unemployment rate after standardisation for differences in age, marital status and skill. Less skilled manual workers were much more responsive to variations in job opportunities than skilled manual and non-manual groups who were relatively insensitive to such variations. This suggests that the latter groups are relatively unconstrained in terms of their search over the urban economy while the former may have much more limited job horizons.

There is probably some scope for a limited trapped worker situation in which unskilled manual workers find that the number of job opportunities within their job search horizon is dramatically reduced for some reason (perhaps a large plant closure); however, it seems that for many other workers job search probably extends over most of the labour market. If this is so any differences in unemployment within urban areas will reflect variations in the composition of the labour force produced by the pattern of residential location.

The dynamics of unemployment

The examination of the levels and changes in the unemployment stock has diverted attention away from the fact that the labour market is in continuous state of turnover (refer back to Fig. 4.1). Consideration of the dynamic behaviour of these stocks and flows in the labour market has two advantages: it emphasises the variety of processes in the labour market and it enables a distinction to be made between inflows and outflows on the one hand, and the duration of unemployment on the other. In the first place, the inflow of workers into the stock of unemployment is made up of a number of components: workers laid off or made redundant; workers who voluntarily quit their jobs; workers who re-enter the labour force after a period of absence (e.g. married women); new entrants into the labour force (e.g. school-leavers or migrants); and unemployed persons who have not previously registered. These flows are the product of different labour market processes, and may be expected to be influenced by different sets of forces. The flow of workers who are laid off by employers will be affected by the level of local labour demand, redundancies and the processes of job turnover described in Chapter 3, whereas the flow of new entrants, especially school-leavers, is largely determined by demographic factors (although the timing of entry will vary according to economic conditions and individual circumstances). Un- fortunately, many of these aspects of the labour market remain undocumented and therefore empirical studies have tended to concentrate upon aggregate inflows rather than its component parts.

The stock of unemployment (U_t) is determined by the product of two forces, the inflow into unemployment (I_t) and the expected or mean duration of unemployment (D_t) i.e.

$$U_t = I_t \times D_t.$$

If U_t and I_t are known then the mean duration can be calculated thus:

$$D_t = U_t/I_t.$$

These identities show that a given stock of unemployment could result from a high inflow and short mean duration, a low inflow and long mean duration or some other combination. It also follows that when unemployment increases, this could have resulted from an increased inflow, an increased mean duration or both. In fact the most striking feature of unemployment inflows is their relative stability; in Great Britain the male monthly inflow rate has followed an almost constant trend throughout the 1970s and 1980s despite the massive increase in the number of unemployed males. Similar results have been found in local labour markets (Hasluck 1982). It seems that the main reason for rising unemployment has been increasing durations rather than increased inflows (female inflows have increased slightly but are still small in comparison to the changes in duration).

Although unemployment inflows are generally stable over time, there are marked differences in inflows and durations between local labour markets. Between 1976 and 1979 Liverpool experienced a relatively low inflow rate compared to Manchester but suffered much higher unemployment because of longer average durations (Armstrong and Taylor 1985).

Unemployment inflows

Of the factors involved in creating variations in unemployment inflow rates, changes in labour demand might be expected to be crucial as falling demand will result in increased redundancies, early retirements and temporary lay-offs. Some urban areas may have a disproportionate amount of secondary employment of a seasonal or short-term nature and this will raise the level of employment instability and hence the unemployment inflow rate. Offsetting these effects, the flow of voluntary quits will decrease and some discouraged workers may defer their entry into the labour force. Inflow variations may also reflect differences in the composition of the labour force as it is known that inflow rates vary systematically with age, occupation and other personal characteristics (Moylan and Davies 1980; Stern 1982). These associations may be interpreted as supply side influences, but they are equally consistent with secondary labour market explanations. Armstrong and Taylor (1985) examined male inflow rates for 28 TTWAs in the North West region and concluded that local variations in unemployment inflow rates are the result of local variations in demand.

The duration of unemployment

While differences in inflow rates are important, it is differences in duration which explain most of the inter-urban variation in unemployment rates and it is lengthening duration which explains the recent increases in urban unemployment. This feature of unemployment is important not only for the light it sheds upon the nature and causes of unemployment, but also because of the obvious welfare and policy implications of lengthening spells of worklessness. The costs of unemployment to the individual are likely to be positively related to the length of time without work, and the same is likely to be true of social costs. Equally important in this respect is the frequency of unemployment; many short spells of unemployment may be as bad as one long period without work.

The main source of data on unemployment durations is the quarterly analysis by the Department of Employment of registered unemployment, categorised by duration and disaggregated by age, sex and locality. Comprehensive as they are, there are a number of problems inherent in the use of these figures, as pointed out by Main (1981). The official figures measure interrupted or incomplete spells of unemployment; completed spells remain unobserved. The average length of a completed spell might be estimated by doubling the average duration of these interrupted spells (on the grounds that, on average, individuals would be halfway through their spell of unemployment) except for the fact that measured uncompleted duration is biased upwards. Short spells of unemployment occurring between counts will not be recorded and there will be an over-representation of long durations. To further complicate matters, in periods of rising unemployment individuals will be less than halfway through their spells of unemployment and the measured duration will be biased downwards. A frequently used measure of duration of unemployment is the proportion of 'long-term' unemployed among the total unemployed. From a normative point of view this may be the best indicator of the cumulative burden of unemployment. The distinction between long-term and short-term unemployment is necessarily rather arbitrary, the current convention in the UK is that it refers to a continuous period of unemployment lasting twelve months or more.

However it is measured, there is no doubt that the average duration of unemployment has increased during the 1980s. The proportion of long-term unemployed has increased from under 16 per cent of the register in 1971, to nearly 25 per cent in 1979 and to 40 per cent in 1985. At the same time the relative importance of short-term unemployment declined; between 1976 and 1985 unemployment of up to four weeks' duration declined from 16.5 to

9.1 per cent. It would appear that the entire distribution of durations has been displaced upwards.

The general increase in long-term unemployment has not been equally distributed across localities. Green (1985) has demonstrated the existence of systematic spatial variations in the incidence of long-term unemployment among local labour markets. The endemic nature of long-term unemployment is evidenced by the finding that the average expected duration exceeded 52 weeks in all areas. Some areas had much higher expected durations, the worst example being 160 weeks in Liverpool. The localities with the largest proportion of long-term unemployed are mainly the largest and oldest urban areas, especially the conurbations (excluding London). Further evidence covering the period 1974–82 is provided by Ball (1983) who, in a novel application of shift-share analysis, shows that such regions as the West Midlands and South East experienced greater than expected increases (positive differential shifts) in long-term unemployment whereas the reverse was the case in more traditionally depressed regions. Not only this, but a detailed examination of changes in local labour markets within the West Midlands revealed that long-term unemployment is heavily concentrated on the metropolitan core. Greater than expected increases in unemployment took place in core areas of the conurbation, while in the rural areas of the region and small urban localities surrounding the conurbation there was a negative local shift. These results not only confirm the previously observed association between high unemployment and metropolitan labour markets but suggest that the recent increases are not temporary or short term but are the result of more fundamental economic problems.

Influences on long-term unemployment

To explain these variations in long-term unemployment it may be useful to consider briefly the factors which influence the duration of unemployment. The probability of re-employment and the duration of unemployment is determined by the outcome of the labour market search process. The length of the period of searching is determined by the reservation wage which, in turn, is dependent on such factors as the distribution of job opportunities, the costs of continued search (including the cost of remaining unemployed) and the probability of receiving a wage offer in any period. From the employers' perspective, applicants may be offered a job, or not, depending upon whether they meet the employers' minimum hiring standard. These hiring standards will determine the likelihood that workers are offered a job. For some workers, job offers may never be received because they fail to meet employers' hiring standards in terms of productivity or some other characteristic.

Studies of unemployment duration have emphasised a variety of characteristics associated with increased durations and long-term unemployment. Age appears to be of particular significance with longer durations experienced by older workers (Mackay and Reid 1972; Nickell 1980; Colledge and Bartholomew 1980; White 1983). This could be a reflection of various factors including unrealistic wage expectations (a high reservation wage), or the association of age and ill health, or obsolescent skills. Unskilled workers also appear to experience more long-term unemployment whatever their age, perhaps reflecting less efficient search or a preference by employers for unemployed skilled workers. This could also be related to the dual labour market hypothesis. Primary employers will seek workers who possess the right characteristics of skill and stable work history. Place of residence may be used as a screening device for this purpose giving rise to intra-urban variations in durations (McGregor 1977). Secondary workers with a low probability of re-employment in good jobs will be forced either to accept longer durations or to take inferior jobs often of an unstable and transitory nature (e.g. seasonal). Such workers experience more long-term unemployment or repeated spells of unemployment.

Most variations in duration will be associated with changes in the level and structure of demand. As the level of labour demand declines the probability of receiving a job offer decreases and all workers in the queue for jobs will experience reduced probabilities of re-employment and the whole distribution of durations will be shifted upwards. Lynch (1983) calculated that for a representative unemployed young person, a decrease of 50 per cent in the arrival rate of job offers increased duration by over three-and-a-half weeks (an increase in duration of 15 per cent). As demand falls the proportion of the register who are long-term unemployed will increase and this increase will tend to be concentrated upon those who have the lowest relative probabilities of re-employment.

Why, then, should the longest durations and greatest increases in long-term unemployment be concentrated in the conurbations? The most likely explanation is that it is a reflection of the decline in job opportunities (demand) in these areas rather than the characteristics of the workforce. Green (1985) showed that even for similar age groups there were great differences between areas. In Liverpool the median duration of uncompleted spells of unemployment for under 25 year olds was 34 weeks as compared to 17 weeks in St Albans (a typical small southern town), and 73 and 31 weeks respectively for those aged 45. On average a young person in Liverpool could expect to be unemployed for a longer period than an older worker over 45 in a southern town. Furthermore, there is a striking correspondence between those areas identified by Green as suffering above-average unemployment durations in 1983 and the urban areas which have experienced the greatest reductions in employment over 1978–81.

Vulnerable groups among the unemployed

The burden of unemployment is not equally shared by groups in the labour force. Not only is the rate of unemployment persistently higher for some but when labour demand is falling their rate rises disproportionately.

Youth unemployment

The rate of unemployment among young people aged 16–19 is almost double the overall rate in most urban labour markets, and is especially acute in urban core areas. In Liverpool the rate among males aged 16–19 was nearly 40 per cent for most of the 1980s and not much below 30 per cent in Birmingham, Manchester and other major towns and cities.

One explanation of these high rates is the growth in the population of young people which has been disproportionately great in inner city areas as Table 4.1 clearly shows. In 1984 the proportion of people aged between 20 and 24 living in London was 24 per cent higher than in the national population. In the inner areas of Birmingham, Liverpool, Manchester and other metropolitan cities equally high proportions of 20–24 year olds can be found. In the latter cases, but not London, there is a similar, but not quite so marked, disparity in the population of young people aged 15–19 years. This large supply of young workers will certainly

Table 4.1 Age composition of the inner
cities: age groups as a proportion of
total population, 1984

	Age	
	15–19	20–24
London	83	123
Birmingham	113	119
Liverpool	107	114
Manchester	110	121
Newcastle upon Tyne	95	122
Leeds	105	117
Sheffield	101	118

England = 100
Source: adapted from *The Times*, 21
Oct. 1985: 4.

have exacerbated the problems of finding employment but it is
unlikely that demographic factors alone are responsible for the
plight of the young jobless.

A high rate of job turnover has frequently been observed among
young people and new entrants to the labour market, and these
frequent spells of unemployment will lead to high rates even
though the duration of these spells may be relatively short. The
reasons for this is that many young people enter the labour market
with no work experience or job-related skills and a high turnover
of jobs is a form of search at the intensive margin. Not all of the
high turnover is the result of quits but is the result of the periodic
and short duration of much work open to young people. This is
particularly the case with entrants who possess few if any
qualifications or skills and are therefore forced to work in the
secondary sector. Even in primary labour markets the internal
labour market and hiring policies of firms may place young
entrants at a disadvantage in the competition for jobs since young
workers are generally recruited at the bottom of the job hierarchy
and are most disadvantaged when firms are cutting back on
employment.

From a neoclassical perspective, youth unemployment has been
blamed on too high a level of wages which has priced young
workers out of jobs. The cause of over-pricing is variously blamed
on trade unions or wages councils (Seibert 1985; Brittan 1985) or on
unrealistically high expectations produced in schools. However,

as Gleave and Sellens (1984) have pointed out, rising wages for young workers could simply reflect the occupational flexibility of new entrants to the labour market who may seek jobs in new fields of employment which offer relatively high rates of pay.

Older workers

The problem of high unemployment among older workers is the reverse of that among the young. While job turnover is low, durations are frequently long and for the oldest workers unemployment may mean never working again. The median duration of uncompleted spells of unemployment among males aged 55–59 years was 74 weeks in 1985 as compared to only 24 weeks for males aged 18–19. The likelihood of leaving the stock of unemployed for the former group was only 12.2 per cent over a three-month period (*Employment Gazette*, Apr. 1985). The reason for becoming unemployed is much more likely to be redundancy than voluntary quitting and the growing incidence of unemployment among older workers may be related to the operation of the Redundancy Payments Act which provides a financial link between redundancy and age, although Nickell and Andrews (1983) find little support for this.

Older workers face a number of difficulties when seeking employment. They may have obsolete skills and their previous experience may be of little value to a new employer. Even if this is not objectively so, older workers may suffer from being stereotyped as inflexible or having unrealistic expectations, which may be partly correct since internal labour markets tend to create vacancies which may be unattractive to workers with long service. Older workers may suffer from poor or deteriorating health. Nearly 40 per cent of unemployed males aged 50 or over in the DHSS cohort study reported a disability or health problems as compared with 10 per cent of those aged under 25 (DHSS 1984).

The unskilled and the unqualified

The unskilled are disproportionately represented among both the unemployed in general and the long-term unemployed. The DHSS cohort study of unemployed males found only 8 per cent of the sample last worked as employers, managers or in a professional occupation as compared to 23 per cent of the general population

Over 40 per cent of the sample last worked in semi-skilled or unskilled manual jobs compared to 19 per cent of the general population (DHSS 1984). This over-representation of the unskilled appears to be the case regardless of age. Among the long-term unemployed the situation is even more marked. Colledge and Bartholomew (1980) found that around 75 per cent of a sample of unemployed had no qualifications of any kind.

The disproportionate presence of the unskilled among the unemployed is often cited as evidence of structural unemployment (Hawkins 1984) with a consequent emphasis on training and retraining as a solution (Metcalf 1975). However, the vulnerability of the unskilled may simply be a reflection of their lack of specific training which reduces the likelihood of their being hoarded by firms during recessions. In contrast, trained workers when made redundant represent a lost investment to firms and will be retained if a fall in demand is thought to be temporary. It is also possible that unskilled workers engage in less effective search, particularly of a formal kind, and would therefore survey fewer job opportunities over a smaller geographical horizon (Parkes and Kohen 1975). If differential demand or search explanations are correct then a programme of improving skills and upgrading qualifications will have little effect other than to cause employers to raise their current hiring standards.

The male–female differential

On the face of it, males appear more vulnerable to unemployment than females. The female unemployment rate in Great Britain is less than the male rate and has been so since 1955. Indeed, until 1975 the ratio of female to male rates decreased and so, too, did the share of unemployment accounted for by females. This is surprising since it is the opposite of the experience of many other industrial countries.

Since the mid-1970s female unemployment has increased quite markedly and at a faster proportionate rate than for males. Nevertheless, even at the bottom of the 1980 recession female unemployment was only two-thirds that of males and since that date the difference has widened again; in 1985 the ratio of female to male unemployment rates was 61 per cent. Despite the considerable proportionate increase in female unemployment rates, the share of unemployment accounted for by females has remained virtually

unchanged since immediate post-war period (around 27 per cent).
However, there are serious problems of measurement relating to
female unemployment as the loss of a job may lead to withdrawal
from the labour force rather than add to unemployment, and even
if a woman continues to seek work she may not be registered as
unemployed. If women had the same propensity to register as men
then the number of unemployed females might increase by around
40 per cent (Hawkins 1984). This would make the male–female
differential more apparent than real.

Employment opportunities for women have expanded greatly
because of the expansion of non-manual and service industry
occupations and relatively low female unemployment over the
past two decades may simply be a reflection of a greater relative
demand for female labour. This trend and the consequent male–
female unemployment differential seems likely to continue for the
forseeable future since the effects of new technology appear to have
had little impact so far on female employment and there is little
evidence of males competing for secondary labour market jobs
which have traditionally been filled by women.

Ethnic minorities

Unemployment rates are much higher among black minority
groups than in the white labour force. A survey of the city of
Leicester in 1983 found that the unemployment rate of all age
groups was substantially greater among those of West Indian and
Asian ethnic origin than among white residents. Most marked was
the rate of 45.5 per cent among West Indians aged 16–19 years of age
(Leicester City Council 1984). Similar results have been reported in
other studies (Showler 1980) although Metcalf (1975) found that
New Commonwealth immigrants tended to be found in towns
with low unemployment rates. Since there is no reason to believe
that members of ethnic minorities are less motivated to find
employment as others in the labour force, their relatively high
unemployment rates can be interpreted as evidence of labour
market disadvantage or racial discrimination.

Language may be a problem (see Smith 1981; Smith 1980)
although apparently more so for Asian groups than for Afro-
Caribbean groups. In Leicester around 10 per cent of the Asian
population could not speak English and a further 13 per cent spoke
only a little. A lack of educational attainment and skills may be

another form of disadvantage which will tend to consign members of ethnic minorities to secondary labour market employment or force them into high-risk entrepreneurial activity. In some instances young workers may react against such a disadvantaged position in the job market and effectively withdraw, at least temporarily, from it. This may, of course, have the unintended effect of compounding their secondary status.

Summary and conclusion

From a consideration of the underlying causes of unemployment, it is concluded that an urban area may experience above average unemployment rates either because of a relatively inefficient local labour market which leads to high levels of frictional unemployment, or structural imbalances in labour demand and supply within the city, or else a local deficiency of labour demand. Although the evidence suggests some role for all three factors, most of the variation in urban unemployment appears to be related to local demand deficiency. The chronic unemployment of metropolitan economies can be explained by the collapse of employment which has occurred in these areas and the inability of the labour market to adjust sufficiently or rapidly enough to this decline in labour demand. Since employment decline is systematically related to the degree of urbanisation this has resulted in the concentration of unemployment in the conurbations, large cities and their inner areas. In addition, because of differential shifts in demand and unbalanced population change this unemployment falls disproportionately on certain groups in the labour force such as the unskilled, the young and the old. The unequal incidence of unemployment is reflected in localities where there is an above-average concentration of such vulnerable workers. This effect is particularly marked within an urban area, where differences in unemployment appear to be symptomatic of the residential segregation of the workforce.

These conclusions have some implications for policy. In the first place, the precise mix of factors responsible for high unemployment may vary from one urban locality to another and the appropriate policy response may correspondingly vary. Second, although local demand deficiency is the main cause of high local unemployment there may be different reasons for such a deficiency. The decline in demand for labour may be a spatial reflection of a national decline in aggregate demand and the implied remedy for this is an expansion of economic activity through appropriate national fiscal and monetary policy, a strategy which lies largely outside the powers of local policy-makers. However, if the decline in local demand is the result of decisions made by firms in the course of organising their production (the so-called supply side of the economy) then the scope for influencing the spatial pattern of labour demand and its level in the local economy is increased. Even so, the scale of such activity may have to be disproportionately great compared to the effects sought because of the very open nature of local labour markets which result in the diffusion of labour demand over neighbouring areas.

Further reading

An introduction to the theory of unemployment can be found in most labour economics textbooks (see Creedy and Thomas 1982 or Joll *et al.* 1983). More detailed analysis is contained in the following: Hawkins (1984) *Unemployment*; Creedy (1981) *The Economics of Unemployment in Britain*; Hughes and Perlman (1984) *The Economics of Unemployment: a comparative analysis of Britain and the United States*; Greenhalgh, Layard and Oswald (1983) *The Causes of Unemployment*. Many of these discuss the spatial pattern of unemployment, but Chapter 10 of *The Urban and Regional Transformation of Britain*, edited by Goddard and Champion (1983), provides a specific examination of recent regional and subregional unemployment change.

5
Economic policy and urban labour markets

The discussion in previous chapters has highlighted the very severe nature of unemployment in metropolitan economies. The question now arises: What is to be done about this problem and by whom is action to be taken? Although the commitment to maintain full employment, first stated in the 1944 White Paper on Employment Policy, still formally exists, the rise of mass unemployment in the 1980s has led to a reappraisal of the role of government in this field. This is most clearly revealed by the Department of Employment's 1985 White Paper 'Employment: the challenge for the nation' which, at the very least; shifted part of the responsibility for achieving full employment to management and to labour, or as the government's critics alleged, effectively abandoned the aim of full employment. One consequence of this is that local authorities have increasingly been drawn into the field of economic development and employment creation in an attempt to reduce unemployment in their local areas. This chapter will examine the changing spatial emphasis of economic policy to reduce urban unemployment. This involves both an examination of the labour market and urban policies of central government and the scope for local employment initiatives.

Policy and the local labour market

In the face of the concentration of unemployment in urban economies, policy-makers have a number of options. They could do nothing and allow the decline of urban economies to continue unabated. This option might be justified on the grounds that such decline represents the inevitable result of market processes and to attempt to deflect or reverse such trends is neither desirable (in terms of economic efficiency) or likely to be effective. It could even be suggested that the process of change should be speeded up in order to mitigate the social costs of adjustment to the new spatial order. Politically, such an option may not be acceptable.

Another option would be to attempt to alleviate the worst effects of urban decline. Such policies do not challenge the underlying trends in urban economies but seek to reduce the social and economic costs of a period of economic transition. From this point of view the need to reduce unemployment in the cities is more to do with achieving an equitable distribution of the burdens of unemployment than it is with the overall reduction of unemployment. Such policy usually consists of the subsidisation of economic activity in the areas most badly affected and transfer payments to offset local need.

Finally, policy-makers may attempt to reverse the loss of jobs and the increase in unemployment by directly confronting the processes of change. In most cases this will involve direct intervention in the local economy because market forces will be leading to a contrary result. Although such direct action to create employment could be taken by either central or local government, as has already been noted it is local government which has taken these initiatives.

The objectives of policy

Whether policy is implemented by central or local government it is likely that the main objectives of urban unemployment policy will be:

(a)   the reduction of the level and rate of unemployment in the urban economy;

(b)   the achievement of a more equitable burden of unemployment among groups and localities in the urban area;

(c)   the provision of support for the unemployed in terms of facilitating their return to work and enhancing their leisure time;

(d)   to monitor and plan the urban economy in order to minimise future unemployment in the locality.

These objectives have to be placed into the context of the policy-makers overall economic and social goals and the weight attached to each one will vary accordingly. Other priorities may be given precedence and this may create conflicts between goals.

Alternative policy perspectives

Policy depends upon an underlying framework of ideas which provide a guide to policy action and, as Keynes himself put it, 'practical men, who believe themselves exempt from any intellectual influences, are usually the slaves of some defunct economist' (Keynes 1936). Previous chapters have examined in detail the economic decline of metropolitan economies and the rise of urban unemployment and it is clear that different economic perspectives have interpreted these events in different ways. Alternative explanations of how labour markets work and what causes unemployment can be expected to be reflected in economic policy. The relationship between theoretical perspective and policy is shown in Fig. 5.1. In practice the relationships may not be as simple as Fig. 5.1 suggests, because policy-makers are not always consistent. Equally, the same policy may be recommended even though the underlying explanation of the problem and the rationale for policy is different.

The neoclassical perspective

According to the competitive perspective, in an economy where wages and prices are flexible, employment and output will tend to settle at their equilibrium (or natural) levels. Unemployment will be mainly the result of labour market frictions which prevent the perfect matching of workers and jobs during the continual turnover of jobs in the economy. Although such unemployment is not costless, insofar as it arises voluntarily and brings about a better allocation of labour it need not be regarded as especially serious although measures which improve the efficiency of the labour market search process are obviously desirable.

The inequality of unemployment rates between localities and its concentration within large urban areas is, according to this view, the result of differences in levels of frictional unemployment. However, unemployment above frictional levels will result if wages in a particular area are too high relative to other localities. The need for relative wage adjustment arises because of changes in the spatial pattern of labour demand and supply and it is the failure of wages to adjust, in conjunction with the immobility of firms and labour, which results in the relatively high levels of unemployment in cities.

The rise of mass unemployment poses a problem for the

Alternative theoretical perspective	Types of unemployment emphasised	Explanations in terms of:	Typical policy advocated	Methods and agency of change
Neoclassical/ Competitive	Voluntary Frictional Seasonal	The individual decisions of workers and firms when faced by imperfect knowledge and costly adjustment. Problems are caused by individual inadequacy or interference with the market by the state or trade unions.	Increase the incentives to individuals to be more efficient in search or to engage in less of it. Remove impediments to competition (especially wage reduction). Reduce state involvement in the labour market. Maintain a 'sound' macroeconomic environment in which enterprise and individual inititative will flourish.	Reliance upon market processes and individual, private enterprise. Role of the state limited to some minimum regulations and investment required to create the conditions for the growth of employment and speedy adjustments to change. Local economic initiatives of limited scope.
Structuralist/Keynesian	Voluntary and involuntary frictional structural demand deficient	The interaction of groups and social institutions with the market. Market failure especially at the macroeconomic level is particularly important	Labour market and other public policies to regulate and modify the negative effects of private enterprise and strengthen the market process. Aggregate level of economic	Strikes a balance between the private and public sector. Emphasis on the management of the economy and of economic change – 'liberal corporatism'.

					local economic development may be given a high profile.
	by the complex and changing nature of the labour market and the inadequate regulation of management of the economy.	Class structure and the social organisation of production. Problems are caused by the dynamics of capitalism and the organisation of production for profit rather than needs. Emphasis may be placed upon evolving labour market structures such as segmented markets and the restructuring of capital.	ted by policies designed to regulate aggregate demand and its spatial/industrial structure. Account to be taken of social as well as private costs and benefits.	Increased state intervention and finance for industry. Extension of public ownership and public employment. Strengthening of trade unions. Opposition to the market criterion of profitability, production for need rather than profit, and a fundamental reorganisation of society.	Change in the social organisation of production; in the short-term seek to change the balance of power between capital and labour. Recent emphasis placed on local initiatives but fundamental change unlikely to be achieved in spatial isolation from the remainder of economy and society.
Radical/Marxist	Involuntary demand deficient secular stagnation reserve of labour				

Fig. 5.1 Alternative perspectives on unemployment

competitive model since such levels of unemployment cannot be easily dismissed as frictional or structural. The main reason for this growth of unemployment is that wage competition is insufficient to maintain an equilibrium in the labour market. Unemployment has increased because wages are 'too high'. Given that the economy is in competition with other countries and that there has been a worldwide recession, the number of jobs which firms are willing to create at current wage levels is insufficient to employ all of the available workforce. Economic policy designed to increase the level of aggregate expenditure will not, however, lead to any increase in employment because the expansion of output is unprofitable without a reduction in the real wage. Any attempt to increase demand will simply lead to increases in prices and inflation.

There are several important policy implications arising from the competitive perspective. First, according to this view, there is little that governments can do directly to reduce unemployment; the expansion of demand will not achieve this but only lead to inflation. If unemployment is in excess of frictional levels, policy should be directed to eliminating the causes of wage inflexibility. The main barriers to wage competition are generally seen to be collective bargaining and institutional wage setting (e.g. Wages Councils), or the effects of the welfare system. Since both factors operate at a national level they can be expected to inhibit wage flexibility between regions and urban areas. Policy to reduce urban unemployment will tend to be non-spatial and represent part of an overall philosophy of reducing state involvement in the economy, encouraging private enterprise and increasing the incentive to work of individuals. This philosophy is most clearly stated in the 1983 White Paper on Regional Industrial Development, where it is stated that 'The Government believe that wage bargaining must become more responsive to the circumstances of the individual enterprise, including location. Their policies of privatisation, together with a reduction in the power of trade unions to set against their own members' interests, should help to achieve this.'

The structuralist perspective

This viewpoint sees the basic cause of mass unemployment as being a deficiency of aggregate expenditure, a deficiency which would in fact be exacerbated by any tendency to cut wages. The perspective casts doubt both on the view that wage reductions are necessary in order to increase employment and the proposition that it is beyond the power of governments to induce a permanent expansion of economic activity. According to this viewpoint, recent growth of unemployment is largely the result of a deficiency of aggregate demand, partly brought about by world recession, but substantially exacerbated by deflationary government policy.

The origin of unequal spatial concentrations of unemployment is to be found mainly in the differential sensitivity of groups of workers and geographical areas to changes in aggregate demand. Recession has reduced the demand for labour, but this reduction is focused to a greater extent on some workers and localities than others, producing spatial consequences. Not all of the differences in unemployment between areas can be explained by demand deficiency, the efficiency of the market as an allocative mechanism is also called into question. Market outcomes are not seen as being necessarily the most efficient or socially desirable.

Policy to reduce urban unemployment revolves around the expansion of demand. As demand is expanded and unemployment falls, so the differences between localities will be reduced. As demand expansion is a fairly blunt economic instrument, there is a case for aiming much of the additional demand on specific localities where social and economic deprivation is greatest through some form of urban policy. An additional justification for this is the belief that the decline of urban areas may be yet another symptom of the inefficiency of market forces. For similar reasons, this perspective also places great emphasis upon the reform of labour market institutions, through manpower policy, in order to overcome the inherent inefficiency of labour markets.

Radical policy

The radical perspective argues that demand deficiency, while an important reason for urban unemloyment, represents only the immediate cause of the problem. The fundamental cause of unemployment is to be found in the nature of capitalist production. In general, unemployment is explained in terms of the periodic crises which beset capitalist economies and the need to maintain a reserve of labour. Recent theoretical developments relating to the spatial restructuring of production have provided a radical view of the process of urban decline and the rise of urban unemployment.

Like the market perspective, radical analysis sees the concentration of unemployment in metropolitan areas and inner-city areas as being the result of market forces. Unlike the former perspective, the radical viewpoint sees such developments as socially devisive, inefficient and fundamentally against the interests of workers. They would reject the policy of wage reduction and increased competition for the same reasons. In contrast, radical policy involves intervention in production, either directly through state ownership or by more indirect means and a fundamental reorganisation of society. 'Elected, publicly accountable authorities must intervene to replace the anarchy of the market economy with justice and fairness' (GLC 1985). Although national policy is an indispensable element of this strategy, intervention in production can, it is argued, often be best achieved on a local basis.

The instruments of policy

Any policy intended to reduce urban unemployment must achieve this objective, either by reducing labour supply or by increasing labour demand, or by improving the efficiency with which the local labour market operates. The reduction of labour supply as a means of reducing unemployment is not generally feasible at a national level but becomes more so at the local economy level when labour can be encouraged to move from one locality to another. Such policy is relatively rare but the Labour Employment Transfer Scheme (see later) is an example of this strategy. Most policy measures to reduce unemployment involve an attempt to increase labour demand or to intervene in the labour market thereby reducing unemployment directly or through the improved matching of workers and jobs. Policy to reduce unemployment is therefore primarily policy to increase employment although the forms which such employment initiatives can take are very varied indeed.

The main influence on the forms taken by employment policies and the instruments chosen to achieve them is the policy-maker's perception of the underlying nature of urban unemployment (see above). The implementation of policy also reflects the powers and resources available and what is politically acceptable. The formulation of an appropriate urban employment policy requires the resolution of a number of dilemmas. Is unemployment best dealt with by general economic instruments or by the use of selective spatial measures? Should policy focus directly on the labour market or work indirectly through other markets? Indeed, should policy support markets or replace them? Because of the different levels of government it is also necessary to decide whether policy should be centrally administered or locally controlled. To a great extent these issues are still in the process of being resolved. As the result, urban employment policy is a complex web of different types of policy, operating in different ways and at different levels. Much national policy relating to unemployment, training and economic development is general in nature but has spatial consequences. Other policy is specifically spatial in character but is operated by central government (regional policy), by local authorities on behalf of central government (urban programmes, enterprise zones), or by independent agencies set up by central government (urban development corporations) or by local government (enterprise boards). To add to this maze of policies local authorities may initiate their own economic development policies.

The impact of policy

The attempt to reduce urban unemployment by increasing employment within a specific locality faces difficulties not normally encountered with more general economic policies. First, the effects of initiatives may spill over into neighbouring local economies (and vice-versa) as economic agents move into and out of the locality in order to take advantage of or to avoid the effects of policy. In addition, the net benefit of initiatives can vary according to the spatial perspective from which it is considered (national, regional or local). These issues make the assessment of the impact of policy on urban unemployment problematic.

Measuring the impact

It is important to distinguish between the gross and net effects of policy measures. The gross effect is the simple direct change in employment induced by policy and consists of any jobs created by the formation of new firms or the attraction of firms into the locality, and the expansion or retention of jobs in existing local firms. The net effect is calculated by subtracting any indirect employment changes attributable to policy from the gross employment effect. These indirect effects consist of the changes in employment among other local firms as the result of the local multiplier or by the displacement of competitors, plus any job loss from firms leaving the locality. In addition, employment change which would have occurred anyway (for reasons unrelated to policy) should also be deducted from the gross effect.

The net impact on employment also depends on the way in which policy affects production processes. If policy measures reduce local costs of production and increase profits then the scale of local employment will increase as existing firms expand, new firms are formed and others move into the area. This is referred to as 'a scale effect'. However, policy can affect relative input prices and firms will respond to this by an increased use of cheaper inputs in their production processes, while new and migrant firms will tend to be those which use the cheaper input more extensively. This 'substitution effect' will tend to reduce the number of jobs for a given level of output if capital is the input which is subsidised and the net change in employment will depend on the relative size of these scale and substitution effects. If labour costs are reduced relative to those of other inputs then both effects will tend to increase employment. The effect of initiatives depends crucially on their effect on the structure of production costs, and this will vary according to the type of policy.

The different stages involved in an assessment of the net impact of policy measures on local unemployment are shown schematically in Fig. 5.2. This highlights the fact that if unemployment is to be reduced, new jobs must ultimately be filled by resident workers. This may not happen if new jobs require skills not possessed by the local unemployed workforce, in which case the jobs may be filled by workers who live outside the area, either by commuting or because relocating firms bring their workforce with them. Similarly, new jobs, especially if part time, may simply attract non-participants (such as married women) back into the labour force. This is particularly likely if there has been a strong discouraged worker response to previous high levels of local unemployment. Finally, jobs may remain vacant, perhaps because they are unattractive in some way (e.g. low wage). If new jobs remain untaken then unemployment will remain unchanged.

The measurement of net employment effects requires a considerable array of information and many of the questions posed in Fig. 5.2 may in practice be unanswerable. An indirect method of measuring policy effects, used in studies of regional policy, is shift-share analysis where the unexpected change in employment

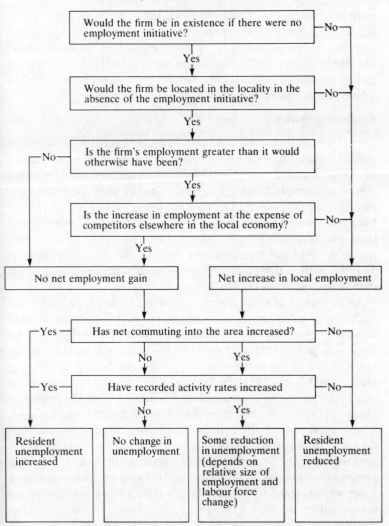

Fig. 5.2 Evaluating the effects of employment initiatives on local unemployment

(the local shift) is interpreted as being due to policy. However, since shift-share analyses of urban economies always reveal a large differential shift (see Ch. 3), this approach offers little scope for studies at the local level. A more direct method involves surveying firms and asking managers to assess the importance and effect of economic assistance (Cameron *et al.* 1982). Such an approach is limited because firms may perceive it to be in their (local political) interests to minimise the apparent impact of local authority assistance (Storey 1983). Measuring the net effects of employment policy remains a difficult exercise and most agencies involved in 'job creation' cite only the gross effects of their endeavours.

Evaluating policy

Even if the net increase in jobs and the reduction in unemployment could be unambiguously quantified, difficulties still arise relating to evaluation and cost effectiveness. A crude measure of relative cost would simply divide the capital cost of a policy measure by the number of jobs created. The cost per job criterion is widely used but overlooks the fact that initiatives bring streams of benefits and costs which stretch into the future. These benefits and costs may spread beyond the revenues and costs of the initiating agency. Taken together, these considerations suggest the need for a social cost-benefit analysis (Willis 1985).

An appraisal of employment initiatives in terms only of local authority or other agency costs and revenues is far too narrow and should be extended to the community level. This might still be limited to purely financial gains and losses in the local economy but it could be extended to a full social cost-benefit study (e.g. Hodge and Whitby 1981). In the latter case, account has to be taken of all relevant social costs and benefits arising from the initiative although in practice the estimation of the net social benefit of such schemes has proved difficult. Studies have tended to assume that the social opportunity cost of employing an unemployed worker is zero, and that any policy which costs no more than the savings on unemployment benefit (plus increased tax revenue) must represent a net welfare gain to society. Willis (1985) has questioned this presumption on two grounds. First, there is a real cost to employing the unemployed because of the existence of an informal economy while, second, since the unemployed have some probability of employment there will be a social opportunity cost in the future.

Whatever the merits of social cost-benefit studies, few have been conducted least of all by the agencies operating employment initiatives in urban areas. Crude financial cost per job is the best that is available in most cases and the evaluation of most forms of policy remains, regrettably, a matter of faith.

The changing emphasis of government policy

Alternative explanations of economic problems compete with one another to capture the minds of Keynes 'practical men'. Shifts and changes in the emphasis of economic policy can be interpreted as the outcome of this theoretical and ideological struggle for influence over policy-makers. Some of the most marked changes in the direction of economic policy have taken place during the 1980s and this section briefly considers these changes in economic philosophy as a background to the subsequent discussion of urban employment initiatives.

Employment policy

In the immediate post-war period the main policy instrument used to keep unemployment at a minimum was the manipulation of aggregate expenditure through a financial strategy which has since become known as 'stop–go'. If unemployment showed signs of increasing then the government would raise public expenditure and cut interest rates and taxes. With unemployment increasing, apparently inexorably from 1966 onwards and accelerating inflation adding to Britain's economic problems, governments of both political parties reduced their reliance on demand management and increased the extent of their intervention in the management of the economy by means of industrial and manpower policy.

The trend away from demand management towards special measures became most pronounced under the Labour government of 1974–79. A large number of programmes were introduced which subsidised employment, encouraged job sharing and early retirement, while simultaneously increasing state support of industry and in particular ailing large-scale employers (most notably British Leyland). During much of this period deflationary fiscal policies were in operation in order to restrain inflation. During this period labour market policy was clearly of a radical structuralist flavour seeing the problem of unemployment as largely the result of the weakness of British industry and of financial markets and solutions were seen in terms of state assistance and intervention in markets.

Since the election of a Conservative government in 1979 the emphasis in policy has swung sharply towards the competitive market perspective. This approach is perhaps best encapsulated in the White Paper 'Employment: the challenge for the nation' (Department of Employment 1985) which argues that: 'The biggest single cause of our high unemployment is the failure of our jobs market, the weak link in our economy.' From this point of view, government is seen as providing the conditions under which an efficient labour market can exist, but being incapable of performing the main task of reducing unemployment. The latter is the responsibility of 'management, employees and the education system working in common understanding and partnership . . . to ensure that the supply of labour meets demand in quality, quantity, cost and flexibility'. The emphasis has shifted markedly from demand management and intervention towards the reform of the labour market, the restoration of competition and changes in the quantity and quality of labour supply. In reality there has been less of a shift in policy than the rhetoric would suggest. While general job subsidies have been phased out, special measures continue (indeed have been enhanced) for young people and the long-term unemployed. While a programme of privatisation of state business has been followed (e.g. British Telecom, Jaguar and British Aerospace) the government is still committed to financial support and incentives to industry. Perhaps most important of all, however, is the general macroeconomic policy of the government. Its overall aim is to reduce the size of the public sector, stimulate private enterprise through tax incentives while maintaining 'sound' monetary policy in order to control inflation and keep interest rates low. In fact it has achieved few of these objectives. Public expenditure remains high because of increased services and benefit payments to the unemployed while taxes have increased for most employees. According to the Institute of Fiscal Studies only 6 per cent of the population have gained an increase in net income between 1978/9 and 1985/6; 87 per cent of the population were worse off (Davis and Dilnot 1985). In addition, by the beginning of 1985 real interest rates had reached their highest post-war level. Only as far as inflation is concerned can any real success be claimed during the early 1980s. Given the chronically deflationary fiscal policy pursued during the early part of the decade (Neuberger 1985), the slowing down of inflation is hardly surprising.

Despite, or perhaps because of, the failure to achieve its stated policy objectives and with unemployment showing no signs of reduction, the Conservative government renewed its efforts to increase competition and reduce unemployment through a market led solution. The 1985 White Paper on employment stressed the inability of governments to create jobs, proposed a number of measures to expand training and community programme schemes and provide incentives for the provision of private sector jobs. In July 1985 these proposals were taken further in a White Paper on business deregulation, 'Lifting the Burden', and by proposals to reform the Wages Councils. The White Paper proposed the establishment of a task force to scrutinize and review new and existing business regulation with the objective of reducing 'red-tape'. Special simplified planning zones extended this idea into the local authority planning arena. The government also announced reforms of the Wages Councils, limiting their role to the setting of minimum hourly wage rates and a single overtime rate (thus excluding references relating to skill differentials, shift working, weekend rates, holiday pay or guaranteed pay for short-time working). More importantly, workers under the age of 21 are excluded from the protection of the councils. This was estimated to affect about 500,000 young people employed in Wage Council industries.

The White Papers on employment and deregulation of business and the reform of the Wages Councils underline the change in direction taken by government policy. Based firmly on the competitive market ideology, such a strategy seeks to create a liberalisation of the business environment, increase competition in the labour market and assist the unemployed into work through work experience and training. Unemployment is seen as being caused by excessive state involvement in regulating the economy, a lack of incentives to enterprise, and wages being too high (especially for young people) while the incidence of unemployment is explicable in terms of the inadequacies of individuals (or their conscious choice) which may be remedied by a combination of training and incentives to work.

The evolution of urban policy

In parallel with the developments outlined above, policies with regard to urban economies have also shifted over the post-war period. Up to the late 1960s central government policy was generally antipathetic to the larger urban economies and the conurbations. Driven by a fear of excessive population growth, congestion and a decline in the social fabric of cities, governments tried to limit the growth of these areas and encourage the dispersal of economic activity by such measures as New Towns and controls on industrial development.

By the end of the decade, the perception of urban problems had changed. Rising unemployment was recognised as being especially acute in the inner-city areas which also had growing concentrations of ethnic minorities, low-skilled and low-paid workers. The policy response was intended to improve the market position of inner-city residents through programmes of education, the provision of social services and improvement of housing. The 1968 Urban Programme, for example, was designed to deal with the shortcomings of individuals and communities in deprived areas which often resulted, so it was believed, from intergenerational cycles of deprivation. It fairly rapidly became clear that this approach offered little prospect of relief from ever-increasing levels of unemployment.

The 1977 White Paper on Policy for Inner Cities and the 1978 Inner Urban Areas marked the introduction of the most ambitious and comprehensive attack on inner-city problems. It embodied the reformist–structuralist view that policy should be directed towards economic development while the agents of change were to be partnerships between central governments, local authorities and private enterprise. The underlying premise of the policy was that inner-city economies had inherent structural weaknesses which market forces alone could not overcome. The programme offered various forms of financial aid for land acquisition, provision of amenities, rent and interest relief and so forth. In addition the programme was intended to 'bend' other development programmes in order to favour the inner cities.

The provisions of the Local Government Planning and Land Act, introduced by the Conservative government in 1980, reinforced the 1978 Act but it also revised it, giving central government greater control over the programme and redirecting its aims. Greater emphasis was placed on attracting private sector investment and the Act established 'Enterprise Zones' (EZs) and 'Urban Development Corporations' (UDCs). The latter would be responsible for economic development in designated metropolitan districts or London boroughs and would have wide powers. The former would consist of areas in which rate relief, local authority planning exemptions and other benefits would exist. The common element in these developments is that they represent experiments with market solutions to urban problems with the EZs representing a more *laissez-faire* approach while the UDC represents a market led, but managed strategy. Both reflect a view that market processes and private enterprise are ultimately the source of new jobs and that local authority regulations and planning represent an impediment to these processes.

With these shifts in central government response to the problem of urban unemployment, it is hardly surprising that the role of local government has changed as well. In the 1970s most local authorities responded to growing unemployment by using their traditional powers relating to planning regulation, land and buildings to attempt to dissuade established firms from migrating and simultaneously promoting inward investment and new indigenous enterprise. This involvement in economic development was encouraged by central government – for example, the Labour government's industrial strategy of 1977 urged local authorities to give priority to the needs of industry in the fields of planning, housing and transport in order to improve the general conditions for industrial confidence and growth. The inner city partnerships and programmes of 1978 provided further impetus towards an economic development role for local councils.

The onset of the 1979–81 recession coincided with changes in political control at national and local level. Although a Conservative government was elected in 1979, many local authorities became Labour controlled around this time. This juxtaposition of events brought about quite substantial changes and tensions in urban policy. As Young and Mason (1983) observed: 'As unemployment has slipped from its pre-eminent place on the national policy agenda in favour of the control of inflation it has, paradoxically, become one of the foremost concerns of local government.' The extent of this concern may be gauged from Table 5.1. For many councils, the development of local economic initiatives was simply a method of signalling their concern about mounting job losses and accelerating local unemployment. In the Labour-controlled metropolitan and city councils more radical alternative economic strategies have been developed. These involve a more pro-active approach which has shifted policy away from traditional property and capital incentives. Emphasis has been placed on direct intervention in the local labour market in order to create or preserve local employ-

Table 5.1 District Council involvement in local
economic Development, England & Wales 1984

Activity	% of replies
Any economic development activity	89
Enterprise trusts	19
Cooperative developments	11
Joint ventures – private sector	32
Joint ventures – public sector	28
Providing rent/rate free periods	42
Making grants	27
Making loans	23
Providing sites	75
Providing premises	62
Providing business advice	37
Providing ITEC's, training workshops etc	43

Source: Association of District Councils (1985)

ment, stimulate employment growth (led by the local public sector), explore new forms of enterprise and socially useful production, and promote greater local democratic involvement in the economic regeneration process.

The growth of local economic initiatives has created something of a dilemma for central government. To some extent such initiatives have been welcomed in so far as they relate to the promotion of private enterprise and small firms. Beyond that level, there is little central government support particularly for the more radical and interventionist approaches. A general antagonism to public expenditure and intervention coupled with fears about the effects of rates upon business and commerce led to the 1984 Rate Act which sought to reduce the ability of local authorities to increase their rates (and introduced 'rate capping'). In addition, the GLC and the metropolitan counties were abolished in 1986. These measures combined with a general squeeze on government grants to local authorities have combined to create an environment in which it has been difficult to find adequate resources for local policy to reduce unemployment.

Government initiatives and the urban unemployed

Policy measures affecting the urban unemployed take a variety of forms. First, there are general measures intended to improve the effectiveness of the labour market and reduce labour market imbalances. There are also measures which are specifically directed towards the unemployed. In neither case are the policies spatial in character but, because of the concentration of unemployment in urban economies, they have a spatial impact. In contrast, other measures are directed specifically towards the regeneration and economic development of particular geographical areas. These measures are not always directly concerned with employment or unemployment but they can have consequences for local unemployment levels. This section examines a number of government policy measures which have an impact upon the urban unemployed.

Training for jobs?

The incidence of high unemployment rates among unskilled workers and young people, together with the spectre of technological change, are frequently cited to support training programmes as a means of reducing unemployment. In addition there is the argument that competitive labour markets tend to under-invest in human capital which, despite providing social returns, is not perceived as a profitable investment by individual firms (Becker 1975; Ziderman 1975, 1978).

The problem of under-investment in training and education may be particularly acute in some core urban areas where the secondary labour market conditions are not conducive to investment in the labour force. Recent changes in urban economies have exacerbated the problem. The provision of training tends to be reduced during recessions because recruitment (a vehicle for training) is reduced and increased uncertainty about the future discourages investment. In addition, the long-term decline of urban economies and de-skilling has led to a greatly reduced demand for traditionally skilled labour.

Reduced training at a time of rapidly rising unemployment is cause for concern on two grounds. First, the unskilled and the untrained will be at a disadvantage in the competition for existing employment and, second, shortages of trained and skilled workers may prevent future expansion. It is clear that the unskilled and the young are more vulnerable to unemployment but it is less clear that this vulnerability can be remedied by training alone. The high unemployment rate in these groups is more a reflection of their secondary labour market position and the differential effects of recession. The provision of increased or new skills in the absence of specific skill shortages or a more general expansion of labour demand may do little more than equalise the incidence of unemployment or, worse, concentrate the burden on those groups who are unable to gain access to training.

The detection of skill shortages is made difficult by the lack of accurate statistics on unfilled vacancies and the evidence is rather partial and often anecdotal. A shortage of labour can be said to exist when there is excess demand for a certain skill at the prevailing wage rate, but this may be due to many other factors than a lack of trained workers. A spatial mismatch of jobs and workers, entry restrictions to occupations, or a failure of wages to rise sufficiently to attract skilled workers from other occupations may all create 'shortages' but it is not clear that increasing the number of trained workers will reduce these or reduce the level of unemployment (Bosworth and Wilson 1980, 1981).

The second aspect of a deficiency of trained labour is that future expansion of output and employment may be prevented by bottlenecks arising from the shortage of key skills or occupations. In this case the shortage is potential rather than actual and therein lies the dilemma; if training is expanded to meet future manpower needs before the jobs are created then the newly trained workers or those they displace will remain unemployed. The problem is compounded by the possibility that human capital, like physical capital, becomes obsolete when unemployed. While this provides a strong argument for more training and retraining it also underlines the need to maintain high levels of demand. As Lindley (1982) observes: 'The evidence indicates that the main constraint on the supply of newly trained craftsmen was not the supply of willing recruits four years or so previously, but the demand for recruits by employers.'

The provision of training in Britain has evolved over the past three decades in a series of training initiatives by government. Prior to the 1964 Industrial Training Act a fairly *laissez-faire* training environment existed with local authorities and employer each making their own provision. Since 1964 there has been increased state intervention beginning with the establishment of the Industrial Training Boards (ITBs) and the establishment in 1973 of the Manpower Services Commission (MSC). While originally set up to coordinate training activities, the MSC quickly expanded its responsibilities to embrace major elements of further education, training, and the special unemployment programmes. Although local participation in the development of MSC programmes has been considerable, the training system has not been very responsive to local needs (Fairly 1983), while the scale of MSC activity has in many instances displaced local training programmes. The extent of MSC activity can be gauged from the fact that more than 2.5 million people are expected to have passed through its employment and training programmes during 1985–1986.

Since 1980 the direction of training policy has shifted in keeping with government emphasis on market solutions to unemployment. A reduction in state involvement in training was signalled by the abolition during the early 1980s of 16 of the 23 ITBs, while the 1984 White Paper on 'Training for Jobs' proposed a loan scheme for the finance of adult trainees. The main thrust of recent training policy has been the Youth Training Scheme (YTS) which came into operation in 1983. YTS provides 16 and 17 year olds with work-related training for up to two years. The objective of YTS is to provide broad vocational skills which will increase employment prospects for the participants and produce a more flexible and capable workforce. Perhaps the most significant element of the scheme is that it provides a massive subsidy to participating firms: £2,050 per year for each trainee while the trainee receives an allowance of £26.25 per week (in 1985).

The evidence, unfortunately, does not support the view that such training drastically improves employment prospects. Of those leaving the YTS between July and September 1984, only 59 per cent entered employment and 30 per cent simply returned to unemployment (figures given in a parliamentary answer by the Secretary of State for Employment, 3 June 1985). Even this overstates the effects of YTS because it is not known what proportion of trainees would have found work in any case, nor is it known to what extent YTS trainees have displaced non-participants. There is no denying that the YTS and similar training programmes have had a considerable impact on measured unemployment but critics of the scheme have suggested that it merely disguises unemployment or, worse, has shifted the emphasis of training away from the acquisition of skills towards the social control of youth (Moos 1983).

Public employment programmes

Public employment schemes represent a direct attempt to reduce the number of unemployed by creating jobs. Previous schemes have included the Job Creation and the Community Enterprise programmes but the most comprehensive scheme of all is the Community Programme which was introduced in 1982. The scheme provides up to 12 months employment for the long-term unemployed on projects of benefit to the local community (with special provisions for priority groups such as the young or the disabled). While working on projects workers are paid the local wage for the job subject to a maximum overall weekly average (£63 per week in 1985).

The programme is administered by the MSC and has had major consequences for urban economies. Although many different projects are eligible for support, 98 per cent of projects up to mid-1985 have been organised by local authorities and voluntary organisations (*Financial Times* 17.7.85). In 1984–85 there were 130,000 programme places (to be increased to 230,000 in 1986) and of these a large proportion were projects located in inner city areas. The cost of the programme has been substantial (£549 million in 1984–85).

The case for the programme is that it directly affects the long term unemployed by creating job opportunities, that the community benefits from its projects, and that the scheme is relatively inexpensive. Several criticisms have been made of the scheme, some general to all such schemes and others more specific. A general criticism of all job-creation programmes is that they merely redistribute jobs among the workforce rather than producing a net reduction in unemployment. The crucial issue concerns the nature of unemployment in the local economy. If demand-deficient unemployment exists then schemes will be able to soak up the unemployed without raising wages and causing displacement effects, but if local labour markets are already at full employment then public job programmes will compete for workers against other employers, raise wages and reduce employment in the private sector (Hughes and Perlman 1984). In addition increased job opportunities may induce an increase in local participation rates with the effect that the fall in unemployment is less than the increase in the number of programme places offered.

The need to avoid displacement effects provides a justification for paying the going local wage rate. In practice there is a wide dispersion of rates and the Community Programme has tended to pay the minimum; according to the MSC the average weekly wage while on the scheme was just £58 in 1985. The scheme is therefore vulnerable to the charge that it only affords low pay and poor conditions (Finn 1985). Another dilemma facing public employment schemes concerns the nature of the projects. If projects compete directly for local demand then the possibility of displacement arises even if demand-deficient unemployment exists locally. Projects need to be non-marketed public services or to meet local demands currently supplied by firms outside the area if they are to avoid displacement effects. The 1985 White Paper on Employment describes Community Programme projects as including 'clearing up derelict land and canals, building scout halls, installing loft insulation and draught-proofing for pensioners'. The MSC has estimated that 40 per cent of projects have been in environmental or building work and it could be argued that such projects are 'make work' schemes of little true long-term value. In part this criticism is answered by attempts to link Community Programme jobs to short-term training but the extent of such training is limited; nearly 70 per cent of participating workers are engaged in unskilled work.

Even if the element of training is small, Community Programme places may provide valuable work experience and this could increase the employment prospects of participants. The Department of Employment has claimed that participants are, on average, between two and three times more likely to secure employment than other long-term unemployed. If this is correct, these improved job prospects for participants can only be at the expense of non-participants unless the total number of jobs is increased overall. If displacement does take place then the effect of the scheme is to change the distribution of long-term unemployment in favour of participants. In this case it becomes important to know who is likely to participate and who, by implication, will be the groups to experience increased unemployment as a result. The composition of Community Programme participants is mainly under 25 years of age (50 per cent), male (70 per cent), and white (94 per cent) (Finn 1985). Not only are older workers, women and ethnic minorities not benefiting from the scheme (as they ought, given their proportionate shares of unemployment) but unemployment among these secondary labour force groups may have been increased by the programme.

On the face of it, the Community Programme appears to represent an interventionist approach to unemployment, but this is not really the case. The programme has been designed to meet the needs of business by producing short-term and part-time employment at low wage levels; the alternative approach of expanding permanent full-time public sector jobs has been rejected. The programme has the added advantage, from this perspective, of increasing competition among workers and adding nothing to wage expectations while simultaneously reducing the number on the unemployment register. The only surprise is that the private sector has not made greater use of the scheme. The expansion of the programme, like the expansion of YTS and other MSC schemes, has also had the effect of 'crowding out' activities formerly carried out by voluntary organisations and local authorities. Many of these agencies are now largely subcontractors for MSC-funded schemes, local autonomy has been eroded and central control increased.

Regional policy and the urban unemployed

The traditional form of government assistance to areas of high unemployment is through regional policy measures. Regional policy has been in existence, in one form or another, for over fifty years since its introduction into Britain by the 1934 Special Areas Act. Over this period regional policy has applied to a varying pattern of areas and used a variety of policy instruments. These have included a number of different types of capital subsidies, a regional employment premium, physical controls on industrial development and a number of other measures. The vigour with which regional policy has been pursued has varied as the result of these changes in instruments and targets. Probably the most active period of regional policy was between the period 1963–79. Between these dates there was a conjunction of measures which appear to have had a substantial effect on the growth of manufacturing employment in peripheral regions (Griffiths and Wall 1984: 347). The extent of regional policy assistance has been significantly reduced since 1979 both in terms of the areas receiving assistance (see Fig. 5.3) and the amount of resources committed to the programme. It is hard to escape the conclusion that regional policy

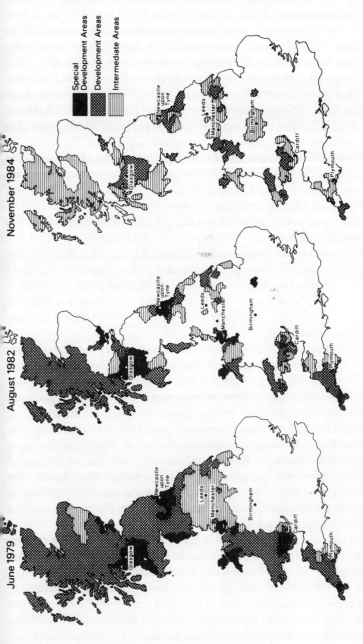

Fig. 5.3 The changing pattern of regional policy. Source: Martin 1985: 382 1.

has now been brought firmly under the austerity programme of the government's monetarist credo and that 'there is more at work here than just cost cutting; the reduced commitment to regional policy reflects the government's neo-market ideology' (Martin 1985: 380).

The present form of regional policy (since November 1984) consists of a two-tier system of assistance to industry located in one of two types of area: Development Areas (DAs) and Intermediate Areas (IAs). The geographical coverage of these two areas is shown in Fig. 5.3; the DAs cover about 15 per cent of the working population, while the IAs cover an additional 20 per cent. Although the geographical coverage was reduced in the 1984 revision, the proportion of the working population actually increased from 27.5 to 35 per cent largely because of the inclusion for the first time of some large urban areas.

Regional policy offers a number of incentives to assist in job creation. These are:

1.   *Regional Development Grant* (RDG). This consists of a grant of 15 per cent of the cost of new capital (excluding replacement investment) in the form of plant, machinery and buildings. This grant is automatically available to qualifying projects in the DAs, but is restricted to these areas alone.

2.   *Regional Selective Assistance* (RSA). This is a discretionary 15 per cent subsidy for capital and training projects which is available in both the DAs and the IAs.

Previous regional assistance was restricted to manufacturing industry only, but since 1984 a number of service industries have also become eligible, although only for RDGs (and therefore only in the DAs). In order to achieve a degree of cost effectiveness in regional assistance, a RDG is subject to a cost-per-job ceiling of £10,000. However, in an attempt to encourage small firms, this limit may be waived for firms employing less than 200 employees. For labour-intensive projects, an alternative grant may be made of £3,000 for each new job created.

In the past, regional policy has not been concerned with the plight of the cities and conurbations. Although a number of major urban areas were included within assisted areas, and some even had (the now abolished) Special Development Area (SDA) status (e.g. Glasgow, Newcastle upon Tyne and parts of Liverpool and Manchester), a great many were excluded, most notably the West Midlands conurbation and Greater London. The disproportionate growth and concentration of unemployment in cities and inner areas (as described in previous chapters) during the 1970s and 1980s meant that there was a growing mismatch between regional policy and the areas with the highest unemployment. Indeed, it is likely that regional policy worked to the detriment of a number of these areas by directing employment growth away from city economies to the assisted regions. Moore *et al.* (1983) estimated that regional policy had the net effect of creating more than 95,000 manufacturing jobs in the SDAs and DAs between 1971 and 1981. Given the parlous state of most urban economies it would seem likely that some of these job gains were at the expense of the unassisted metropolitan areas. These adverse effects should not be exaggerated; the extent to which the relocation of firms was responsible for urban decline was small, as Chapter 3 showed. However, regional policy may have had the effect of drawing the growth of new firms away from the urban areas, but this is more difficult to establish. What has become clear during the 1980s is that the traditional aim of regional policy to redistribute employment from regions of low unemployment to areas of high unemployment is not an appropriate response to mass unemployment. In some respects the recent geographical realignment of regional aid has been to the advantage of the urban economies. Regional policy in its present form is more spatially selective and attempts to relate regional aid more closely to the geographical incidence of high level of unemployment. This has resulted in the inclusion, for the first time, of parts of the West Midlands (Birmingham, Wolverhampton, Walsall, Coventry and Telford). It is the addition of these areas which accounts for most of the increase in the proportion of the working population covered by assistance. The removal of vast rural tracts of northern England, Scotland and Wales has meant that regional policy has become much more of an urban policy. However, there are still many cities and urban inner areas which have severe unemployment and social deprivation, but which do not have assisted status. Inner London is an obvious example of this, but there are many more. The main reason for this is that such cities are still judged on the basis of the more prosperous regional economies within which they are located.

In other respects, present regional policy is less satisfactory. The changes introduced in 1984 laid great stress on the cost savings which were to be achieved. These savings were made, first, by reducing the level of RDG to 15 per cent in all areas by means of abolishing the SDAs (within which the RDG had been at the rate of 22 per cent). Second, the reduced coverage of assistance meant that the proportion of the working population eligible for a RDG fell by 30 per cent. This reduction of resources has been estimated to be around £312 million, representing a cut of over 70 per cent in RDG (Martin 1985; see also Chisholm 1985). When introducing the 1984 scheme, the government forecast a 43 per cent reduction in RDG expenditure.

In so far as savings in regional policy resources are achieved by a redistribution from rural and small towns to previously unassisted cities and urban centres, then their impact on urban unemployment can only be favourable. It is an interesting question whether a capital grant of 15 per cent will be sufficient (in the absence of other measures such as physical controls) to retain jobs in the urban economies in the face of spatial restructuring and cumulative decline within these local economies, and in an unfavourable macroeconomic environment. The narrow spatial focus of policy may well lead to the creation of distortions in economic development, with urban areas outside the assisted areas carrying the double burden of urban decline reinforced by regional policy. A more fundamental criticism of regional policy is that it may deflect attention away from urban unemployment and any examination of alternative strategies for its reduction. As Martin (1985) has observed: 'Ultimately, sound and sustained local economic development is the key to overcoming the problems of high unemployment, inferior jobs, low incomes and the deterioration of the social and physical infrastructure.'

The Urban Programme

The schemes described so far are measures which have had an impact on urban unemployment but which are not specifically focused on urban or inner-city areas. In contrast the Urban Programme, as its title implies, is an example of a spatially selective approach to employment generation. The Urban Programme consists of a number of different schemes which have evolved since the original Urban Programme was launched in 1968. The main aim has been to improve the physical and economic environment of inner-city areas by supporting projects which:

(a)   are designed to regenerate economic activity, for example by improving or providing commercial or industrial premises, advice or training;

(b)   are designed to improve the physical environment by renovating buildings, clearing unused land and improving rundown housing;

(c)   are designed to meet social needs by providing community facilities for deprived social or ethnic groups.

The programme represents a major source of economic development funds for local authorities. The programme budget grew quite rapidly during the early 1980s, from £165 million in 1979–80 to a peak of £348 million in 1983–84 but a diminished emphasis on urban aid has led to reductions in the size of the programme by about 15 per cent in real terms to the level of £338 million in 1985–86.

The programme is intended to concentrate resources for development in those areas of most need. The largest share of resources goes to the 7 Inner Area Partnerships and 23 Programme Authorities designated under the 1978 Inner Areas Act (over a third of the budget); other designated districts under the Act are eligible for more limited assistance. Local authorities not covered by the 1978 Act must apply for grants under the Traditional Urban Programme. The assistance provided under the programme consists of 75 per cent grants from central government for approved projects. In addition urban development grants are available for schemes designed to attract substantial private sector funds.

The basic strategy of the Urban Programme is to regenerate inner city areas by means of environmental improvement and capital investment in permanent productive assets; nearly 70 per cent of the programme has been devoted to capital investment schemes. As the result major reductions in urban unemployment are likely to be achieved only in the long term and only small effects can be expected in the short term as the result of any additional local expenditure and employment arising directly from the projects. Even the achievement of these long-term objectives is open to question because of the deficiencies of the programme. The objectives of the programme are not explicitly concerned with the reduction of unemployment but include land reclamation and property development, both of which could lead to a conflict between differing goals. Second, grants under the programme require a 25 per cent contribution from local authorities or other organisations. In practice this has used up a large slice of council funds, the effect of which is to reduce other development activities and increase central control over local economic initiatives. In many respects the provisions of the Inner Urban Areas Act are idiosyncratic and provide inadequate support, for example, by limiting financial support to cooperatives to just £1,000. Perhaps the most fundamental criticism is that they may actually reduce employment and increase unemployment since the majority of projects amount to capital subsidies.

In addition to the problems identified above, the programme has proved to be difficult to implement. Central funding and approval of projects has made the process time-consuming and imposed a degree of uniformity on the scheme which may be inconsistent with wide variations in local economic conditions and it has proved difficult for some local authorities to act in partnership with central government for political reasons (see Parkinson and Wilkes 1985 on partnership in Liverpool). There is now also doubt about whether the designated areas really do have the worst urban problems since deprivation often appears to be as great in non-designated cities as in the designated ones, a result that Bentham (1985) puts down to successful political lobbying in the past. Even if areas are correctly identified, they represent only a small subarea of the local labour market and spillover effects from policy will be experienced.

More recently, the programme has become even more spatially selective. In 1981 Urban Development Corporations were established in London and Merseyside (in both cases covering dockland areas) while in 1985 five City Action Teams (CATs) were established to cover the areas of Birmingham, Liverpool, Merseyside–Salford, London (Hackney, Islington and Lambeth) and Newcastle–Gateshead. The CATs report directly to the Department of Employment and this has been interpreted as signalling an increased orientation towards job creation and the use of the Urban Programme as a means to reduce inner-city unemployment. They may also signal the intention to direct resources into inner-city economies while by-passing the local authorities in these areas.

Enterprise zones

Introduced in the 1980 Budget by Sir Geoffrey Howe, enterprise zones (EZs) are small designated areas within which planning controls are streamlined and financial assistance is available. The benefits of EZ status (which apply for 10 years) are:

(a)   exemption from general rates on industrial and commercial property (reimbursed to the local authority by the Treasury);

(b)   100 per cent allowances from corporation and income tax for capital expenditure on industrial and commercial property;

(c)   exemption from development land tax;

(d)   priority to be given to applications from firms for certain customs facilities;

(e)   exemption from industrial training levies;

(f)   speedier administration of any controls remaining in force;

(g)   reduced requests for statistical information.

Initially 11 EZs were designated on 15 sites but these were followed by a second round of designations which brought the total number to 25. According to the Department of the Environment the purpose of the EZ is: 'to see how far industrial and commercial activity can be encouraged by the removal of certain tax burdens, and by relaxing or speeding up the application of certain statutory or administrative controls' (cited in R. Tym and Partners 1984). The zones are clearly a product of the competitive market ideology but are far from the original freeport concept of Hall (1977). Hall proposed a package of unorthodox measures which he referred to as 'the freeport solution' to inner-city decline. This idea was taken up by Sir Keith Joseph and Sir Geoffrey Howe who proposed the establishment of deregulated zones called enterprise zones (a history of the development of these ideas can be found in Butler 1981 and Jordon 1984).

The difference between these seminal ideas and their implementation as EZs is quite marked. Many of the zones are not inner-city areas at all but are suburban (e.g. Speke) or even rural (e.g. Invergorden). The number of zones is greater than originally proposed and extent of de-regulation has been small. Rate relief and capital allowances provide an element of financial assistance not previously envisaged. This divergence between the original idea and its implementation was ascribed by Jordon (1984) to the pluralistic nature of liberal democracies (departmental wrangles, pressure group activity and the divided aims of government) and the practical problems of devising schemes which avoid fraud and deadweight spending.

EZs are administered by the local authorities in which they are located and in most cases have simply been absorbed into these authorities' overall economic development programme. This, together with the large public landholding in EZs has meant that EZs have been marketed as just another form of inner city or urban assistance to industry. In their second monitoring report on EZs, the consultants Tym and Partners (1982) commented: 'the public sector is taking a much more prominent role than might have been expected in an experiment directed at the private sector.'

As far as the job creation potential of EZs are concerned the main problem is likely to be a displacement effect as it is unlikely that the effects of policy can be localised. If local firms move into an EZ there is no net gain in local employment unless the number of jobs in firms is greater than it would have been had firms not moved to the EZ. Similarly, if new firms are created, they could be in competition with other firms located outside the EZ but still within the local labour market; this is particularly likely if they are firms serving the local (and therefore static) market.

It is fortunate that the EZ experiment has been closely monitored thus enabling a fairly accurate assessment to be made of the employment effects of the policy. An examination of the evidence confirms the worst fears concerning displacement effects. The number of firms and jobs which were 'incoming' (i.e. new and relocating firms) in the eleven originally designated EZs are shown in Table 5.2.

Table 5.2 The job-creation effects of enterprise zones: the first two years

Period	Firms	Jobs
1981–82	295	2,884
1981–83	474	5,035
1981–83	769	7,919

Source: derived from figures in Tym and Partners (1984) Figures relate to new and relocating firms in the eleven first designated enterprise zones.

At first sight the results appear quite impressive, with an average of more than 500 jobs per EZ during 1982–83 and over 1,000 jobs in each of Clydebank, Swansea and Corby. Further investigation reveals that 40 per cent of firms had simply relocated from other areas, and of these 86 per cent had moved from within the same county as the EZ. Furthermore, 75 per cent of incoming firms would have operated in the same county in the absence of the EZ and only 4–12 per cent would not have existed but for the EZ (Tym and Partners 1984). It appears that the net job creation effect of EZs is probably less than 10 per cent of the gross effect and the main impact of the policy has been on the location of jobs within the local labour market.

The policy may have had other effects on the pattern of jobs, and indirectly on unemployment, because it offers capital subsidies and, more importantly, rate relief. The latter provides the most advantage to industrial and commercial activities which are extensive users of property such as warehousing and large-scale retail operations. In 1982–83 more than 30 per cent of incoming firms in EZs were in the transport and distributive industries while 14 per cent were in other services. These kinds of activities would not be expected to create the sort of jobs which would match the characteristics of unemployed residents of these areas. Such jobs would probably be largely part-time and female employment. There is also evidence that in some of the more successful EZs a large proportion of incoming plants are branch plants (Bromley and Morgan 1985). The risk of employment instability inherent in this tendency was discussed in Chapters 2 and 3; it is an interesting question as to what will happen to the branch plants when the benefits of EZ status run out after ten years.

It can be concluded that the EZ is really a failed experiment. Supporters of the original zone of de-regulation idea will no doubt blame the implementation of the policy which has turned the EZs into just another example of old style regional policy dressed up in a modern guise (Taylor 1981). Certainly the EZs are not havens of *laissez-faire*; they are small geographical areas in which highly discriminatory subsidies are paid to capital. Massey (1982) has argued that the most important aspect of EZs is their ideological significance, as they promote a specific view of the causes of urban decline, foster the notion of free enterprise and create the 'political space' in which to attack local government and local services. Whatever view of EZs is accepted, they are expensive. Between 1981 and 1983 the total cost of EZs was £132.9 million; £16.8 million in rate relief, £39.8 million in public sector land development, £38 million in capital allowances and £38.3 million in other costs. This works out at a cost of £16,782 per gross job created. However if the net effect is less than 10 per cent of the gross effect (as estimated above) the cost per job rises to a staggering £168,000 per job.

Freeports and simplified planning zones

The EZ represents one attempt to implement Hall's idea of a freeport, but it seems to have emerged in practice as rather a different policy to that originally envisaged. The freeport idea is to be given another try in the form of six areas which were designated for freeport (FP) status in 1984. These areas are:

1.   Liverpool port
2.   Southampton port
3.   Birmingham airport
4.   Prestwick airport
5.   Cardiff port
6.   Belfast airport

Within these areas goods are exempted from the payment of all customs duties and value added tax (VAT) unless the goods are removed from the zones into the UK. A number of advantages are claimed for the FP. First there are a number of possible financial savings to be gained by firms located in the FP; for instance, improved cash flows as the result of non-payment of duties and VAT. There would also be some benefits from reduced administrative costs and less government form-filling. Employment may be increased both directly by attracting investment into the FP (from both home and foreign sources) and as the result of the growth of warehousing, storage, security and other related activities. In many respects these areas are more like the original concept but bereft of the general de-regulation which Hall intended.

The crucial issue as far as FPs are concerned is: Will they be successful in attracting new investment? This issue is too complex to be pursued in detail here, but Balasubramanyam and Rothschild (1985) conclude that this is not likely. In fact these authors conclude that 'it is hard to conceive of any advantages to be derived from such a development' although they quite fairly point out that FPs are in their infancy and it is too early to provide any firm conclusion. The problem with FPs, as with EZs, is that if they are successful they may damage the employment prospects of workers located outside the zone, whereas if they are unsuccessful they are a waste of effort and resources and deflect policy away from its proper objectives.

Just as FPs and EZs have each extracted a part of the original unorthodox package, so too the 1985 White Paper 'Lifting the Burden' selects just part of the *laissez-faire* strategy. In addition to more general measures relating to small companies and taxation, it was proposed to establish 'simplified planning zones'. These would enable local authorities to specify certain kinds of developments which would not need planning permission. It even suggests that private developers might be able to establish such zones for development purposes. So far this has not been attempted.

Job Search and Employment Transfer schemes

If employment cannot be created in urban economies, perhaps workers could be persuaded to move to other localities where employment opportunities are better. Two schemes exist to enhance labour mobility. The first, the Job Search Scheme, provides travelling expenses and subsistence for workers who are unemployed or under threat of redundancy. The second, the Employment Transfer Scheme, provides grants to enable workers to move to another area in order to fill job vacancies which cannot be filled by unemployed people in that area. The schemes have mainly been directed to workers in areas assisted by regional policy.

As a means of making the labour market more responsive to market conditions, the schemes may have some attractions. However, workers themselves do not seem to share this view and the numbers involved have been minute. In 1983–84, only 4,104 people benefited from the Job Search Scheme while the number benefiting from the Employment Transfer Scheme over the same period was only 3,780. On this basis such schemes do not appear, at present, to contribute very much to the reduction of urban unemployment.

The scope for local initiatives

A local employment initiative may be defined as any action taken by a local authority to alleviate a perceived employment problem

(JURUE 1980), a broad definition which makes it clear that a great deal of local authority activity is potentially a vehicle for employment initiatives. The emphasis placed on these initiatives has increased in recent years, for obvious reasons. For similar reasons local employment initiatives have come to embrace both 'industry-based' policies and 'people-based' schemes (Gregory 1984). The former initiatives aim to remedy the major causes of job loss and lack of job creation while the latter seek to channel resources to particular groups who experience high unemployment. Employment initiatives has become a 'catch all' term covering both kinds of activity.

The organisation of local initiatives

A local authority intending to take action to alleviate an employment problem has considerable scope for action, but is constrained in a number of ways; e.g.

(a)   the extent of its legal powers;
(b)   the resources available;
(c)   directives from central government.

The legal powers under which local authorities operate are derived from many different Acts of Parliament. Many of these place a statutory duty on the authorities to provide services ranging from employment services through education to welfare provision. When carrying out these statutory duties local authorities have some discretion about the location and scale of provision and have increasingly taken the consequences for employment and unemployment into account.

Supplementing their statutory duties, councils have permissive powers under which they may raise revenue for a variety of purposes. From the point of view of economic development activity the most important general powers available to local authorities are granted by the 1963 Local Government (Land) Act, the 1971 Town and Country Planning Act and the 1972 Local Government Act. These allow the authorities to engage in a wide variety of transactions in land and property, provide financial assistance to industry, conduct promotions and many other forms of development activity. The single most significant permissive power arises under Section 137 (s.137) of the 1972 Local Government Act. Popularly known as the '2p rate', this permits each local authority to incur expenditure up to the proceeds of a 2p rate where this is 'in the interests of their area or any part of it or all or some of its inhabitants'. The 1982 Local Government (Miscellaneous Provisions) Act explicitly extended s.137 to provide for industrial and employment initiatives and s.137 has been used extensively by local authorities for these purposes.

Local authorities may be granted additional powers through special or local Acts. The most important example of the former is the 1978 Inner Urban Areas Act. This is limited to designated inner-city authorities and provides powers to declare improvement areas, assist local industry and encourage cooperatives. In the case of local Acts, over thirty authorities have sought local powers to assist industry (e.g. the 1976 Tyne and Wear Act). Although extending their powers, these local Acts have inadvertently acted as a constraint on the authorities involved because they render many economic activities ineligible for s.137 finance, because that provision cannot be used to extend or modify another power. Ironically both the West Midlands CC and Greater London Council were unsuccessful in their attempts to obtain significant powers for employment initiatives by local Acts, and have therefore been left free to become the largest users of s.137 funds for economic regeneration.

Most local authorities have made organisational innovations to facilitate a greater role in local economic development, including the establishment of economic development units (EDUs) and unemployment units. In some cases legally separate development corporations or boards have been established such as Greater Manchester Economic Development Corporation Ltd or the Greater London Enterprise Board. Teams of economic and industrial development officers and other specialists have been recruited and this area of local government at least appears to offer good employment prospects! These organisational developments are discussed by Mawson (1983, 1984a,b) and Young (1983). As with all new organisations teething problems have emerged; newly established EDUs have sometimes come into conflict with departments more traditionally concerned with these matters such as planning and estates departments. Since economic development and unemployment policy impinge on many local authority departments such as education, housing and environmental health, issues have arisen concerning inter-departmental rivalries, status, and access to elected members. More fundamental issues are concerned with coordination and conflict in policy since different departments have differing policy objectives and do not always consider the wider implications of their own contribution to local government economic policy. This problem is compounded by the differing relationships which departments have with outside agencies and central government.

These organisational problems may be resolved by the formulation of an explicit economic development and employment strategy. The advantages of a local economic strategy are, first, that it requires an explicit statement of the aims of economic initiatives. In so doing it may also assist in identifying possible conflicts in goals. Given the complexity of much local authority organisation, a strategy may help to identify the responsibility for the different aspects of policy implementation and indicate the means by which coordination is to be achieved. Most important of all, a strategy provides a guide for tactical decision making which enables small-scale decisions to be placed in context by reference to the overall strategic policy.

The new orthodoxy

The essential feature of what Boddy (1983a) has termed 'the new orthodoxy' is that reductions in unemployment, in so far as they can be achieved at all, are seen as coming about by private sector employment growth in response to the creation of profitable investment opportunities in the local economy. Such conditions, it is argued, require a flexible and competitive local labour market supported by the appropriate provision of social capital and infrastructure and the removal of impediments and bottlenecks in other areas of the local economy. In particular, local authorities have sought to promote economic development by use of their traditional planning powers and their role as landowners and property developers. The main strategy pursued has been that of capital investment subsidies targeted, along with other assistance, on mobile firms and the small-firm sector.

Local investment subsidies

Local authorities have the powers to make and guarantee loans, make grants and provide other financial assistance to promote economic development. It is beyond the scope of this discussion to consider the details of local authority involvement in the property market (for a useful discussion of this see Boddy 1983b) but it may be noted that such property-led initiatives have increased in number to a considerable degree; in 1972 only 5 per cent of local authorities had new factory schemes (Camina 1974) whereas by 1978 this had risen to 57 per cent overall and 68 per cent of London boroughs (Falk 1978). Perry and Chalkey (1984) noted that by 1982 more than 20 per cent of all small factory units (under 5,000 sq. ft) in England had been built by local authorities.

Investment subsidies have taken a variety of forms:

1. Site acquisition and preparation.
2. Factory construction.
3. Grants to firms establishing in new factories.
4. Grants and loans for the acquisition of new equipment.
5. Subsidised rentals.

Clearly such initiatives involve considerable capital costs for the initiating authority although these will be recouped in whole or part upon disposal of the premises or from rent revenues. JURUE (1980) estimated that apart from administrative costs, site acquisition and preparation was virtually costless. In contrast, advance factory schemes can be expected to be expensive with construction costs not being covered even when market rentals are charged. Subsidised rentals and cheap loans also raise the costs of initiatives while direct grants are the most expensive of all forms of assistance. JURUE argue that such factory provision rarely yields a commercial rate of return, a conclusion supported by Willis (1985). However, many local authorities have developed innovations such as lease-back arrangements in order to foster a closer and more mutually profitable association with the private industrial property development sector.

The crucial issue concerning these initiatives is whether or not they are capable of creating jobs. There seem to be few grounds for optimism in this respect. The basic premise on which such policy is based may be erroneous. It has been argued that employment growth is constrained by a shortage of suitable premises or capital equipment, a suggestion forcefully put by the small-firm lobby. It is difficult to reconcile this argument with the overwhelming evidence that unemployment results from a shortage of demand; firms facing falling sales are unlikely to be influenced by policies designed to increase productive capacity. Investment subsidies and cheap industrial premises may simply displace old capital and premises without creating additional jobs; private capital is displaced by public capital. Ironically, investment subsidies will probably have most effect in prosperous areas (where capacity constraints are present) and least effect in the metropolitan economies (where there is excess capacity). These effects are compounded by the negative substitution effect on employment that is a common feature of all capital subsidies.

Important distributional issues are raised by the operation of policies involving industrial property. Many authorities have developed green-field and suburban industrial estates. This is partly a reflection of the lower development costs of such sites and partly an attempt to increase the attractiveness of the area to mobile firms. The result has often been to reinforce the suburbanisation of existing employment; inner-city firms may move to the more attractive suburban location with no net employment effect although the reduction in employment in the inner areas may be substantial (Cook and Harrison 1984). This effect may be partly offset by refurbishment of inner-area property but this is usually expensive and not suitable for many industrial processes. Therefore even if factory construction and investment subsidies increase employment in the whole urban economy they risk reducing employment in the inner areas. The residents of these inner areas, having low incomes and being constrained by the housing market, may be immobile and unable to fill new suburban jobs while the reduction in inner-area jobs adds to an already high level of unemployment.

As with most initiatives, monitoring and evaluation is sparse but it must be concluded that many of the above reservations appear to be borne out by experience. Cameron *et al.* (1982) suggest that up to 70 per cent of jobs created between 1976 and 1979 by the advance factory programme in Tyne and Wear would have existed without assistance. The gross employment increase was estimated at 950 jobs which is relatively small and results in a cost per job of nearly £41,000 (in 1981 prices) once deadweight is taken into account. Willis (1985), reviewing the evidence from three areas of Britain including Tyne and Wear, concluded that initiatives only become financially viable when exchequer financial flows (savings on benefits and increases in taxes) were taken into account and even then only after 25 years had elapsed.

Although striking at the heart of the traditional estates and property development role of local authorities, the analysis and evidence point to the relative failure of this type of traditional initiative. Although the gross number of jobs involved may be larger than most other initiatives it is disappointingly small in comparison with the resources involved. It is quite possible that the same level of resources devoted to other forms of employment initiative would have yielded a greater number of jobs. The initiatives have frequently accelerated decentralisation of employment and exacerbated inner-city decline.

Small firms and job creation

It is probably true to say that most traditional local authority employment initiatives rely largely and in some cases exclusively on support for existing and new small firms. This emphasis may be partly explained by the promotion and support of small firms by central government through the Small Firm Service, and the Business Start-Up and Loan Guarantee schemes. Local authority support has gone far beyond this with the provision of grants and loans, rent and rate holidays for newly established firms, and the provision of industrial and commercial premises in small units. This local commitment to small firms can largely be explained by the powerlessness of local authorities to prevent employment loss from plant closures and *in-situ* employment decline in large firms. Encouraged by the ideology of individual initiative and local enterprise, the promotion of small firms at least has the virtue of demonstrating that something is being done to regenerate the local economy and, it is believed, provides the basis for future employment growth.

Leaving aside the interesting question of the definition of a small firm and the confusion which often exists between small firms and new firms, it appears from new company registrations that the number of new firms in Britain has been increasing quite steadily since the mid-1970s (Bannock 1981; Binks and Coyne 1983). The stock of small firms has correspondingly increased, for instance the number of firms employing less than 100 employees increased from just under 18 per cent of employment in 1971 to around 22 per cent in the early 1980s. This is still some considerable way short of the employment role played by such small firms in the inter-war years when they accounted for over 30 per cent of employment. Nevertheless, the case for the support of small firms rests on their employment growth prospects. It has been observed in a number of studies that the rate of employment growth has been faster in the smaller firm size bands, indeed in recent years it is only in small firms that any net employment growth has taken place; in large plants net job losses have occurred. Macey (1982) found that, on average, only firms employing between 10 and 20 employees had increased employment between the years of 1972 and 1975. Similar results have been found in regional and local studies (Fothergill and Gudgin 1979; Storey 1980; Coyne and Lincoln 1982).

Despite the general picture of growth, there is considerable variation in the importance of small firms both between and within large urban areas. This is partly a reflection of the industrial structure of areas as there are differences between industries in the employment share of small firms, being as high as 44 per cent in printing and 22 per cent in machine tools but only 18 per cent for manufacturing overall. It is also a result of the differing net rate of new firm formation which can also be related to the existing industrial and size structure of the local economy since the rate of new firm formation seems to be lowest in areas which have a large proportion of employment in traditional heavy manufacturing industries and in large plants. This association appears to relate to the low probability of an individual learning the broad range of skills required to start a firm, the lack of contact which production workers have with customers and the general unconduciveness of the urban economic environment to the creation of new enterprise (Johnson and Cathcart 1979a; Fothergill and Gudgin 1982). The evidence tends to suggest that the inner areas of urban economies play a diminished role in generating new firms although there are differences between cities in this respect.

The renewed growth of the small-firm sector could be attributed to a number of factors of which technological change is a front runner. Bollard (1983) has demonstrated how electronic innovations and automation have reduced the minimum efficient scale of production in printing and machine-tool manufacturing. Such changes in the size structure of industries need not necessarily be associated with increased employment unless the smaller enterprises have a competitive advantage which enables them to obtain a larger market. This is unlikely in most cases because small firms predominantly serve local and regional markets (Johnson and Cathcart 1979b; Storey 1982) and are therefore dependent upon local consumer demand and intermediate demand from larger local companies for whom they supply goods or services or perform subcontract work. For this reason much attention has focused on innovating firms in the high-technology sector where the rapid growth of markets seems to present a better prospect of sustained output growth. There is little evidence on the pattern of innovative new firms, but Lloyd and Mason (1984) suggest that most such enterprises are located in the south of England; over half were located in the South West region but, significantly, few in Greater London. The prospects of large industrial cities experiencing employment growth from this quarter seems remote.

There are other reasons for being cautious about the wisdom of relying on small firms for economic regeneration. In the first place the survival rate of new firms is very low. The Department of Trade and Industry estimated that 50 per cent of new firms did not survive longer than two and a half years (DoI 1983). In Manchester and Merseyside the death rate of firms over their first 10 years has been estimated to be in excess of 60 per cent (Lloyd and Dicken 1983). This raises doubts about the long-term benefits of supporting small or new firms and also poses a dilemma for policy-makers. If death rates are very high then support will inevitably be given to a large number of failures which increases the cost of support. Alternatively, if support is to be given on a selective basis it is unclear as to how the successful firms of the future are to be identified. Some selectivity is desirable because not all new firms add to the total of local employment. In some cases firms are set up in competition with existing local firms, often by ex-employees and this can have serious employment displacement effects. Even worse, the subsidised new firm during its brief life may under-cut established firms and drive them out of business (Gilbert 1984).

Looked at realistically, it seems that the small-firm sector is unlikely to make a major contribution to the reduction of urban unemployment. It has been argued that social and economic change has created a situation in which there will be no growth in employment in Britain until there is a massive shift of resources to the small-firm sector (Bannock 1981) but even if this were true such growth is likely to take place outside the conurbations and the major metropolitan areas. On the evidence even this seems unlikely.

Local enterprise agencies

Another presumption of the new orthodoxy is that enterprise would flourish were it not for a lack of communication between economic agents in the local economy. The difficulties are seen as being greatest in the case of small firms and individuals wishing to start businesses. In an effort to overcome these problems, local authorities operate a variety of schemes and agencies designed to increase and facilitate the creation of new jobs by offering advice on government assistance, sources of finance, market research and so forth. Such activities are not without problems, there is a traditional antipathy between small business and local government while questions have been raised concerning the quality of the advice.

A private solution to the provision of advice has taken the form of local enterprise agencies (EAs). EAs need to be distinguished from the interventionist Enterprise Board discussed in the next chapter. The latter, while legally separate from its parent council, is nevertheless an extension of it. EAs, in contrast, are independent organisations funded by private sponsors whose aim is to mobilise local business resources to meet the needs of the community. These agencies may be wholly private sector initiatives but in the main are partnerships between public and private sectors. The number of such agencies has grown rapidly. Whereas up to April 1981 only 23 EAs were in existence, in June 1984 the number was 180 (*The Guardian* 1.3.85). Later surveys have put the number as high as 240 and there are expected to be more than 300 agencies by 1986 (Turner 1985).

The concept of the EA emerged around 1979 with the encouragement of the newly elected Conservative government. In 1981 Business in the Community (BIC) was set up by a number of business corporations (e.g. Marks and Spencer, ICI, Shell and others) together with the Department of Industry, the Department of the Environment and the Manpower Services Commission. BIC has operated with an executive seconded from industry and a brief to bring together business, local authorities and other organisations to identify and meet economic needs. It has been largely responsible for stimulating the growth in EAs. Central government has also encouraged this self-help approach to economic development by publishing a guide to establishing and running EAs and by offering tax concessions.

EAs carry out a number of activities in the main concerned with business advice. This may take the form of technical advice, e.g. marketing feasibility studies or it may involve acting as intermediary between entrepreneurs and other organisations such as the Small Firm Service (Department of Trade and Industry), Local Authority Economic Development Units and estates departments, or other institutions such as universities and polytechnics, local banks, etc. Financial assistance is rarely, if ever, provided although one of the functions of the EAs is to advise small or potential business on how they may obtain this from elsewhere. It is clear from surveys of enterprise agency clients and associated organisations that EAs are regarded as a great success. A survey of the clients of twelve agencies found that 11 per cent of those starting businesses and 9 per cent of those already in business stated that they would not have started or would have closed without the assistance provided. A further 53 and 34 per cent respectively, felt that it would have been more difficult to start their business or their employment would have been less without help from the agency (CEI 1985). It has also been claimed that such partnerships change attitudes and modify the behaviour of local organisations.

Publicity and promotion

Although there is something of the 'begger thy neighbour' approach to many local initiatives it is never more clear than in marketing and promotional activity. Such promotion and advertising could be classed as an employment initiative since it is aimed at attracting mobile industry to the local economy. Middleton (1981) showed that 86 per cent of local authorities surveyed were actively trying to attract firms from elsewhere in Britain and 77 per cent from abroad. The wisdom of sometimes substantial promotional budgets has been doubted by many, but for any local authority it is a classic example of the prisoner's dilemma; no authority can afford to stop unless the others do likewise. In the absence of such forebearance, the effects of promotion are largely offsetting.

Summary and conclusion

The approach taken in policy to alleviate urban unemployment depends on the underlying ideological perspective of the policy-makers. It has become increasingly apparent that central government is committed to a view of unemployment as arising from the weaknesses of the competitive labour market. This has led to a retreat from intervention, with the possible exception of the market for young workers, and to the introduction of policies designed to increase competition, incentives to work and to overcome institutional impediments to labour market adjustment. This has taken place in the context of a general economic approach which emphasises the virtues of private enterprise and a reduction of state involvement in economic affairs. The effect for urban areas is that there has been little new policy support for urban economies during the 1980s despite their massive job losses and unemployment. Where new policies have been introduced to assist urban areas they exclusively rely on the creation of a highly competitive market environment within a very small area. The analysis of labour markets in earlier chapters would suggest that such an approach is unlikely to be successful and the experiment with enterprise zones certainly bears out this expectation.

As spatial aspects of unemployment have moved further down the national agenda, local government has increasingly become involved in employment initiatives and unemployment policy. While local authorities have powers to promote economic development their impact has been limited for two reasons. First, most initiatives are inevitably modest because of constraints on local authority spending. Second, and more important, the traditional forms of economic development activity are not capable of dealing with problems of the scale of recent urban decline. Local authority powers mainly relate to land and property development with the result that most initiatives seek to regenerate the local economy by providing the conditions in which private enterprise can flourish through the provision of subsidies for capital investment, particularly in the form of industrial premises. Small firms are the main target for this activity in the expectation that they hold the prospect of future job growth. But the size of the employment effects of these policies is very small in comparison with the scale of urban unemployment, while the cost per job when displacement and deadweight spending is taken into account is very high and can hardly be justified even on a social cost–benefit basis. This result is hardly surprising when one considers that the main reasons for job loss and unemployment has been the closure of large plants and massive *in-situ* decline. When firms are faced by a lack of demand or are intent on abandoning the urban areas as part of a restructuring exercise, then capital subsidies and the promotion of small firms are unlikely to make much of an impact on the local economy.

Further reading

An examination of alternative policy responses to unemployment is contained in *Unemployment: policy responses of Western democracies* edited by Richardson and Henning (1984). The evolution of urban and local economic policy can be found in the following: Lawless (1981) *Britain's Inner Cities: problems and policies*; Young and Mason (1983) *Urban Economic Development: new roles and relationships*. Details of the wide range of central and local government assistance to industry and labour is contained in the periodic review *Financial Incentives and Assistance for Industry: a comprehensive guide* (5th edn, Aug. 1985) produced by the chartered accountants Arthur Young.

6
Radical local employment initiatives

Dissatisfaction with the traditional form of local employment initiatives led a number of local councils, notably the metropolitan authorities but also a number of city councils, to adopt more radical and interventionist policies during the 1980s. This change represents more than an escalation of pragmatic responses to rising urban unemployment. It reflects a fundamentally different political and ideological approach to the problems of urban economies which links the reduction of unemployment to increased local democracy and community involvement in local policy-making. The 1981 Labour GLC manifesto, for instance, stressed the need to

> increase the elements of democratic control over industrial decisions: control by elected authorities so that investment decisions are taken with regard to the wider interests of the community and controlled by workpeople in the workplace.

The underlying philosophy of radical policy is that the problem of urban and inner-city unemployment cannot be solved by market processes or traditional policies. There is a need to plan the local economy and to intervene directly in local industry and the local labour market in order to create jobs for local workers. This intervention should take account of the broad interests of the workforce, the community, and the disadvantaged rather than the narrow, sectional interests of industry and capital.

Ironically, this approach, while urging greater intervention in the local economy, views the roots of the unemployment problem and ultimately its solution as lying outside the local arena.

> It is important to bear in mind that intervention by the County will not necessarily overcome national trends which have an over-riding influence on the local economy. Nevertheless, the implementation of selective initiatives to assist local people and

industry can positively support the development of the economy and demonstrate to the Government that there are alternatives to its present economic policies. (WMCC 1984)

Even the staunchest of supporters of radical local employment initiatives would not see such policies, in the form that they are presently implemented, being sufficient to reduce urban un-employment in the absence of appropriate action by central government. However, opinions differ as to how far such local strategies are merely symbolic and 'educational' or, alternatively, are the means of making a real contribution to the reduction of unemployment.

The distinctive features of radical initiatives

The broad objective of radical employment initiatives is to directly intervene in the local economy in order to increase the quantity and quality of jobs for local people thereby reducing the level of local unemployment and its concentration among vulnerable groups. This objective is often associated with a secondary one of ensuring that production is to satisfy social need rather than the narrow objective of profit. In more specific terms, the objectives of such initiatives are:

(a)   to provide the means for immediate and direct intervention in the local economy in order to prevent the loss of jobs by plant closures or *in-situ* redundancies;

(b)   to plan for the long-term development of the local economy in order to secure future employment and production to meet social needs;

(c)   to support the unemployed, breaking their isolation from the world of work and facilitating their return to employment by means of training, advice and other support;

(d)   to improve the quality of employment and to increase the job opportunities for disadvantaged groups in the local labour market;

(e)   to explore, through examples, alternative forms of business organisation and to extend workers control.

In practice there are differences in the means by which local authorities have sought to achieve these objectives and in the priorities which they have attached to individual aspects of radical

policy. Despite this, a number of distinctive common features can
be identified.

Direct intervention in production

According to the radical perspective, the reason for the concentration of unemployment in metropolitan areas is the national and
international restructuring of production and a deficiency of
aggregate demand caused by government policy. It follows from
this that the decisions affecting local employment are taken by the
owners and managers of the production process and by the
government. Influencing the latter may not be possible, even
though it may be a prerequisite for the restoration of full
employment. Therefore, attention is shifted to decisions in
production. The spatial restructuring of production has resulted
in the movement of jobs away from the metropolitan economies
while the general decline in economic activity has meant that
many local firms have faced and may still face financial collapse. If
job losses are to be avoided or reduced, then intervention in
existing local production is required to maintain or even increase
the local level of labour demand and this can only be achieved by
direct involvement in the decisions about local employment. It is
clearly impractical to be involved in every such decision and it will
not be possible where control resides outside the local economy.
Therefore, policy measures tend to focus on medium- to large-sized
indigenous firms rather than small firms or 'footloose' branch
plants of large corporations.

Another aspect of radical intervention in the private sector is its
strategic nature. Certain sectors may be identified as strategically
important to the local economy and employment initiatives
directed to those sectors. Most local authorities pursuing radical
initiatives have conducted 'sector studies' to obtain the detailed
knowledge required for successful intervention. To some extent
this is making a virtue of a necessity. Because of the limited
resources available to local authorities they have been forced to use
them in a manner which secures the greatest effect. However, it is
also the case that attempts have been made to coordinate
intervention in order to avoid adversely affecting other local firms
or other industrial sectors. The strategic approach to intervention
is also a dynamic one; it emphasises change. It is recognised that
urban economies will be restructured by market forces in the

absence of intervention and that it is not possible or desirable to wholly prevent change. Instead, employment strategies seek to plan and guide such change so that it is more in accord with the interests of the people who live in the urban centres. As the London Industrial Strategy puts it, intervention 'is intended to provide a cushion to the process of restructuring' (GLC 1985: 45). In the face of inevitable change, an emphasis must be placed on the development of alternative forms of employment, measures to promote new and socially useful products and to train labour to cope with the effects of new technologies.

The role of the public sector

The local public sector plays a pivotal role in radical economic initiatives. The public sector can exert an influence on the local economy and the labour market in a number of ways. The public sector is a very large employer – for example, in London nearly one-third of all waged labour is employed in the public sector and of this about half is under local control. The local authority is often the largest single employer; for instance, Sheffield City Council employs over 30,000 people which is five times as much as the city's largest private sector employer. This in itself allows the local authority to affect directly the level and conditions of local employment. In addition to public sector employment, the local authority is also a major purchaser of locally produced goods and services and a major investor in the locality. In 1985 the GLC spent around £500 million on the products of about 20,000 different firms and for some of these firms the GLC was their largest customer. Similarly, in Sheffield, where total expenditure is about £80 million per year, some £20 million is spent on the goods and services of nearly 900 local firms. The importance of the public sector in the local economy means that it can affect, both directly and through the local multiplier, labour demand and employment. In addition the public sector can influence the operation of the local labour market through its own employment, recruitment and training policies as well as by means of 'contract compliance' and 'enterprise agreements'. In the former case firms supplying goods or services to the local authority must comply with conditions concerning employment, pay and trade union recognition while in the latter case the receipt of financial or other assistance is made conditional upon meeting similar stipulations.

Democratic planning

Whereas the competitive market perspective sees trade unions as being responsible for much of the failure of markets to adjust to conditions of excess supply, the radical perspective sees the trade unions as playing an important role along with other groups in the local community in the planning and implementation of employment initiatives. The trade unions are particularly important in two respects. First, they provide inside knowledge of firms and sectors where intervention may be required. Second, they can provide additional leverage for the implementation of policy in large, especially multinational, corporations where the local policy-maker is in a weak position to influence decisions. To increase this leverage, and as an end in its own right, most initiatives encourage the extension of trade union membership to areas of employment where membership has traditionally been low (such as women workers) and seeks to strengthen trade unions where they already exist. This mutual dependence of trade unions and radical initiatives is illustrated by the existence of many local 'early warning' systems, such as 'Jobwatch' in Merseyside, which are intended to provide local authorities and trade unions with an early warning of impending redundancies and plant closures. In the two and a half years up to mid-1985, the early warning system of the GLC identified more than 120 possible closures, of which a number subsequently received assistance from the Greater London Enterprise Board (GLEB).

Labour market policies

Employment initiatives are concerned with creating and retaining jobs. But not jobs at any price (or in this case, any wage or conditions). The quality of work and the equality of access to employment are equally important. The view is taken that a modern enterprise should offer decent and satisfying jobs. Thus it is usually a condition of receiving assistance from, or of supplying to, the local authority that firms must observe the provisions of the Health and Safety Acts, the Employment Acts, the Equal Pay and the Race Relations Acts. In addition, stipulations may be made regarding trade union membership (this is a condition for all GLEB assistance), training, equal opportunities and so forth. In addition, exceptional treatment may be accorded to vulnerable groups such as ethnic minorities or women in the implementation of the initiatives, as well as the initiating of projects specifically designed to facilitate the employment of these groups. Many local authorities also provide grants and other support to local groups and organisations which are concerned with employment and unemployment matters.

Employment initiatives in practice

Broad trends rarely manifest themselves in a uniform manner in every locality. As Chapter 3 has pointed out, local factors influence the way in which national trends operate in the local economy. In a similar manner the movement towards radical intervention in the local economy has not taken the same form in every area. Considerable variation exists in the emphasis placed on different elements of the radical approach and in the way in which employment initiatives have been implemented. These differences are the result of many factors including the economic structure of the local economy and its particular experience of employment decline, the differences which exist in the powers of local authorities and their organisational structure and, not least, the political perspectives of local policy-makers. Combined with the momentum gained by existing traditional initiatives, these factors have meant that the move towards radical solutions has partly taken the form of creating new policy measures but has also consisted of redirecting existing schemes to accord more with the overall radical strategy. The result has been a complex pattern of local authority agencies and forms of intervention, not all of it clearly distinguishable from 'the new orthodoxy' except in its underlying philosophy. The remainder of this chapter will examine some of the more significant aspects of the radical approach to local employment initiatives but it is important to remember that such developments need to be seen as operating in parallel with more traditional forms of economic development activity and local authority assistance which in many cases have been bent to fit in with the overall radical philosophy.

Enterprise boards

Undoubtedly the enterprise boards are the flagships of local authority interventionist strategy. The first of these boards was established in January 1982 by West Midlands County Council and this was rapidly followed by other metropolitan authorities. The largest enterprise boards are:

West Midlands Enterprise Board	(WMEB),	established 1982
Lancashire Enterprises Ltd	(LEL),	established 1982
Greater London Enterprise Board	(GLEB),	established 1982
West Yorkshire Enterprise Board	(WYEB),	established 1982
Merseyside Enterprise Board	(MEB),	established 1983

These enterprise boards have been used as models for smaller scale enterprise boards set up by a number of district councils and some London boroughs.

Although they vary in their scope and style of operation, all the boards have the same broad objectives; to act as a catalyst for the regeneration of the local economy by strategic intervention to create and preserve jobs. The strategic role is crucial because the resources which can be brought to bear are modest in comparison with the scale of the problem. By focusing resources on key industrial sectors it is hoped that a disproportionately large job-creation or preservation effect will result from industrial linkages and job dependency in the local economy (see Ch. 2).

The main instrument of intervention has been the provision of long-term development capital for investment in local companies. The aim of the boards has been to attract investment funds from financial institutions such as pension funds in order to create financial leverage which will multiply the impact of public sector investment. This not only spreads the risks between the private and public sectors but also means that a board can secure a role in the control of local enterprise for a relatively small stake. Examples of this financial leverage are provided by the GLEB which funded more than three-quarters of its investments by private finance, while an investment of £875,000 by the MEB (up to 1985) secured a further £1 million in private funds and government grants. The accountability of firms receiving assistance is achieved by securing directorships for representatives of the enterprise board, and the entering into investment and planning agreements with the companies concerned. By these means, at relatively small cost, the enterprise boards are able to participate in and guide the formation of local corporate strategy.

Enterprise boards are independent private companies set up by a local authority and financed mainly from s.137 money. Independent status has been sought because of the controversy which still surrounds the direct acquisition of the equity investment in local companies by local authorities. While some authorities have been prepared to invest without involving an external company (most notably Sheffield City Council), most have preferred an 'arms length' agency whose powers are more clearly defined and legitimate. Such an arrangement does bring other incidental advantages relating to a freedom from some of the restrictions of local government finance.

In part the differences which exist between boards are a reflection of the differing organisations of local authorities rather than fundamental differences in objectives. Both the GLEB and LEL are the main agents through which economic initiatives are carried out on behalf of the local authority and inevitably their activities involve the full range of economic initiatives. In the case of the WMEB, the WYEB and the MEB, initiatives are restricted to investment activity and other development functions are carried out by other departments of the local authority. Even so, there are differences in philosophy and practice between the boards. The WMEB, for example, has been primarily concerned with intervention in the traditional industries of the economic base of the West Midlands conurbation. Its objective has been to stabilise employment in existing local companies and assist in their reorganisation whether by financial restructuring, mergers or management buy-outs. The perception of the nature of the problem facing local companies is of a failure by the British financial system to provide the right sort of long-term finance on the right terms for companies facing the need to reinvest and re-equip for modernisation. This view of the problem can be contrasted with that of the GLEB which has seen the situation facing the Greater London economy not so much in terms of an 'equity gap' but in terms of a shortage of attractive opportunities for profitable private investment. The role of the GLEB has therefore been to act as a catalyst to new enterprise which, once initiated, will be able to secure investment funds. One result of this has been a considerable effort to create and support of firms involved with new technology, especially microelectronics and energy conservation, and with the promotion of new types of enterprise including ethnic minority businesses and cooperatives. Other enterprise boards have been rather more pragmatic in their approach, simply providing assistance as and when worthwhile projects have arisen.

It is probably not necessary to choose between alternative rationale for public intervention. The enterprise boards are essentially local in character and reflect their economic and social context. Differences between regions in the supply of capital may mean that both the GLEB and the WMEB are correct; nevertheless it does seem that the WMEB perspective is more akin to the experience of the metropolitan and northern industrial areas where unemployment is most heavily concentrated. The experience of these localities has been one of rapidly declining employment as the result of the closure of firms. Many of the traditional industries of the conurbations have experienced increased competition, especially from overseas, and faced with this loss of competitiveness there has been a need for increased investment. However, when profits are low or losses are incurred, firms face the unhappy choice of short-term borrowing to finance modernisation or steadily becoming less and less competitive. Many choose the latter course, but it is one of the ironies of the recession that many of the firms which suffered from financial collapse were those which attempted to modernise while firms using antique plant and equipment lingered on. The role of the enterprise board is to cut into this vicious circle of declining competitiveness, falling profits, stagnation, increasing indebtedness and financial collapse. The provision of equity capital and long-term loans enables firms to reduce their gearing (the ratio of debt to equity) and set their business on a more secure financial footing.

It is not surprising that differences between the boards are reflected in the type of enterprise receiving assistance. In the case of the WMEB, nearly 90 per cent of financial assistance has been equity investment in medium to large firms in the manufacturing sector mainly in the strategically important metal and foundry sector. This financial support has been limited to firms which employ more than fifty workers; smaller companies may be eligible for assistance if they 'have strategic importance to the West Midland economy or significant growth prospects' (WMEB 1983, s.2.2). The average size of assisted firm has 100 employees. This contrasts sharply with the other enterprise boards which have invested in a broader range of sectors and often in smaller companies. LEL has a number of investments in the fishing industry as well as in the service sector and manufacturing, and

Table 6.1 Job creation and preservation by enterprise boards

Enterprise board	Number of jobs	Number of enterprises	Cost per job (£)
GLEB	2,600	179	3,624–5,234*
WMEB	2,750	30	2,965
WYEB	2,000	31	2,220
LEL	600	21	4,100
MEB	733	9	1,193

The period covered is from the date of establishment until April 1985
*The lower figure assumes that half of the investment costs are written off; the higher figure assumes that all investment funds are written off.
Source: Various

although ostensibly concerned with medium-sized companies it has investments in firms employing less than ten persons. The GLEB has a minimum size of forty employees for firms within which it invests, but the average size of firm assisted by the GLEB is actually much smaller (twenty employees). This apparent contradiction results from the fact that the GLEB also has responsibility for the promotion of cooperatives, black businesses, and other small ventures.

There are other contrasts between the operation of the boards. The WMEB is concerned with the long-term growth prospects of companies and these are assessed on a commercial basis. LEL, however, provides subsidised finance in the form of loans at 2 per cent less than the bank basic rate. The GLEB goes even further in departing from commercial criteria and adopts a set of broad guidelines involving the nature of control within the company, the training provided and levels of local unemployment. Both the WMEB and the GLEB require companies to enter into planning and investment agreements covering such matters as the management of the company, salaries of managers and directors, industrial relations, health and safety and training programmes.

Evaluating the economic effects of the boards is difficult. On the positive side it may be claimed that the boards have been directly responsible for preserving or creating several thousand jobs (see Table 6.1) during a period of major job losses and rising unemployment. Enterprise boards (leaving aside the contribution of other local authority economic development units) have been credited with the preservation or creation of over 20,000 jobs since their inception (Benington 1985). In addition, there may be indirect employment gains, since the boards have chosen to invest in strategically important sectors. These jobs have been created at a cost which is small in comparison with many other forms of industrial aid. Most estimates of the cost per job of enterprise board investment suggest a figure which is very low in comparison to other forms of employment creation measures. Although the cost per job varies between boards, even the most expensive (GLEB) is only a fraction of the £50,000 and the £65,000 cost per job, respectively, of regional aid and enterprise zones.

The use of gross cost per job as the basis for judging the merits of enterprise boards may be misleading. Unlike regional aid, enterprise board assistance provides an equity stake in companies and this increase in the value of the boards' investment portfolio should be offset against the costs of job creation as should any repayments of loans. Equally, the most appropriate way in which to assess the cost of employment schemes is not the gross cost per job but the cost per job-year. In this way, the cost of job creation or job saving can be contrasted with the alternative cost of unemployment. The average direct cost to the exchequer of each person unemployed ranges from around £5,000 for a single person to £7,500 for a person with an adult dependant and two children. These estimates are only the direct financial costs and take little account of the indirect and social costs of unemployment; social audits carried out by some local authorities have revealed even higher costs arising from plant closures and redundancies. In Merseyside, for example, the cost of redundancies has been estimated at approximately £5,700 per redundancy within one year (with central government bearing about three-quarters of the costs) and in excess of £10,000 per redundancy after five years (MERCEDO 1985). Compared to these costs, the net cost of enterprise board investment seems small.

Critics have alleged that the enterprise boards are unnecessary, wasteful of public resources and distort industrial development (see Taylor 1985). If investments are commercially viable, it is argued, private funds will be forthcoming and public investment is unnecessary. If companies seek public funding in order to make investments which they would have carried out anyway, or if enterprise boards invest in economically non-viable companies, then such investment is clearly wasteful. It can also be argued that the industrial development of the local economy is distorted because assisted companies have an 'unfair' advantage. These criticisms are general to all interventionist strategies. More specific criticism alleges that the boards lack the financial expertise to make a proper assessment of the prospects of firms applying for investment funding. In fact, despite some well-publicised failures, the investment record of the boards is probably rather better than other organisations such as the Industrial and Commercial Finance Corporation which expects around 30 per cent of investments to fail (representing 10 per cent of its portfolio). In 1984 the GLEB was embarrassed by the failure of a computer company called London Microtech which cost the board nearly £480,000; nevertheless this still represented only 6 per cent of total investment. By 1985 the GLEB had incurred lost investments of slightly less than £4 million, but these were more than offset by increases in the value of the investment portfolio (Palmer 1985). By commercial standards such risks are unexceptional. In any case, even in the cases where firms closed down after receiving assistance from the GLEB the cost per job-year was still substantially less than other forms of job-creation schemes or the cost of maintaining an unemployed worker; the independent consultants to the GLEB, Thornton Baker, estimated that the cost per job-year in the twenty-seven investments which had ceased trading by 1985 was £3,300 (figures cited in GLEB, 1985).

The boards have been criticised on other grounds than cost. Those favouring the market economy argue that the boards have simply attempted to turn back the inevitable process of industrial and spatial change which must take place if Britain is to become more efficient and internationally competitive. More radical critics see the boards as just another form of municipal assistance to capital during the worldwide recession; they would question the value of trying to rescue failed capitalist enterprises. The former viewpoint would recommend the dismantling of the boards whereas the latter would prefer to see their powers widened in order to alter the form and balance of power in the local economy. A more technical criticism, but still important, is that the enterprise boards attempt to create jobs by subsidising capital rather than labour costs. As Chapter 5 has pointed out, this leads to partially offsetting substitution effects on employment. The substitution of capital for labour occurs rapidly because the firms receiving assistance use such funds for re-equipment and modernisation. There may be situations in which firms are rendered more profitable and expand output through the use of new capital but do not expand but reduce the number of jobs.

The future of the enterprise boards is uncertain following the abolition of the Greater London Council and the Metropolitan Counties in 1986. The independent status of the boards allows them to continue in existence, but they face difficulties in securing enough finance to continue their operations. The GLEB is particularly vulnerable because it was previously funded entirely by the GLC using s.137 funds. The government has provided funds for the year 1986–87, but it remains to be seen what will happen to the board after this period. In the metropolitan areas, boards will be funded by district councils. This almost certainly implies a cut in funding for two reasons: first, the districts are fully committed to their own economic development initiatives and, second, there is no longer any county council funding. The response by boards has been to look for institutional funds to replace s.137 money. The WMEB has set up the West Midlands Regional Unit Trust with Lazard Securities (a merchant bank) and by the end of 1985 had obtained subscriptions amounting to over £4 million from over fifteen separate pension funds, including those of Cadbury–Schweppes and London Transport.

The continued existence of the enterprise boards seems to depend crucially upon the government's attitude to them in the future, the financial state of the district councils, the continuation of the powers granted by s.137, and the capacity of the boards to generate other sources of funds. Unless the government changes its attitude towards the boards, and increases their funds, it seems likely that they will remain, for the time being, merely symbolic of an alternative approach to urban economic policy.

Local employment subsidies

With a few exceptions (such as the regional employment premium of 1967–76), the traditional form of industrial, regional and local assistance to industry has taken the form of grants and other measures designed to reduce the cost of capital, whether in the form of machinery or as property and buildings. Such indirect attempts to create employment can be counter-productive as the effect of such measures may be to increase the capital intensity of firms and reduce their employment. Radical initiatives are not immune to this criticism although they attempt to overcome these difficulties by measures designed to secure some degree of control over the way in which the restructing of production takes place. An alternative approach attempts to increase the demand for labour by means of employment subsidies which reduce the cost of labour, or the relative cost of specific groups in the labour force.

Employment subsidies were first introduced on a major scale in 1975 when the Labour government introduced the Temporary Employment Subsidy (TES). This was followed by a variety of other special measures including the Short-Time Working Compensation Subsidy, and the Small Firm Employment Subsidy (SFES). In a parallel development, subsidy schemes were introduced which aimed to tackle the rapidly worsening problem of youth unemployment. Initially such schemes were pure subsidisation but they quickly became entwined with the issues of work experience and training. Since the election of the Conservative government in 1979 all general employment subsidies have been phased out, but youth employment subsidies have been maintained and strengthened, first by the Young Worker Scheme (introduced in 1982) and, second, by the Youth Training Scheme which began in 1983. YTS was discussed in the previous chapter, but in the present context it can be noted that the scheme amounts to a universal school-leaver subsidy. In 1985, a subsidy of £2,050 was payable to employers while the trainee received an allowance of £26.25 per week.

The general case for wage subsidies has been presented by Layard (1976) and Layard and Nickell (1976, 1980) who argue that such subsidies will lead to an expansion of output and employment at less cost in terms of inflation, balance of payments deficits and public sector borrowing than other more traditional methods of expanding demand. Mukherjee (1976) has claimed that savings on unemployment benefit and gains in tax receipts will make such schemes self-financing, although more cautious assessments suggest only that the net cost (in terms of public borrowing) will be less than other policies for the same effect (Metcalf 1982). Critics of subsidy schemes have cast doubt on these claims and have alleged that substantial employment displacement effects will result from subsidies (Burton 1977; Addison 1979). The receipt of subsidy will give some firms a competitive edge over their unsubsidised rivals and, as a result, job gains in the former will be offset by job losses in the latter. Although such displacement effects cannot be ruled out, employment subsidies may produce net job gains if they can be provided to industries with high elasticities of demand – in particular, export industries and those in competition with imports.

All employment subsidies have the same basic objective of reducing the marginal real cost of labour and thereby inducing firms to employ more labour than otherwise would have been the case. A number of different types of employment subsidy may be distinguished according to their affect on employment. Subsidies may be designed to stimulate the creation of new jobs and expand employment (job-creation subsidies) or alternatively to encourage firms to delay or defer job losses and redundancies (job-preserving subsidies). In either case, there will be a net increase in the number of jobs compared to the level of employment in the absence of the subsidy. An alternative form of subsidy is aimed at lowering the relative costs of employing a particular group in the labour force, such as the young or the long-term unemployed, and encouraging firms to increase their recruitment from that group. In this case, while it is likely that employment of the target group will be increased, it is not so clear that employment will increase overall. Firms receiving the subsidy may substitute the cheaper subsidised labour for that of other workers, leaving net employment unchanged. This will not matter if the aim of policy is to secure a more equitable distribution of the burden of unemployment. Even if substitution does take place, a net increase in employment is still likely because subsidies reduce costs of production and encourage some substitution of labour for capital; both effects work in the same direction to enhance the net employment effect (see Ch. 5). In addition, since the marginal cost of employment is reduced relative to hours of work, employment may be expanded at the expense of the hours of existing employees. Subsidies, in effect, may promote a degree of work-sharing. Although this is good from the point of view of reducing unemployment it can lead to problems of over-manning and reduced labour productivity. A problem of a longer term nature is that subsidies may inhibit structural change in an economy by providing support for activities which have little or no economic future. This is a problem mainly associated with job-preserving rather than job-creating subsidies. In fact, the latter could be used to promote growth by encouraging employment in areas of the economy which have good growth prospects but which face short-term difficulties for one reason or another. In either case there is a risk of political lobbying both to make activities eligible for subsidies and to maintain such financial assistance.

The direct impact of any subsidy, either on recruitment or redundancies, will depend upon the level and form of the subsidy and the elasticity of labour demand. The larger the ratio of subsidy to the current wage and the greater the short-run elasticity of demand, the larger will be the employment gain. It can be expected that the effect of a given subsidy scheme may vary between firms, industries, and types of labour with the largest job gains being made in sectors with a high elasticity of demand and relatively low wages (particularly if the subsidy is a flat-rate payment per employee). Rajan (1985) has suggested that the impact of subsidies will be felt in two different ways. Initially, the impact of the subsidy has more to do with its effect on an employer's awareness of the plight of the subsidised group than upon its effects on costs. This produces a significant but short-lived response from firms; a year or so after introduction this effect of a subsidy has evaporated. The real benefits of job subsidies will only be felt after sufficient time has elapsed to enable reduced labour costs and prices, and changes in production processes, to create new jobs. Unfortunately, job subsidies in Britain have had a life span of between one and five years and therefore much of the benefit of this type of policy measure has been wasted.

Given the scale of subsidisation which has been taking place (albeit often dressed up as training) it may be wondered what scope remains for locally initiated employment subsidies. In fact there has been a rapid growth in local employment subsidy schemes during the 1980s. Cleveland County Council is often credited with introducing the first such scheme (a youth recruitment subsidy) in 1981 and since then the number has increased very rapidly. Botham (1984) estimated that by 1983 over thirty local authorities (including Greater Manchester, West Yorkshire, Tyne and Wear, Merseyside, Cleveland, Strathclyde and many lower tier authorities) were offering employment subsidies. A number of factors may be responsible for this growth in the number of local schemes. It may have become politically expedient for local authorities to subsidise local employment particularly because national subsidy schemes exclusively relate to young workers. In some localities the problem of unemployment is just as severe for groups such as older workers as it is for young workers. In addition, the national schemes appear to be primarily concerned with the short-term objective of redistributing the incidence of unemployment and reducing the numbers on the unemployment register. Employment subsidies could, alternatively, be used to promote the aims of a long-term local economic development strategy by supporting employment in strategic sectors, be they local firms, small firms, high-technology or any other sector with growth potential. Finally, it has been claimed (Packham 1983) that subsidy schemes can be administered more efficiently by local authorities than by central government. Firms may find local authorities more approachable, while local knowledge can assist the effective and efficient scrutiny of applications for assistance.

The main source of funds for local employment subsidies has been a combination of s.137 money and grants from the European Community Social Fund (ECSF). Three schemes are available, although the last two apply only to local authorities in assisted areas:

1. A grant of £35.00 (in 1985) to firms who wish to recruit unemployed people aged under 25.
2. A grant of 30 per cent of gross earnings to firms employing less than 25 people who wish to recruit unemployed people regardless of age.
3. A grant of 30 per cent of gross earnings to firms employing 25 or more people who wish to recruit persons from one or more of the ECSF priority groups (these include the long-term unemployed, ethnic minorities and the disabled).

In each case the maximum period of assistance is 26 weeks. Although local authorities have considerable discretion as to how they implement employment subsidy schemes, a considerable degree of similarity has emerged. In most cases service sector firms as well as those in manufacturing are eligible for assistance. Both stock and flow subsidies have been used, but where grants are made to large firms they are aimed at increasing the recruitment of the long-term unemployed. Jobs which are supported by subsidy are monitored to ensure their permanence and conditions may be attached to the provision of subsidies (relating to union recognition or minimum wages). Firms may be required to repay any grants received if they breach these conditions or if they move out of the area.

The selective application of employment subsidies to urban areas with high unemployment has a number of advantages. It partially offsets the overwhelming bias towards capital in most traditional urban and regional policies and by restoring relative factor prices promotes both additional employment and increased economic efficiency. In addition, local labour subsidies may have a greater effect on employment than schemes applied nationally because local firms will face more price elastic demands for their products than is the case for whole industries. A given reduction in the marginal cost of labour will generate a relatively large output response as local firms gain an advantage over competitors located in other areas. Equally, the prospect of employment subsidies may attract firms into the local economy. In either case the total level of local employment will increase and the level of unemployment will fall.

Whatever the merits of employment subsidies in principal, there are a number of practical problems which arise in any implementation of such schemes. The major difficulty is that of minimising deadweight spending which arises when subsidies are paid to firms for jobs which would have been created in any case or to avoid redundancies which would not have occurred. Such a waste of resources may be partly avoided by careful and detailed investigation of every application for assistance; this raises the administrative costs of schemes, reduces the speed at which they can be processed and may ultimately reduce the number of applications received. Alternatively, administration can be kept to a minimum but only at the cost of allowing deadweight spending to increase. Offsetting this, local knowledge of the firms involved and of the conditions in the local economy may enable reasonably effective scrutiny to be carried out by the local authority departments administering the schemes.

In support of local employment subsidies it can legitimately be claimed that local authorities operating such schemes have been able to support a large number of jobs within a short period of time. The scheme operated by the Greater Manchester CC was supporting nearly 500 jobs within six months of its commencement, while a similar scheme in Strathclyde was supporting 2,175 jobs after only twelve months. However, a much smaller response has been experienced by other local authorities such as Cleveland where, after nearly eighteen months, only 82 jobs had received support (Botham 1983). The cost of employment subsidies does not appear great, being about £500 to £1,000 per job on average. Unfortunately it is impossible to know what proportion of these jobs are net gains. Evidence relating to earlier national subsidy schemes such as TES and SFES suggest that deadweight spending could be as much as 50–60 per cent of gross job gains (Layard 1979; Deakin and Pratten 1982) but, for the reasons discussed above, this may be less likely for spatially selective and locally administered schemes. Significantly, the industries receiving most support from local employment subsidies are much the same as those which received support from the TES, namely textiles, footwear and leather goods, and clothing. Perhaps more worrying is the support which has been given to activities such as construction and retailing which are sectors likely to produce high levels of job displacement through competition for local customers. More positively, surveys of firms which have received support suggest that the jobs created have remained in existence after the subsidy has ended, often with the original recruit in employment.

Although employment subsidies have created jobs their impact on the long-term unemployed appears to have been fairly limited. Few large firms have taken advantage of the schemes and where small firms have done so they were not obliged to, and generally did not, recruit the long-term unemployed. It seems that employment subsidies have been of most help to small firms. Similarly, Botham (1983) has shown that areas with the highest unemployment have been least successful in securing employment subsidies. In Greater Manchester, the inner-city areas of Manchester and Salford accounted for 35 per cent of unemployment but only received 14 per cent of subsidies, largely because of a lower rate of application for support. It would seem, in this case at any rate, that the operation of the subsidy scheme has served to reinforce the underlying process of employment suburbanisation, which is part of the original cause of urban unemployment.

Workers' Cooperatives

The ideals and philosophy embodied in workers' cooperatives and similar common ownership enterprises are particularly attractive to local policy-makers who favour greater planning in a more democratic local economy. Such enterprises, owned and controlled by those who work in them, are hardly a new idea (they date back more than 150 years to the nineteenth-century socialist Robert Owen) but they have assumed a renewed significance within the context of local employment initiatives. In the ten years between

1975 and 1985 the number of cooperatives has grown from 30 (the majority of which were in Greater London) to more than 1,000 in many locations within Britain. More than 10,000 workers are employed in cooperatives and common ownership enterprises.

In principle, a cooperative has a number of advantages over more conventional private enterprise. As the workforce own the enterprise, their motivation and productivity is increased, while their involvement in decision-making and identification with the goals of the enterprise may reduce alienation and require a lower level of remuneration. Taken together, higher productivity and/or lower wages may mean that some activities which are not economically viable when undertaken by private enterprise become so when carried out by cooperatives. Common ownership has other advantages. For the employee it may bring greatly increased security of tenure, for the enterprise the benefit comes from the increased flexibility of the workforce as traditional demarcation of jobs may be reduced and communications improved, while the local community may gain a socially responsible locally controlled enterprise. In practice, cooperatives are to be found in a great many forms in different activities and of varying size. Most tend to be fairly small in size and are usually new ventures established to exploit a gap in an existing market or to respond to new technological or market opportunities. Larger cooperatives often, but not always, have their origins in failing or failed businesses where the existing workforce are able to rescue the business through the establishment of a cooperative.

Despite the advantages of common ownership it remains the case that cooperatives have remained, until recently, a relatively rare form of business organisation. The reason for this is that cooperatives face two related problems: their legal status and finance. Until 1976 cooperatives had a somewhat ambiguous existence, being covered neither by company law nor the law relating to provident societies. This situation was rectified by the 1976 Industrial and Common Ownership Act which established a legal definition of common ownership and industrial cooperative enterprise. Because of these legal complications, prior to 1976 it was very difficult for cooperatives to secure finance from the usual commercial sources. Attempts to overcome this problem led to the establishment of the Industrial Common Ownership Finance Ltd (ICOF) in 1972, the Scottish Cooperative Development Committee (SCDC) in 1976 and the National Cooperative Development

Agency (NCDA) in 1978. The Cooperative Bank, a subsidiary of the Cooperative Wholesale Society has also provided some financial assistance.

The scale of the support at a national level has been minimal. The NCDA has a relatively small budget and restricts its activities to promotion and advice. The ICOF, in addition to giving advice, operates a revolving fund from which loans have been made to start new cooperative enterprises and to recover failed businesses. However, the main impetus towards the development of co-operatives has been from local authorities. This support has taken the form of grants and loans provided under the Inner Urban Areas Act (although limited to £1,000) and from s.137 money. To encourage and provide material assistance to common ownership enterprise many local authorities have set up local Cooperative Development Agencies (CDAs).

Local authority CDAs typically offer a comprehensive range of services to cooperatives. They provide feasibility studies, financial forecasts, market research, financial advice and other services to assist in the establishment of cooperative enterprises. In addition, many CDAs have links with the ICOF. By 1984, West Midlands CC had made grants totalling £500,000 to the ICOF to be channelled through three CDAs in Birmingham, Coventry and Wolverhampton. Once cooperatives have been established many CDAs provide assistance with training for management because, as one local development agency has observed, 'most cooperatives are formed by unemployed people with particular skills but no business knowledge' (MERCEDO 1985).

Under the active support of the CDAs the number of cooperatives has grown rapidly. A wide variety of activities are covered ranging from engineering and electronics to wholefood warehouses and restaurants. In the West Midlands, between 1981 (when the cooperatives initiative was launched) and 1984, more than 40 cooperatives were created involving more than 200 jobs. In Sheffield, over a similar period, 30 cooperatives and 140 jobs were created. Perhaps the most energetic promotion of cooperatives has been by GLEB which provided assistance to 25 cooperatives (out of a total of 27 assisted enterprises) in its first six months of existence, a number which had risen to 95 by 1985. In a number of cases these 'new' enterprises were rescues of non-locally owned branch plants which faced closure as the result of corporate restructuring. Altogether, cooperatives account for approximately half of all

GLEB investments (although only accounting for 10 per cent of funds).

Despite these impressive results, the number of jobs created by cooperatives remains small in comparison with the scale of urban unemployment. In terms of cost per job, cooperatives are relatively cheap; the average size of grant received by West Midland cooperatives has been £8,650 per cooperative, or £1,817 per job in gross terms, while in Sheffield the cost per cooperative was £11,240 and £2,400 per job. In Merseyside the cost per job has only been £640 (although the number of jobs was only 50). These costs compare favourably with other initiatives since much of the assistance consists of loans which will eventually be repaid (and recycled back as further aid to cooperatives). Net employment effects are difficult to assess and in some cases new cooperatives may simply legitimate work previously carried out in the informal economy. This would be a good thing from many points of view, not least for the gain in tax revenue, but would not add to total employment. In addition, displacement effects can be expected from cooperatives which are in competition for local customers, for example in the printing, retailing or building sectors. It has been alleged (Abel, 1985) that radical local authorities favour cooperatives over other small businesses and that any cooperative regardless of activity or viability will obtain assistance. If so, this would be wasteful of resources and damaging to the credibility of local initiatives, but the proposition is difficult to verify. A somewhat facetious refutation of this charge was made by the Director of GLEB in response to an equally facetious and hypothetical application for assistance invented by a journalist. The application was assessed thus: 'Black, that is a plus. Lesbian? Small additional plus. Engineering, we're in favour. Cooperative? Very much. Yes. But you are going to lose money for ever? Sorry, sisters, we are not a charity. We can't help you' (quoted in *The Guardian* 2.2.84). It seems that cooperatives are to be favoured, but only if they can demonstrate that they will produce economically viable and socially useful jobs.

A more fundamental criticism argues that cooperatives contribute little to long-term economic regeneration. There is little evidence so far that small cooperatives grow into large ones. Cooperatives in Sheffield have only maintained a static level of employment in contrast to private firms receiving assistance which managed to increase their employment on average by three new employees per enterprise. While this is a valid criticism to make, it ignores the significance of cooperative enterprise for workers whose secondary labour market status normally condemns them to employment instability and a high probability of unemployment. Traditional forms of business organisation may not be accessible to such marginal workers. Cooperatives may offer the only genuine route to an increased control over their working lives. Although the impact of such new forms of enterprise on the total number of local jobs may be small, their impact on particular social groups should not be underestimated.

Local government fiscal policy

The notion of using the local public sector to lead the economic regeneration process has formed an important element in many of the more radical strategies adopted by local councils. Quite apart from an ideological attraction, the expansion of the local public sector appears to offer a number of advantages as a route to reduced levels of local unemployment:

1.   Public employment has a direct and measurable effect on local employment.
2.   By appropriate recruitment and selection the impact of employment expansion can be focused on local residents and the long-term unemployed.
3.   Increases in public spending will increase jobs in local firms which supply goods and services.
4.   A reduction in unemployment may be engineered while at the same time increasing community welfare by the provision of public goods for collective consumption.
5.   An expansionary fiscal policy can be implemented through the normal course of council activity without the need for special schemes or additional administration.

Critics of such an approach point to the financial requirements of such a policy and argue that higher local taxation will lead to offsetting employment losses. The crucial question concerning local fiscal policy thus concerns the relative employment impacts of local public expenditure and local taxation.

An increase in local government expenditure can be expected to increase employment in the urban economy directly through increases in the public sector workforce and indirectly through the increased employment of local firms providing goods and services. In addition, there will be secondary employment effects as the result of the operation of the local multiplier process. The precise size of the increase in employment will depend upon the scale of the fiscal stimulus, the form which it takes and the size of the local multiplier (see Ch. 2). However, the net effect of an increase in local government expenditure is affected by the prevailing state of urban markets; displacement or 'crowding out' effects may arise if spare resources are unavailable. When this happens the effect of increased public expenditure is to transfer resources from the private to the public sector with only a limited or even a zero net effect on employment.

Crowding out will occur if an expansion of local demand encounters markets which are supply constrained; these might be labour submarkets for occupations or skills, or might be local land, property or capital markets. Any attempt to expand demand in these circumstances will cause prices to rise in the markets which are fully employed and this, in turn, will cause some reallocation of resources away from the private sector. The extreme case is where a fixed ratio of inputs is required in production and no cooperating factors of production are available for labour to use. In this case, despite an increase in demand, no increase in employment can take place until there is an increase in the supply of other factors. For instance, an expansion of a local authority housing programme might be expected to increase the number of jobs in the building trades and reduce unemployment as unemployed workers were hired. However, if there is already local full employment (i.e. only frictional levels of unemployment) in the building trades then any reduction in unemployment will be temporary; wages will be bid up in the competition between private and public sectors and labour costs and house prices will rise. The effect of increased house prices will be to reduce private sector demand for housing. The ultimate effect of the fiscal expansion will be to switch employment from the private sector to the public sector with little net job gains. A similar effect might occur if there was a shortage of other factors such as building land.

The critical factor determining the effectiveness of an expansionary local fiscal policy is the absence of local supply constraints. As far as labour is concerned, this condition is likely to be satisfied in most metropolitan labour markets as the evidence of Chapter 4 has clearly shown. While there may be a small number of occupations in short supply (generally in the field information technology) there is chronic excess supply in most urban labour markets and it seems unlikely that an expansion of labour demand could not be accommodated. In contrast, it has been argued that the absence of cooperating capital will prevent any public sector led expansion (Scott and Laslett 1978). This is a real danger particularly in view of the large number of plant closures which have been experienced in urban economies in recent years. Such closures deplete the capital base of local economies. Once such industrial capacity has been lost it is extremely difficult to replace and the expansion of employment to former levels may be inhibited. This is an incentive to provide support for local firms and the maintenance of local levels of aggregate demand has a part to play in such a strategy. Without such fiscal support there may be further shedding of excess capacity and further constraints on the possibility of future economic recovery.

Any increase in local public expenditure has to be financed, and in order to do so rates may be raised. As rates represent a cost to business (albeit a rather small proportion of total costs) it has been argued that increased taxation will lead to some reduction in employment among local firms while causing other firms to move jobs out of the area. The counterview is that the incidence of rates (as a tax on land) will be borne entirely by landowners, in which case the effect of rates on business costs may be minimal and limited to a reduction in the capital value of industrial property in the case of firms which own their own premises. The accumulating evidence relating to enterprise zones lends some support to this proposition. In many of the zones, where no rates are charged, property rents have increased to an extent which has offset the benefit of not having to pay rates (Cadman 1981; Norcliffe and Hoare 1982). The evidence relating to the employment effects of local taxation was discussed in Chapter 3 where it was concluded that the limited available evidence on this matter does not support the view that high levels or increases in rates have a negative net effect on local employment (see Gripaios and Brooks 1982 and Crawford *et al.* 1985). However, even if business rates were shown to have a negative effect on employment it must be remembered that only half of all rate revenue is raised this way (the remainder being levied on domestic property) while around 55–60 per cent of total expenditure is financed by grants from central government. Thus, on average, only a quarter of any increase in local expenditure will fall on local businesses and any reductions in employment will be correspondingly less.

The most direct method of expanding local employment and providing a fiscal stimulus to the local economy is by means of an expansion of direct labour. This also has the advantage of allowing control over the recruitment of workers to new jobs enabling employment expansion to be directed to the local and possibly long-term unemployed. However, there is little evidence of any massive expansion of local government employment in response to increased urban unemployment. Although large increases in local authority employment took place in the 1960s, since the recession of 1979–83 the total number of people employed by local authorities has declined with only the police, social services and the housing sector recording any expansion in the number of jobs. The most likely reason for this is simply that local authorities have experienced considerable financial difficulties during the 1980s and have sought to streamline their own operations. This, plus the effects of government policy on the privatisation of local authority services has meant that local government employment has fallen alongside that in the private sector. Of course there are exceptions, most notably the West Midlands CC which increased its full-time workforce by 14 per cent and its part-time workforce by 95 per cent over the period. A number of notably radical London boroughs – including Islington, Hackney and Lambeth – also increased their employment substantially during this period and the possibility that this was a direct response to mounting metropolitan unemployment cannot be ruled out.

Employment initiatives and the quality of work

While poverty and low pay are not restricted to urban areas, there is a concentration of poverty in many inner-city areas of Britain (see Holterman 1975). As has already been shown in previous chapters, these areas also contain the greatest concentrations of urban unemployment and this is a reflection of the association which exists between poverty, low pay and unemployment. The residents of urban-core and inner-city areas often experience poverty as the result of a mixture of intermittent employment and periodic spells of unemployment (although the duration of these spells is likely to have increased dramatically during the 1980s) coupled with low pay and poor conditions while in work (for non-spatial evidence of these associations see DHSS 1984). Those groups in the labour force most likely to experience unemployment (such as the young, the unskilled, ethnic minorities, and women) are also those most likely to experience low pay.

Explanations of unemployment which emphasise the role of market processes tend to see the reduction of concentrations of urban unemployment and an improvement in pay and conditions as mutually exclusive goals, in the short term at any rate. Unemployment persists because the wage rates of some groups in the labour force are too high. Because the young or the unskilled, for instance, have low productivities they only have a low value to employers and will only be employed if their wages are low enough to make their employment worthwhile. If low pay and un-employment continue to coexist, the reason must be that wages are not low enough. In the long term, according to this perspective, low pay may be eliminated only by raising the productivity of workers, perhaps through training but also by means of technological change and capital investment. In contrast, more radical views of the labour market which stress the importance of labour market structure suggest that unemployment and low pay are just two aspects of the same problem, namely the secondary labour market status of some workers and the shortage of good jobs. The segmentation of the labour market was discussed in Chapter 2 and suggests that the labour market consists of a number of non-competing submarkets. Good jobs are in relatively short supply and some groups in the labour force are crowded into poor, low-paying jobs in the secondary sector where they meet the employers' needs for a flexible and cheap reserve of labour. From this point of view it may be possible to reduce unemployment and improve pay and conditions if the supply of good jobs can be increased and if such jobs can be made more accessible to disadvantaged groups in the labour force.

Changes in the nature of employment and in employers' labour market practices are not likely to take place spontaneously; instead they must be pursued through intervention in the labour market. Local authorities which view the employment problems of their local labour markets in these terms see themselves, in the absence of central government policy, as having a new role, 'one that explicitly attempts to compensate for the failure of the local labour market to create and sustain genuine employment opportunities for many groups of workers' (GLC 1986). Radical local employment initiatives thus regard changes in the nature and conditions of employment and increased job opportunities for secondary labour market groups as being as important as job creation. In practice the latter tends to dominate employment initiatives simply because of the urgency of the need to reduce local unemployment but also because it may be easier to achieve these changes when employment is increasing.

The local authority as employer

The sector of employment over which local authorities have most control is their own labour force. As the largest employer in many local labour markets the local authority can, at the very least, set an example to other employers in the locality by means of its employment, recruitment and training policies. It could go further and seek to positively discriminate in favour of disadvantaged groups. It is certainly true that the local public sector has not always lived up to high ideals in its employment policy, especially as far as black and other ethnic groups are concerned. MERCEDO (1985) cites the examples of Merseyside County Council which employed only some 30 black people on a workforce of 6,000 and Liverpool City Council which employed about 300 black people on its workforce of 36,000. As far as equal opportunities for women are concerned, the problem is one of access to senior positions rather than access to employment *per se* since local authorities are among the largest employers of women workers. There are many different forces responsible for differing employment opportunities and many of them are beyond the reach of local authorities. Most have responded by organisational measures designed to monitor their own employment practices, encourage staff development and to take more active measures where possible. Action on low pay is complicated by the difference in hours of work which often exist between local authorities and private employers. Hourly rates of pay are generally much higher in the public sector but hours of work are shorter. As the result, many local authority employees earn less than their counterparts in the private sector and low pay can be found among the employees of both sectors.

Contract compliance and enterprise agreements

The problem of secondary employment outside the local authority has been tackled by means of financial leverage involving contract compliance and enterprise plans. The latter requires that firms which receive financial and other assistance from a local authority must agree to certain conditions relating to employment involving the implementation of existing legislation regarding employment protection, health and safety, equal opportunities and racial discrimination. Other conditions may be imposed relating to trade union recognition and the target groups for any resulting recruitment. Similar conditions are sought through contract compliance which involves an attempt to influence the employment practices of firms which supply goods or services to local authorities by inserting appropriate clauses in contracts and by vetting firms which apply to be included on approved lists for tendering. To some extent this has always been the case because all government contracts, whether central or local, contained a 'fair wages' clause designed to ensure that employees of government contractors received reasonable wages. However, this practice was abandoned by central government in 1983, one consequence of which was to leave the local authorities with no mechanism for dealing with breaches of their fair wages clause, although such measures have always faced problems of definition and implementation. As the result many local authorities have turned to contract compliance. The difference between this and the fair wages clause is that contract compliance makes contracts conditional with the compliance with existing legislation. Firms which do not agree to abide by such legislation will not be awarded contracts nor be placed on the council's list of approved suppliers. Such an approach obviously relies upon the financial leverage provided by the size of local authority budgets. Its effectiveness in changing the conditions of employment in the local labour market depends upon a number of factors. In the first place much depends upon the volume of business carried out with local firms and the extent to which they rely on council business. In the case of larger firms less leverage may be exerted if council contracts represent only a small fraction of business or if the supplier holds a local monopoly so that the local authority has little option but to contract business. Local monopolies can be undermined by the threat of competition from direct labour but this possibility may be limited in the case of many goods and some services.

Both contract compliance and enterprise agreements face a similar dilemma. Improvements in pay and condition may raise costs of production in general and in relation to other locations. If financially weak firms are forced to change employment practices and pay levels, there is the risk that such firms may not be able to survive without drastic restructuring and investment. Imposing the conditions may mean that the firm goes out of business altogether. Alternatively the firm may be able to increase productivity by reorganising production in order to pay for the improved pay and conditions. This may result directly in job losses and in some cases firms may feel that if they have to restructure they may as well reconsider all aspects of production, including location, with the result that some firms may prefer to move to more favourable locations rather than remain where they are and meet the conditions imposed by the local authority as the price of its assistance. Links between firms must also be borne in mind. The imposition of conditions on firms, whether by means of contract compliance or by enterprise agreements, may have consequences as far as suppliers or customers are concerned. There have been instances of hostile reactions from customers to changes in employment practices and the extention of worker democracy and unionisation, and where this happens there is a conflict between the preservation or creation of jobs and the achievement of goals relating to the quality of work.

Local training programmes

Training programmes have come to be more or less monopolised by the Manpower Services Commission with the result that local authorities are little more than agents of the MSC. Nevertheless, there is scope for a distinctive local approach to training and a number of authorities have attempted to develop such local schemes although the scale of such efforts is inevitably small. A number of problems with MSC training programmes were identified in Chapter 5, namely that such programmes often provide low-quality pre-vocational training geared to meet the need by industry for low-waged but experienced labour. Other criticisms relate to the overwhelming emphasis on youth training when adults and the long-term unemployed may have as great a need and the possibility that training has perpetuated existing patterns of disadvantage in the labour market.

In order to carry out local training programmes and to bend existing training schemes towards more radical ends many authorities have established training organisations, of which the Greater London Training Board and Merseyside Education,

Training, Enterprise Ltd are two examples. These and similar training agencies have developed local training strategies often in conjunction with other aspects of employment initiatives such as the development of cooperatives and small firms. Training can also be used as a support for an equal opportunity policy by facilitating access by women to non-traditional areas of employment in the local economy, increasing job opportunities for ethnic minorities in the public sector and by encouraging the formation of black businesses.

Support for the unemployed

Unemployed workers may be forced to take poor, low-paid jobs simply because they have few financial reserves, poor information about the local labour market and other consequences of a relatively weak labour market position. Alternatively, they may become alienated from the world of work and drift into patterns of living which make re-employment more difficult. To assist in the overcoming of these problems support in a wide variety of forms is given to organisations and community groups which work with the unemployed or seek to promote employment issues. This support often consists of the funding of unemployment centres or similar organisations which offer advice on matters of welfare benefits, training, education and the constructive use of leisure time. Local authorities also offer financial assistance to voluntary organisations which promote many different types of projects ranging from the employment of disabled people to combating racial or sexual discrimination. From the radical perspective these diverse activities are required in order to support local people when their position in the local labour market is at its weakest.

Summary and conclusion

Faced with rapidly mounting numbers of job losses and unemployment many metropolitan and city councils have developed a distinctive form of local economic policy. The objective of this new approach to the problem of urban unemployment is probably best summarised as follows:

> to intervene in a process of capital restructuring with deliberate policies – not of protection – but of *restructuring for labour*, building on what remains of firms and work groups, factories,

plant and machinery (GLC Industry and Employment Branch, Social and Economic Study Pack No. 3, Pt II: *italics* in the original).

The fundamental goal of long-term economic development and the creation of worthwhile and meaningful jobs for local people are translated into action in a number of distinctive ways. Intervention is democratic, it is claimed, being based upon the needs and wants of local people. This is achieved by various means, not least the accountability of local government in local elections, but also the process of popular planning and the extension of industrial democracy at work. Interventions are strategic, both in the sense of relating to an overall conception of the direction in which the urban economy should develop, and in the sense of concentrating interventions into key sectors where the maximum leverage on employment and the restructuring process can be achieved. The skills and expertise of local labour should be developed in order to take advantage of economic change, whether in the form of new technology, new and socially useful products or new forms of business enterprise. In particular, economic change must not be allowed to perpetuate or even accentuate the unequal job opportunities and low pay which characterise much of current employment in urban labour markets.

There has been considerable variation between local authorities in the extent to which they have embraced these radical ideals and the manner by which they have implemented the policy. In some respects these initiatives have been remarkably successful, creating or retaining quite large numbers of jobs at a relatively low cost per job. Yet it is important to retain a sense of proportion regarding these initiatives. In proportion to the scale of urban unemployment the job-creation effect of radical initiatives is minute. GLEB, at a time when the recorded number of unemployed in London was 400,000, could only claim to have saved or created 4,000 jobs. Similarly, the West Midlands can claim to have created between 4,000 and 5,000 jobs in about 30 enterprises between 1981 and 1985, but this has to be set against the loss of more than 250,000 jobs in the county between 1978 and 1983 and a total of unemployment of nearly 220,000. It can, of course, be claimed with some justification that matters would have been even worse without these jobs which may actually understate the true impact of intervention because of its strategic nature. Nevertheless, it has to be recognised that such radical employment initiatives on their own will not achieve any dramatic reduction in urban unemployment. The reasons for this minimal impact and the lessons to be drawn are considered in the next and concluding chapter.

Further reading

The clearest explanations of the radical perspective and the strategy of restructuring for labour are contained in 'The London industrial strategy' and 'The London labour plan' published by the GLC in 1985 and 1986 respectively. Documentary and case study material relating to the decline of the London economy, multinational firms, and the role of the GLEB can be found in GLC Social and Economic Study Packs. The Annual Reports of the various Enterprise Boards contain detailed information on the nature, scale of investments and the job-creation effects of such intervention. The political case for a radical approach to local economic development is presented by Blunkett and Green (1984) *Building from the Bottom: the Sheffield experience* and Murray (1984) *From the Market to the Factory: new directions in municipal socialism.* An analysis of local labour market policy and job creation is provided by Davies and Mason (1984) *Government and Local Labour Market Policy Implementation* and by Chandler and Lawless (1985) *Local Authorities and the Creation of Employment.*

7
A more coherent policy for urban employment

The main aim of this book has been to examine the reasons for the concentration of high unemployment in Britain's cities and their inner areas. Attention has been focused on the nature and operation of urban labour markets and the impact of economic and social change upon them. The analysis has been partial in that many important aspects of the urban economies have been referred to only in passing, but the justification for this is the need to concentrate the analysis on those factors and processes which are central to the issue of urban unemployment.

Much of the discussion has concerned the reasons for the decline of employment in the core of the urban areas and alternative policies, national and local, which have impinged upon the urban labour markets. An underlying theme in these discussions has been the contrasting analyses of competing perspectives. These theoretical and ideological frameworks provide distinctive interpretation of urban decline and they underpin differing policy prescriptions. Shifts in the emphasis of policy can be interpreted as being the outcome of competition between economic ideas, and the ebb and flow of urban policy reflects such an ideological struggle. The novel aspect of the 1980s has been the increasing dominance of the competitive or market perspective at the national level while more radical interventionist strategies have been developed at the local level. This is all the more remarkable because of the gradual loss of independence by local authorities in recent years.

In this concluding chapter some of the lessons to be drawn from recent policy will be considered and some suggestions for a more coherent approach will be made. However, before assessing urban policy the prospects for urban unemployment will be briefly examined.

The prospects for urban unemployment

One lesson that can be drawn from an examination of the economic decline of urban economies and the rise of urban unemployment is that the fundamental causes of change originate outside the urban areas themselves. It follows that any attempt to predict the likely course of unemployment in cities is conditional upon events and policies at a national level, although the precise way in which national trends affect localities will vary according to each area's own particular local economic, social and political characteristics.

It is quite clear that there is very little prospect of a reduction in the overall national level of unemployment in the foreseeable future. One factor leading to this conclusion is the expectation that the labour force will continue to grow in size. Between 1985 and 1990 there are expected to be around 800,000 extra participants in the labour force and it is not until 1993 that any reduction in the labour force will occur. This growth of labour supply means that an equivalent number of jobs are required simply in order to maintain unemployment at its present levels. Changes in participation rates will affect this prediction. Much of past labour force growth has resulted from the increased participation of married women, but future trends in married women's participation are uncertain. Several institutional changes may adversely affect married women's participation rates and these include the abolition of the wages councils which may reduce female pay, proposed changes in personal tax allowances which may penalise working women, reductions in the number of places available in further and higher education, and the exclusion of women from the Community Programme. Offsetting this is the continued expansion of part-time job opportunities in the service sector and the added worker effect of high levels of male unemployment.

While future participation rates of females is uncertain it is rather more certain that the number of young entrants into the labour market will decline. By 1993 it is projected that the number of 16–17 year olds in the labour force will have fallen by 30 per cent to around 800,000 compared to 1.2 million in 1985. This will clearly ease the problem of youth unemployment in general although, as Chapter 4 has shown, there may still be above-average concentrations of young people in inner-city areas and youth unemployment could continue to be a problem in these localities. Furthermore, it has to be recognised that the youth unemployment

of the 1980s could become the adult unemployment of the 1990s, as
a hard core of long-term unemployed may persist who have never
actually had a job. This group, in their late twenties and early
thirties, will be too old for (predominantly youth) training
schemes and job-creation programmes, lack work experience and
skills, and are likely to be wholly alienated from the world of work.
This group could constitute a continuing problem for years to
come, a constant reminder of the unemployment of the 1980s.

Important though labour supply changes may be, the main
determinant of future unemployment levels will be trends in
employment. Chapter 3 demonstrated how the rapid decline of the
urban economies can be largely accounted for by the collapse of
manufacturing industries and the future course of urban unemployment will depend very much on what prospects exist for
new job growth. Prediction of future levels of employment is
subject to a considerable degree of uncertainty because it depends
on factors such as government policy and economic events external
to Great Britain. Uncertainty over the effects of the eventual
running down of North Sea oil production and fluctuating oil
prices are examples of the latter, while a change of government or a
switch of economic policy could affect employment trends in the
long term.

The most likely course of manufacturing employment is that of
slow but continued decline. Although by the middle of the 1980s
manufacturing was no longer experiencing job losses on the scale
suffered during the depths of the recession, employment has
continued to decline. In 1985 manufacturing jobs were still being
lost at a rate of around 700,000 per year. The highest rates of
redundancies continued to be, as before, in the engineering and
vehicle sectors together with metal manufacturing and chemicals.
These are, of course, the industries which form the economic base
of the old industrial cities which have suffered so badly during the
recession. On this basis alone it could be expected that cities
currently experiencing high unemployment because of the decline
in their manufacturing employment will continue to suffer high
rates of job loss.

However, the decline in local labour demand may be exacerbated
by the effects of a restructuring of production in manufacturing.
The fundamental reason for the poor performance of British
manufacturing industry appears to be inadequate and inefficient
investment which has resulted in low productivity, high unit

labour costs, and a lack of competitiveness in international markets. Matters have not been improved by government policy, especially the medium-term financial strategy which has involved high interest rates and high exchange rates (see, for example, House of Lords 1985). The diagnosis of inadequate investment matches quite closely the experience of the West Midlands Enterprise Board (see Ch. 6). If manufacturing industry is to improve its international competitiveness, which many see as vital to Britain's economic recovery, this will involve a consequential programme of new investment in plant and equipment. Record (1985) argues that so much capacity has been lost during the recession that manufacturing industry would not be able to expand output without such investment. The importance of this is two-fold. First, new investment raises labour productivity and gives rise to 'jobless growth', a situation where output and sales increase but employment remains the same, or even falls. Second, if a recovery takes place in manufacturing industry the resulting investment creates the most fluid situation as far as the spatial restructuring of production is concerned. Chapter 3 demonstrated that in such circumstances firms may engage in a combination of relocations, plant closures and new plant openings and, as the metropolitan economies often offer less profitable locations than those elsewhere, such restructuring of production will worked to the disadvantage of the cities. Any future expansion of manufacturing industry could very likely take place outside the cities and even result in accelerated job losses in the urban areas.

If the manufacturing industries offer little prospect of employment growth, what of the service sector? The service sector has long been regarded as the source of the jobs required to replace those lost in manufacturing. During the 1960s and early 1970s this was the case; employment increased overall because of the rapid growth of service industry jobs. Despite a slight fall during the period 1980–82, employment has continued to increase during the 1980s at an average of about 140,000 jobs per year. This is much less than at the peak of service sector growth and is certainly insufficient to reduce unemployment by any significant amount (bearing in mind the possible growth of the labour force). It is important to note that these additional jobs have been mainly part time and filled by married women. This may be desirable in its own right, but it obviously raises some important questions about the impact on the unemployed. There are grounds for being rather cautious about predicting continued service sector employment growth. Gershuny and Miles (1983) have argued that the present period of de-industrialisation, in which services grow at the expense of manufacturing, may eventually give way to a period of transition to the 'new service economy' or, as it is sometimes called, the self-service economy'. The new service industries will be those which provide products and services which replace the more traditional and labour-intensive (and therefore expensive) services. This process has been exemplified by the replacement of laundry services by the domestic washing machine and the substitution of the video recorder for the cinema.

A more immediate impact on service sector employment is created by technological and organisational change. In effect (although for different reasons) the service industries are beginning to experience the same kind of corporate restructuring which the manufacturing sector experienced a decade or so earlier. In the past the service industries have been relatively immune from technological change, but this situation has altered dramatically with the evolution of information technology. In insurance and banking virtually all previously labour-intensive routine activities are now automated. Employment losses have been avoided because of the creation of new jobs and the expansion in the volume of business. A situation has now been reached where a 12 per cent increase in business is required each year if employment levels in these industries are to be maintained (Rajan 1984). Part of the reason for the expansion of business in the business services sector is that firms in this sector have diversified into a wide range of activities; for example, building societies have become more general financial institutions. As this growth has taken place, so too has a reorganisation of the service sector by means of mergers and acquisitions. Combined with changing information and communications technology, such reorganisations have led to rationalisation and spatial reorganisation. Whereas earlier periods saw the growth of service employment in all areas, the 1980s has been an increased spatial division of service labour and a concentration of service employment. The upper tiers of management, computing services, research and marketing have increasingly been relocated (often during rationalisation following a merger) in suburban and rural locations in the southern parts of England (Marshall 1985). Even if there are good national prospects for employment growth in the service sector, it seems increasingly likely that such growth will pass by many northern cities despite their traditional strengths as regional service centres (Harrison *et al.* 1984). The recent limited extension of regional policy to include selected service industries may have only limited results for these reasons.

Overall the prognosis is not very optimistic. Few economic forecasters suggest that there will be sufficient employment growth, if any, to reduce the national level of unemployment below 3 million, even by the early 1990s. What this brief review of trends suggests is that the major urban areas, the cities and the conurbations, are not even likely to share in any employment growth that is taking place. Indeed the contrary may be the case, an expansion of economic activity may actually produce the conditions under which further metropolitan job losses take place and urban unemployment yet further.

The limitations of present policies

One crucial conclusion to be drawn concerning policy to reduce urban unemployment is that whatever form is taken by policy measures, and no matter who implements them, their impact depends crucially upon the general macroeconomic environment. In the absence of national economic growth and an increase in the demand for labour, policies will simply amount to redistributions of jobs and a sharing of the misery of unemployment. Chapter 3 has demonstrated how the economic decline of the conurbations has been largely due to the collapse of employment in their manufacturing sectors and, more recently, reductions in public sector services. It is these reductions in labour demand which are the immediate cause of the job shortfalls and high unemployment rates which are discussed in Chapter 4. To a considerable extent localised demand deficiency in the urban economies was a spatial reflection of the massive lack of demand for output during the 1979–83 recession. Layard and Nickell (1985) have estimated that as much as three-quarters of the increase in unemployment between the periods 1975–79 to 1980–83 was the result of demand deficiency. Government policy during the 1980s has consistently rejected the expansion of demand as a means of reducing unemployment preferring (as Ch. 5 has shown) to emphasise the need to increase labour market competition and reduce real wages. Even on their own evidence the scope for this seems limited, a 10 per cent reduction in the real wage and a larger reduction in money wages being required to increase employment by 1 million with the initial effect of the wage cut being to reduce employment and a net increase in employment only after four or five years (HM Treasury 1985). Policy measures cannot hope to make very great inroads into the unemployment problems of the cities within such a hostile economic environment. An essential prerequisite for tackling urban unemployment must be an expansion of aggregate demand and the level of national economic activity.

Although an expansion in demand and a growth of the national economy is a necessary condition for reducing urban unemployment it is unlikely to be sufficient on its own. There are several reasons for this. First, although an expansion in demand can be expected to 'trickle down' through the labour market, its effects will vary considerably from one group in the labour market to another. The structured and segmented nature of the labour market concentrates unemployment among workers in the secondary jobs market, and these workers will be at the back of the queue when an increase takes place in the number of jobs. This effect will be particularly marked in the inner cities because many disadvantaged groups are residentially segregated into these localities. Any jobs which are created may simply be filled by recruitment of workers resident outside the urban core, leaving inner-area unemployment relatively unchanged. Furthermore, as was discussed in the section above, the spatial structure of jobs which emerges in any economic recovery may be quite different from that which existed prior to the recession. The decentralisation of employment and the emergence of a new spatial division of labour (see Ch. 3) has shifted jobs away from the cities. In addition, years of deficient demand, low output, and high unemployment may have rendered demand expansion less efficient than was the case in the past. Spatial restructuring of production, rationalisation of industrial capacity, and the virtual non-participation in the labour market of the long-term unemployed could mean that an expansion of demand will produce production 'bottlenecks' and labour shortages despite the existence of chronically high levels of unemployment in some local labour markets. This poses the threat of inflation and a worsening balance of payments, both of which might cause national growth to be prematurely stopped. These factors clearly provide a case for demand management and the maintenance of a high and stable level of demand, but in so far as this has not been the case in the past the dilemma remains.

Industrial, spatial, and labour market policies are the means of dealing with the sort of 'supply side' structural problems which macroeconomic policies cannot directly affect. Chapter 5 discussed a number of such policies which impinged upon the urban economies. Consideration of those policies suggests that they contain some inherent contradictions. Much of industrial and spatial policy is concerned with the provision of incentives to firms to increase capital investment in plant and buildings, usually by means of tax allowances, capital subsidies and by capital expenditure on infrastructure. The effect of such policies, although only partially successful, has been to increase the capital intensity and scale of production plant and to cause or facilitate the relocation of production. In conditions of static or falling output this has inevitably led to job losses, particularly in the old traditional urban areas, despite the ostensible job-creation aim of these policies. Labour market policies have, in effect, been left with the task of attempting to ameliorate the effects of other economic policies. As such they are aimed at job creation for the most vulnerable groups in the labour market and particularly at young workers. In fact, with depressed levels of demand and high levels of unemployment, much of what such policies achieve is simply a more equitable distribution of unemployment, although the evidence in Chapter 5 suggests that schemes such as the YTS may actually perpetuate or even accentuate existing inequalities in the labour market.

The most important criticisms of existing policies are that they are essentially short-term and largely uncoordinated expedients. They provide blanket measures, often administered on an inflexible and arbitrary basis, with little regard to any overall economic strategy. Apart from the inherently conflicting aims of industrial and employment policies, there has been little attempt to relate national policies to their spatial consequences with the result that the cities and conurbations have often suffered adverse consequences of policy. In cases where measures have been specifically directed towards urban and inner-city areas the effects have been dwarfed and offset by the spatial effects of other policies. Spencer (1985) in a study of the West Midlands, notes the inconsistency of the policies of the Department of the Environment which supports the inner areas and the objectives of the Department of Trade and Industry which are to support industry within a region regardless of location. The latter, supported by greater resources, has drawn employment away from the centre of the conurbation to the detriment of employment in the inner areas.

One of the most marked trends during the 1980s, described in the previous two chapters, has been the increasingly local character of policy. While national policy in general has tended to take a much reduced interventionist stance, attempting to create competitive conditions instead, industrial policy has become more spatially selective, first through the inner-area partnerships and programmes, then the introduction of enterprise zones and urban development corporations and finally in the form of freeports. Regional policy has also been realigned on a more selective, and more urban basis. Alongside these developments, local authorities have devised their own forms of employment initiatives – in some cases little more than local reflections of national policy but in others of a radically different nature. While these developments might appear favourable to the urban areas and the prospect of reducing urban unemployment, in fact there are severe limitations to the impact on the problem which local policy can achieve. In their traditional form such local initiatives lack adequate resources; for example, the real value of the Urban Programme has been falling, in real terms, in recent years. Local authorities lack the legal and territorial power to exert any great influence on the local economy. In addition to the general criticisms of traditional forms of industrial and employment policy listed above, local initiatives have the additional failings of relying too heavily on incentives to new and small firms and of creating job displacement effects. The small firm myth was examined in Chapter 5; small firms offer the prospect of a small number of jobs only, such jobs are often in the secondary sector (poor-quality jobs) and the long-term prospects may not be good as such firms are often not innovative. Furthermore, jobs 'created' by local policy can lead to displacement as firms change location in order to benefit from incentives (the enterprise zones exemplify this effect) or as they recruit labour which has been targeted under a local employment policy. In either case, the gross employment gains grossly overstate net gains and it is conceivable that employment could be reduced if firms use relocation as an opportunity to shed labour.

Radical employment initiatives of the type examined in the last chapter overcome some of these difficulties by means of the development of a strategic approach and their attempts to secure greater control over local production. However, these initiatives also have their limitations. As before, the main limitations are legal and financial. To some extent the legal problems have been overcome by the establishment of the enterprise boards and other 'arm's length' agencies. The most severe limitation is financial; the distinctive core of radical initiatives are largely financed from revenue raised under s.137 of the 1972 Local Government Act and this represents a very small amount of funds for most authorities. This source amounts to only £8 million for the West Midland CC and £40 million for the GLC and for many city councils the amount of revenue raised by s.137 is very small indeed. This financial difficulty will be exacerbated by the abolition of the metropolitan counties and the GLC since their abolition removes another tier of local government finance. Although there may be some compensating increase in rate support grant to district councils it seems less likely that such authorities, who are more tightly restrained by statutory main programmes, will be able to devote the same level of resources to radical initiatives. Many councils will be forced to rely on the Urban Programme and other government controlled measures for the regeneration of their local economies.

A more fundamental limitation of the radical initiatives is that by their local nature they are often incapable of exerting influence on those sectors which their sector studies have revealed to be the most important strategically. In London and elsewhere much of the restructuring of production has been initiated by multinational companies over which the enterprise boards have little control. On the other hand, successful local companies are not likely to seek any involvement with their local authority and the main sectors over which the authority will be able to exert control will be in declining sectors and in badly managed firms. Given the small size of the available funds there is a danger that strategic intervention may get locked into such sectors rather than the potential areas of employment growth as originally intended.

The limitations of localised employment initiatives are reflected in their achievements. Radical initiatives have been credited with the creation of around 20,000 jobs while a slightly smaller number have been attributed to enterprise zones (in gross terms at any rate). In comparison with the scale of the problem, such initiatives must be regarded as having made only a marginal contribution to the reduction of urban unemployment. In view of this it may be wondered why such local initiatives have attracted so much recent attention. The reason for this, as Duncan and Goodwin (1985) have pointed out, is that these initiatives are best seen as localised experiments with alternative economic policy. The main significance of such experiments is as propaganda for one theoretical and ideological perspective or another. Seen from this point of view such experiments are not expected to lead to any massive increases in jobs but are intended to change people's ideas and expectations. They are exemplars of the competition between competing perspectives on urban unemployment.

Future directions in policy

Future developments in policy affecting the urban economies must take account of the limitations and contradictions outlined above. The simplest approach would entail the reform of present policies to improve their implementation and to secure better coordination of government departments and local authorities and the reconciliation of national, regional and urban policy objectives. From some points of view, such a reconciliation is not feasible because policy has been attempting the impossible, namely to reverse the process of decentralisation and the suburbanisation of employment. According to this view, policy should attempt to work with the grain of social forces and not against them. If market forces are responsible for the job losses in cities, it will be very difficult to reverse this spatial process and resources will be wasted by any attempt to do so. Worst of all, if measures succeed in preventing employment decentralisation then the result will be an inefficient allocation of resources. This being so, policy should aim to speed up the process of adjustment and minimise the social cost to the residents of the inner cities. The aim of urban policy should be, as Moynagh (1985) puts it rather bluntly, 'to concentrate on making the inner city a good place for commuting to work elsewhere'. Resources should be spent on environmental and housing projects but not directly on job creation. In order to deal with high levels of inner-city unemployment a different strategy is required. Employers in outer-city areas should be encouraged to employ more inner-city residents, either by means of a marginal wage subsidy for each inner-city resident recruited (Gudgin *et al.* 1982) or by means of schemes similar to the 'affirmative action' programme in the United States where outer-city employers would be expected to recruit a proportion of their workforce from inner-city residents. Labour mobility should be encouraged if the residents of urban areas with high unemployment are to be able to take up jobs elsewhere, and this might involve the subsidisation of transport, measures to facilitate council house transfers, and the relaxation of rules relating to building society and local authority mortgages in order to encourage owner occupation and residential movement. In its most extreme form this critique of urban policy suggests that much of present policy is misguided and should be abandoned, although regional policy may be necessary as a means of ensuring an adequate demand for labour in a region as a whole.

The main deficiency of the above approach is that it fails to take account of the inherent imperfections of markets in the urban economy. These mean that job losses and concentrations of unemployment in urban areas may be unrelated to the efficiency of the urban economy as a location for production. These problems may be more related to the short-term effects of the recession, the unintended effects of government policy or even inefficient management. There are many examples from the past of companies which have been rescued by government intervention, turned around and now form profitable enterprises. Even if urban or inner-city locations are less profitable, it may be argued that corporate decisions which result in the abandonment of city locations fail to take account of the full social costs of such decisions and the social benefits of direct intervention. From this perspective an altogether different approach is required to urban employment generation. This approach would involve a much greater national involvement in local economic development but would reverse the usual relationship of national and local government so that action was initiated from the bottom or local end of the relationship rather than the top. The wide variety of experiences of local economies and the diversity of local resources can only be fully taken account of by local employment strategies, but the aims of these local strategies can only be achieved, ultimately, by drawing upon the power and resources of national government. The solution to this dilemma lies in the development of a national economic strategy. This strategy, like the local versions, should proceed to identify on a sector by sector basis the strategic long-term needs of the British economy and policy should seek to provide for these needs by means of direct intervention in key industrial sectors. Investment strategies should be developed, with joint public and private sector participation designed to secure efficient long-term economic development which takes full social account of the needs of industry and society as a whole. Although there may be an important role for short-term job-creation programmes focused upon the social groups and localities most in need, the main aim of employment policy should be to provide support to the industrial strategy through training and the improvement of job opportunities and the quality of work.

The crucial role of local initiatives in such a strategy would be recognised by the creation of a legislative and institutional framework which gives local authorities a duty to intervene in the local economy in order to reduce local unemployment and which provides them with the resources for the task. Thus free of the distorting effects of their present limited legal powers and the constraints of s.137 finance, local authorities would be able to make use of their expertise and detailed local knowledge to intervene in their local economies, taking account of local variation in economic experience and the preferences of local people. The implementation of the policy would be by means of local enterprise boards linked in a federal relationship to a national investment board. This structure would enable local initiatives to be coordinated while at the same time providing a framework for implementing national strategic policy. The national investment board would be provided with the necessary powers, the staff and the funds to enable it to control the most strategically important sectors of the economy. In this way urban or local economic policy would form the foundation of national economic planning with policy being formulated 'from the bottom up', rather than 'from the top down' as with previous experiments with national economic planning.

As with other aspects of urban unemployment, it seems that there are different directions in which policy might develop. The choice is ultimately dependent not on factual matters or empirical evidence but upon values, attitudes and beliefs. In terms of economic policy, the 1980s will be reviewed as a decade of experimentation, pioneered at the local economy level, in which alternative economic strategies were put to the test. No doubt vigorous debate will continue concerning the causes and appropriate policy for urban unemployment and the struggle between competing perspectives will continue to be played out. The modest objective of this book is to contribute towards an understanding of that debate.

References

Aaronovitch, S. *et al.* (1981) *The Political Economy of British Capitalism: a Marxist analysis.* McGraw-Hill, London

Abel, P. (1985) 'Shelling out the cash in Sheffield', *Town and Country Planning*, June, 194–5

Addison, J. (1979) 'Does job creation work?' in I E A Readings No.20 *Job Creation – or Destruction.* Institute of Economic Affairs, London

Armstrong, H. and Taylor, J. (1985) 'Spatial variations in the male unemployment inflow rate', *Applied Economics*, Vol.17, 41–54

Arthur Young (1985) Financial Incentives and Assistance for Industry: a comprehensive guide (5th edn), Aug.

Association of District Councils (1985) 'Economic development by district councils: a series of papers on best practice', No.6 (Revised)

Azariadis, C. (1975) 'Implicit contracts and underemployment equilibria', *Journal of Political Economy*, Vol.83, No.6

Balasubramanyam, V. N. and Rothschild, R. (1985) 'Free port zones in the United Kingdom', *Lloyds Bank Review*, Oct.

Ball, R. M. (1983) 'Spatial and structural characteristics of recent unemployment change: some policy considerations', *Regional Studies*, Vol.17, No.2, 135–140

Bannock, G. (1981) 'The clearing banks and small firms', *Lloyds Bank Review*, Oct.

Baron, P. A. and Sweezy, P. M. (1966) *Monopoly Capital.* Pelican Books

Bassett, K. (1984) 'Corporate structure and corporate change in a local economy: the case of Bristol', *Environment and Planning A*, Vol. 16, 879–900

Bayldon, R., Woods, A. and Zafiris, N. (1984) 'Inner city versus new town: a comparison of manufacturing performance', *Oxford Bulletin of Economics and Statistics*, Vol.46, No.1, 21–9

Becker, G. S. (1975) *Human Capital* (2nd edn). National Bureau of Economic Research, New York

Beesley, M. (1955) 'The birth and death of industrial establishments: experience in the West Midlands conurbation', *Journal of Industrial Economics*, Vol.4, 45–61

Benington, J. (1985) 'Local economic initiatives', *Local Government Studies*, Sept./Oct.

Bentham, C. G. (1985) 'Trends in the relationship between earnings and unemployment in the counties of Great Britain, 1978 to 1983', *Area*, Vol.17, No.4, 267-75

Bentham, C. G. (1985) 'Which areas have the worst urban problem?', *Urban Studies*, Vol.22, No.2, April

Berger, S. and Piore, M. (1980) *Dualism and Discontinuity in Industrial Societies*. Cambridge University Press

Berthoud, R. (1980) 'Employment in a changing labour market' in Evans and Eversley (eds) (1980)

Beveridge, W. H. (1909) *Unemployment – a problem of industry*. Longman, London

Binks, M. and Coyne, J. (1983) 'The birth of enterprise', Hobart Paper No.98, Institute of Economic Affairs, London

Birdseye, P. and Webb, T. (1984) 'Why the rates burden on business is a cause for concern', *National Westminster Bank Quarterly Review*, Feb.

Blackaby, F. (ed.) (1979) *Deindustrialisation*. Heinemann, London

Blunkett, D. and Green, G. (1984) *Building from the Bottom: the Sheffield experience*. Fabian Society

Boddy, M. (1983a) 'Planning for employment regeneration – practice review; *The Planner*, Vol.69, No.5, Sept./Oct., 175-6

Boddy, M. (1983b) 'Changing public-private sector relationships in the industrial development process', in Young and Mason (eds) (1983), Ch. 3

Bollard, A. (1983) 'Technology, economic change and small firms', *Lloyds Bank Review*, Jan. No.147

Bosanquet, N. (1983) *After the New Right*. Heinemann, London

Bosanquet, N. and Doeringer, P. B. (1973) 'Is there a dual labour market in Great Britain?', *Economic Journal*, Vol.83, 421-35

Bosworth, D. L. and Wilson, R. A (1980) 'The labour market for scientists and technologists' in Lindley R. M. (ed.) (1980)

Bosworth, D. L. and Wilson, R. A. (1981) 'Does Britain need more engineers?' *Journal of Industrial Affairs*, Vol.9 No.1 1-11

Botham, R. (1983) 'Local authority employment subsidies', *The Planner*, Vol.69, No.5, 165-7

Botham, R. (1984) 'Employment subsidies: a new direction for local government economic initiatives', *Regional Studies*, Vol.18, No.1, 84-8

Braverman, H. (1974) *Labor and Monopoly Capital: the degradation of work*. Monthly Review Press, New York/London

Brittan, S. (1985) 'Abolish, not "reform" these job-killing bodies', *Financial Times*, 13 May

Bromley, R. D. F. and Morgan, R. H. (1985) 'The effects of enterprise zone policy: evidence from Swansea', *Regional Studies*, Vol.19, No.5, 403-15

Brown, A. J. (1967) 'The Green Paper on the development areas, appendix on regional multipliers', *National Institute Economic Review*, Vol.40, 33

Brown, A. J. (1972) *The Framework of Regional Economics in the U.K.* Cambridge University Press

Brown, W. (1981), *The Changing Contours of British Industrial Relations.* Blackwell, Oxford

Burridge, P. and Gordon, I. (1981) 'Unemployment in the British metropolitan labour areas', *Oxford Economic Papers*, Vol.33, 274–97

Burton, J. (1977) 'Employment subsidies – the cases for and against', *National Westminster Bank Quarterly Review*, Feb. 1977, 33–43

Butler, S. M. (1981) *Enterprise Zones: greenlining the inner cities*, Heinemann Educational Books, London

Cadman, D. (1981), 'Urban changes, Enterprise Zones, and the role of investors', *Built Environment*, Vol.7, 13–19

Cameron, G. (1980) *The Future of the British Conurbation.* Longman, London

Cameron, G. C. (1980), 'The inner city: new plant incubator? in Evans and Eversley (eds) 1980

Cameron, S. J., Dabinett, G. E., Gillard, A. A., Whisker, P. M., Williams, R. H. and Willis, K. G. (1982) 'Local authority aid to industry: an evaluation in Tyne and Wear', Department of the Environment, London

Camina, M. M. (1974) 'Local authorities and the attraction of industry', *Progress in Planning*, Vol.3, No.2

Carmichael, C. and Cook, L. (1981) 'Redundancy and re-employment', *Employment Gazette*, May

Centre for Employment Initiatives (1985) 'The impact of local enterprise agencies in Great Britain', CEI, London

Champion, A. G. (1983) 'Population trends in the 1970s', Chapter 8 of Goddard and Champion (1983)

Chandler, J. A. and Lawless, P. (1985) *Local Authorities and the Creation of Employment.* Gower Press, London

Cheshire, P. C. (1973) *Regional Unemployment Differences in Great Britain*, Regional Papers II. Cambridge University Press/NEISR, London/Cambridge

Cheshire, P. C. (1979) 'Inner areas as spatial labour markets: a critique of the inner area studies', *Urban Studies*, Vol.16, 29–43

Chisholm, M. (1985) 'Better value for money? Britain's 1984 regional industrial policy package', *Government and Policy*, Vol.3, 111–19

Church of England (1985) *Faith in the City.* Church House Publishing, London

Colledge, M. and Bartholomew, R. (1980) 'The long-term unemployed: some new evidence', *Employment Gazette*, Vol.88, 9–12

Cook, G. and Harrison, C. (1984) 'Factory strategy in need of study', *Town and Country Planning*, Sept., 240–42

Cook, G. and Rendall, F. J. W. (1984) 'Industrial structure and the process of employment decentralisation in Greater Leicester', School of Economics and Accounting, Discussion Paper No.9, Leicester Polytechnic

Cooke, P. (1983) 'Labour market discontinuity and spatial development', *Progress in Human Geography*, Vol.7, No.4, 543–65

Coombes, M. G., Dixon, J. S., Goddard, J. B., Openshaw, S. and Taylor, P. J. (1982) 'Functional regions for the population census of Great Britain' in Herbert and Johnson (eds) (1982), Vol.5, 63–112

Corina, J. (1972) *Labour Market Economics: a short survey of recent theory*. Heinemann Educational Books, London

Corkindale, J. T. (1980) 'Employment trends in the conurbations' in Evans and Eversley (eds) (1980)

Coyne, M. A. and Lincoln, I. C. (1982) 'An analysis of the small firm in the Leicester economy', Leicester Economic Study Report No.5, Leicester City Council and Leicestershire County Council, Oct.

Crawford, P., Fothergill, S. and Monk, S. (1985) 'The effect of business rates on the location of employment', Industrial Location Research Group, University of Cambridge

Creedy, J. (1981) *The Economics of Unemployment in Britain*, Butterworth

Creedy, J. and Thomas, B. (eds) (1982) *The Economics of Labour*. Butterworth

Crouch, C. S. (1982) 'Trends in unemployment – a comment', *Area*, Vol.14, No.1, 56–9

Cuthbertson, K., Foreman-Peck, J. and Gripaios, P. (1979) 'Local authority fiscal policy and urban employment', *Applied Economics*, Vol.11, 377–87

Danson, M. W. (1982) 'The industrial structure and labour market segmentation: urban and regional implications', *Regional Studies*, Vol.16, 225–65

Danson, M. W., Lever, W. F. and Malcolm, J. F. (1980) 'The inner city employment problem in Great Britain, 1952–76: a shift-share approach', *Urban Studies*, Vol.17, 193–210

Davies, T. and Mason, C. (1984) *Government and Local Labour Market Policy Implementation*. Gower Press, London

Davis, E. H. and Dilnot, A. W. (1985) *The I.F.S. Tax and Benefit Model*, Working Paper No.58, The Institute of Fiscal Studies

Deakin, B. and Pratten, C. (1982), *Effects of the Temporary Employment Subsidy*, Occasional Paper 53, Dept of Applied Economics. Cambridge University Press, Cambridge

Dennis, R. (1978), 'The decline of manufacturing employment in Greater London 1966–74', *Urban Studies*, Vol.15, 63–73

Department of Employment (1977) 'Employment in metropolitan areas', Unit for Manpower Studies

Department of Employment (1985) 'Employment: the challenge for the nation', CMND 9474, March

Department of the Environment (1977) 'Inner London: policies for disposal and balance', Final Report of the Lambeth Inner Area Study

Department of the Environment (1985) 'An inquiry into the condition of the local authority housing stock in England: 1985'

Department of Health and Social Security (1984), 'For richer, for poorer?, DHSS cohort study of unemployed men', Research Report, No.11, HMSO

Department of Industry (1983) 'Lifespan analysis of business in the UK 1973-82', *British Business*, 12-18 Aug.

Dex, S. and Perry, S. M. (1984) 'Women's employment change in the 1970s', *Employment Gazette*, Vol.92, 151-64

Dicken, P. and Lloyd, P. E. (1978) 'Inner metropolitan industrial change, enterprise structures and policy issues: case studies of Manchester and Merseyside', *Regional Studies*, Vol.12, 181-97

Dicken, P. and Lloyd, P. E. (1981), *Modern Western Society: a geographical perspective on work, home, and well-being*, Harper and Row, London

Drewitt, R. (1974) 'Standard metropolitan labour areas and metropolitan economic labour areas. Definitional notes and commentary', Working Paper No.1 (Urban Change in Britain 1961-71), Dept of Geography, London School of Economics

Duffy, F. (1980) 'Information technology, organisation and the office', DEGW Architects and Space Planners, London

Duncan, S. S. and Goodwin, M. (1985) 'The local state and local economic policy: why the fuss?, *Policy and Politics*, Vol.13, No.3, 227-53

Ehrenberg, R. (ed.) (1981) *Research in Labor Economics IV*, JAI Press Connecticut

Evans, A. (1980) 'A portrait of the London labour market' in Evans and Eversley (eds) (1980)

Evans, A. and Eversley, E. (eds) (1980) *The Inner City, Employment and Industry*. Heinemann, London

Evans, A. W. and Richardson, R. (1980) 'Urban unemployment: interpretation and additional evidence', *Scottish Journal of Political Economy*, Vol.28, No.2, 107-24

Fagg, J. J. (1980), 'A re-examination of the incubator hypothesis: a case study of Greater Leicester', *Urban Studies*, Vol.17, 35-44

Fairly, J. (1983), 'Training policy – the local perspective', *Regional Studies Vol.17, No.2*, 140-43

Falk, N. (1978) 'Local authorities and industrial development – results of a survey', Paper presented to the Association of Industrial Development Officers' Conference

Finn, D. (1985) 'The community programme – a poor substitute for a real job', *The Guardian*, 19 May, 23

Firn, J. R. and Hughes, J. J. (1973) 'Employment growth and decentralisation of manufacturing industry: some intriguing paradoxes', Paper to the CES Urban Economics Conference, University of Keele (10-13 July)

Firn, J. R. and Swales, J. K. (1978), 'The formation of new manufacturing establishments in the central Clydeside and West Midlands conurbations 1963-1972: a comparative analysis', *Regional Studies* Vol.12, No.2, 199-213

Fothergill, S. and Gudgin, G. (1979) 'The job generation process', Research Series 32, Centre for Environmental Studies, London

Fothergill, S. and Gudgin, G. (1982) *Unequal Growth: urban and regional employment change in the UK*. Heinemann, London

Friedman, M. (1968) 'The role of monetary policy', *American Economic Review*, Vol.58, March, 1-17

Fuchs, V. R. (1968) *The Service Economy*. Columbia University Press

Garside, W. R. (1980) *The Measurement of Unemployment: Methods and Sources in Great Britain 1850-1979*. Allen and Unwin, London

Gershuny, J. and Miles, I. (1983) *The New Service Economy*. Pinter, London

Gilbert, C. (1984) 'The anatomy of decline: the gold, silver and allied trades in Birmingham 1962-1982', Occasional Paper, Dept of Sociology and Applied Social Studies, Birmingham Polytechnic

Gillespie, A. E. (1983) 'Population and employment decentralisation and the journey to work' in Goddard and Champion (1983), Ch. 7

Gillespie, A. E. and Owen, D. W. (1981) 'Unemployment trends in the current recession', *Area*, Vol.13, No.3, 189-96

Gillespie, A. E. and Owen, D. W. (1982) 'Trends in unemployment - a reply', *Area*, Vol.14, No.1, 59-61

Gleason, D. (1983) *Youth Training and the Search for Work*. Routledge and Keegan Paul

Gleave, D. and Sellens, R. (1984) 'An investigation into British labour market processes', Economic and Social Research Council, London

Goddard, J. B. and Champion, A. G. (eds) (1983) *The Urban and Regional Transformation of Britain*. Methuen, London

Goddard, J. B. and Smith, I. J. (1978) 'Changes in corporate control in the British urban system, 1972-77', *Environment and Planning A*, Vol.10, 1073-84

Gordon, I. R. and Lamont, D. (1982) 'A model of labour market interdependencies in the London region', *Environment and Planning A*, Vol.14, 237-64

Gordon, I. R., Vickerman, R. W., Lamont, D. W. and Thomas, A. M. (1983) 'Opportunities, preferences and constraints on population movement in the London Region', Final Report to the Dept of the Environment, Urban and Regional Studies Unit, University of Kent

Greater London Council (1985) 'The London industrial strategy', GLC Industry and Employment Committee

Greater London Council (1986) 'The London labour plan', GLC Industry and Employment Branch

Greater London Enterprise Board (1985) Annual Report and Accounts, 31 March 1985

Green, A. E. (1985) 'Unemployment duration in the recession: the local labour market area scale', *Regional Studies*, Vol.19, No.2, 111-29

Greenhalgh, C. A. (1977) 'A labour supply function for married women in Great Britain', *Economics*, Vol.44, 249-67

Greenhalgh, C. A. (1979) 'Male labour force participation in Great Britain', *Scottish Journal of Political Economy*, Vol.26, 275-86

Greenhalgh, C. A., Layard, P. R. G. and Oswald, A. J. (eds) (1983) *The Causes of Unemployment*. Oxford University Press, Oxford

Gregory, R. (1984) 'Local government response to unemployment in the UK' in Richardson and Henning (eds) (1984)

Greig, M. A. (1971) 'The regional income and employment multiplier effects of a pulp and paper mill', *Scottish Journal of Political Economy*, Vol.18, 31-48

Griffiths, A. and Wall, S. (1984) *Applied Economics: an introductory course*. Longman, London

Gripaios, P. (1977) 'The closure of firms in the inner city: the South-East London case 1970-75', *Regional Studies*, Vol.11, 1-6

Gripaios, P. and Brooks, N. (1982) 'The determination of employment in counties: some evidence on the importance of local authority fiscal policy and government regional policy in England and Wales', *Applied Economics*, Vol.14, 211-18

Gudgin, G., Moore, B. and Rhodes, J. (1982) 'Employment problems in cities and regions of the UK: prospects for the 1980s', *Cambridge Economic Policy Review* Dec., Vol.18, No.2

Hall, P. (1977) 'Green fields and grey areas', in *Proceedings of the Royal Town Planning Institute Annual Conference, Chester*, Royal Town Planning Institute, London

Hall, P. (1981) 'Issues for the eighties', *The Planner*, Vol.67, No.1, 4

Hall, P. *et al.* (1973) 'The containment of urban England', Political and Economic Planning

Hall, P. and Metcalf, D. (1979) 'The declining metropolis: patterns problems and policies in Britain and mainland Europe' in C. L. Leven (1979)

Hamilton, F. E. I. and Lugo, G. J. R. (eds) (1979) *Spatial Analysis, Industry and the Industrial Environment*. Wiley

Harrison, P. (1983) *Inside the Inner City: life under the cutting edge*. Penguin

Harrison, C. R., Hasluck, C. and Holmes, I. J. (1984) 'Office employment and accommodation in Leicester's private business service sector',

Leicester Economic Study Report No.7, Leicester City Council and Leicestershire County Council, Oct.

Hasluck, C. (1982) 'Monitoring the local labour market: the uses of unemployment and vacancy data', Leicester Economic Study No.6, Leicester City Council and Leicestershire County Council, Oct.

Hausner, V. and Robson, B. (1986) 'Changing cities' (revised edn), Economic and Social Research Council

Hawkins, K. (1984) *Unemployment* (2nd edn). Penguin Books

Healey, M. J. and Clark, D. (1985) 'Industrial decline in a local economy: the case of Coventry, 1974-1982', *Environment and Planning A*, Vol.17, 1351-67

Herbert, D. T. and Johnson, R. J. (eds) (1982) *Geography and the Urban Environment; Progress on Research and Applications*, Vol. 5. Wiley

HM Treasury (1985) 'The relationship between employment and wages: empirical evidence for the UK.'

Hodge, I. and Whitby, M. C. (1981) 'Rural Employment: trends, options, choices', Methuen, London

Holterman, S. E. (1975) 'Areas of urban deprivation in Great Britain: an analysis of 1971 Census data', *Social Trends*, Vol.6

House of Lords (1985) *Report from the Select Committee on Overseas Trade*. HMSO, London

Hughes, J. J. (1975) 'How should we measure unemployment?' *British Journal of Industrial Relations*, Vol.13, No.3

Hughes, J. J. and Perlman, R. (1984) *The Economics of Unemployment: a comparative analysis of Britain and the United States*. Wheatsheaf Books

Hughs, S. (1981) 'The mistaken belief that rates cost jobs', *Municipal Review*, Oct.

Hughs, S. (1983) 'Do rates really constitute a major burden on industry?', *Municipal Review*, Oct.

Hunter, L. C. and Mulvey, C. (1981) *Economics of Wages and Labour*. Macmillan, London

Hunter, L. C. and Reid, G. L. (1968) *Urban Worker Mobility*, OECD, Paris

Johnson, P. S. and Cathcart, D. G. (1979a) 'The founders of new manufacturing firms: a note on the size of their "incubator" plants', *Journal of Industrial Economics*, Vol.28, 219-24

Johnson, P. S. and Cathcart, D. G. (1979b) 'New manufacturing firms and regional development: some evidence from the Northern Region', *Regional Studies*, Vol.13, 269-80

Joll, C., McKenna, C., McNabb, R. and Shorey, J. (1983) *Developments in Labour Market Analysis*. Allen and Unwin, London

Jordon, G. (1984) 'Enterprise zones in the UK and the USA: ideologically acceptable job creation' in Richardson and Henning (eds) (1984)

JURUE (1980) 'Local authority employment initiatives', Joint Unit for

Research on the Urban Environment, University of Aston in Birmingham, May

Keeble, D. E. (1978) 'Industrial decline in the inner city and conurbations', *Transactions of the Institute of British Geography* (New Series), Vol.3, 101-14

Keeble, D. E. (1980) 'Industrial decline, regional policy and the urban-rural manufacturing shift in the United Kingdom', *Environment and Planning A*, Vol.12, 945-62

Keynes, J. M. (1936) *The General Theory of Employment Interest and Money*. Macmillan, London

Lawless, P. (1981) *Britain's Inner Cities: problems and policies*. Harper and Row, London

Layard, P. R. G. (1976) 'Subsidizing jobs without adding to inflation', *The Times*, 28 Jan.

Layard, P. R. G. (1979) 'The costs and benefits of selective employment measures: the British case' *British Journal of Industrial Relations*, Vol.15, 187-204

Layard, P. R. G. and Nickell, S. J. (1976) 'Using subsidies as a means of cracking the unemployment nut', *The Guardian*, 2 April

Layard, P. R. G. and Nickell, S. J. (1980) 'The case for subsidising extra jobs', *The Economic Journal*, Vol.90, 51-73

Layard, P. R. G. and Nickell, S. J. (1985) 'The causes of British unemployment', *National Institute Economic Review*, No.11, Feb.

Leicester City Council (1984) 'Survey of Leicester 1983: Initial Report of Survey'

Leven, C. L. (1979) *The Mature Metropolis*. D. C. Heath, London

Lever, W. F. (1974) 'Changes in local income multipliers over time', *Journal of Economic Studies*, Vol.1, No.2, 98-112

Lever, W. F. (1979) 'Industry and labour markets in Great Britain' in Hamilton and Lugo (eds) (1979)

Lever, W. F. (1981) 'The measurement and implications of employment concentration ratios in British local labour markets', *Papers of the Regional Science Association*, Vol.47, 139-54

Lindley, R. M. (1980) *Economic Change and Employment Policy*. Macmillan, London

Lindley, R. M. (1982) 'Occupational choice and investment in human capital' in Creedy and Thomas (eds) (1982), Ch. 4

Lloyd, P. E. and Dicken, P. (1982) 'Industrial change: local manufacturing firms in Manchester and Merseyside', Inner Cities Research Programme, Dept of the Environment, London

Lloyd, P. E. and Dicken, P. (1983) 'The components of change in metropolitan areas: the events in their corporate context' in J. B. Goddard and A. G. Champion (eds) (1983)

Lloyd, P. E. and Mason, C. M. (1984) 'Spatial variations in new firm formation in the United Kingdom: comparative evidence from

Merseyside, Greater Manchester and South Hampshire', *Regional Studies*, Vol.18, No.3, 207-20

Lloyd, P. E. and Reeve, D. E. (1982) 'N.W. England 1971-1977: A study in industrial decline and economic restructuring', *Regional Studies*, Vol.16, No.5, 345-59

Loveridge, R. and Mok, A. (1979), 'Theoretical approaches to segmented labour markets', *International Journal of Social Economics*, Vol.7, No.7, 376-411

Lucas, R. E. (1981) *Studies in Business Cycle Theory*. MIT Press

Lynch, L. M. (1983) 'Job search and youth unemployment' in Greenhalgh, Layard and Oswald (eds) (1983)

Macey, R. D. (1982) 'Job generation in British manufacturing industry: employment change by size of establishment and by region', Government Economic Service Working Paper No.55, Regional Research Series No.4, Dept of Industry

Mackay, D. I. *et al.* (1971) *Labour Markets under Different Employment Conditions*. Allen and Unwin

Mackay, D. I. and Reid, G. L. (1972) 'Redundancy, unemployment and manpower policy', *Economic Journal*, Vol.82, No.328, 1256-72

Madden, M. and Batey, P. W. J. (1983) 'Linked population and economic models: some methodological issues, analysis and policy optimisation', *Journal of Regional Science*, Vol.23, 141-64

Main, B. G. M. (1981) 'The length of employment and unemployment in Great Britain', *Scottish Journal of Political Economy*, Vol.28, 146-64

Manley, P. and Sawbridge, D. (1980) 'Women at work', *Lloyds Bank Review*, Jan., No.135

Marshall, J. N. (1985) 'Business services, the regions and regional policy', *Regional Studies*, Vol.19, No.4, 353-63

Martin, J. and Roberts, C. (1984) 'Women's employment in the 1980's: evidence from the women and employment survey', *Employment Gazette*, Vol.92, 199-209

Martin, R. L. (1982) 'Britain's slump: the regional anatomy of job loss', *Area*, Vol.14, No.4, 257-64

Martin, R. L. (1984) 'Redundancies, labour turnover and employment contraction in the recession: a regional analysis', *Regional Studies*, Vol.18, No.6, 445-58

Martin, R. L. (1985) 'Monetarism masquerading as regional policy? The government's new system of regional aid', *Regional Studies*, Vol.19, No.4, 379-88

Mason, C. M. (1980) Intra-urban plant relocation: a case study of Greater Manchester, *Regional Studies*, Vol.14, 267-83

Massey, D. B. (1982) 'Enterprise zones: a political issue', *International Journal of Urban and Regional Research*, Vol.6, 429-34

Massey, D. B. (1983) 'Industrial restructuring as class restructuring:

production decentralisation and local uniqueness', *Regional Studies*, Vol.17, No.2, 73–90

Massey, D. B. (1984) *Spatial Divisions of Labour: social structures and the geography of production.* Macmillan, London

Massey, D. B. and Meegan, R. A. (1978) 'Industrial restructuring versus the cities', *Urban Studies*, Vol.15, 273–88

Massey, D. B. and Meegan, R. A. (1982) *The Anatomy of Job Loss: the how, why and where of employment decline.* Methuen, London

Massey, D. and Meegan, R. (eds) (1985), *Politics and Method: contrasting studies in industrial geography.* Methuen, London

Mawson, J. (1983) 'Organising for economic development: the formulation of local authority economic policies in West Yorkshire' in Young and Mason (eds) (1983)

Mawson, J. (1984a) 'Local responses to unemployment – the Leeds approach', *Local Government Policy Making*, March, 13–21

Mawson, J. (1984b), 'Bradford's experience', *Local Government Policy Making*, March, 28–36

McGregor, A. (1977) 'Intra-urban variations in unemployment duration: a case study', *Urban Studies*, Vol.14, 303–13

McNabb, R. (1977) 'The labour force participation of married women', *Manchester School*, Vol.45, 221–35

Meager, N. (1984) 'Job loss and the regions: how important is redundancy?', *Regional Studies*, Vol.18, 459–67

Merseyside Economic Development Office (1985) 'Review of MERCEDO operations 1981–1985', Report of the Chief Economic Advisor, MERCEDO, April

Metcalf, D. (1975) 'Urban unemployment in England', *Economic Journal*, Vol.85, 578–89

Metcalf, D. (1982) 'Special employment measures in Britain', Policy Studies Institute, Sept.

Metcalf, D. and Nicholl, S. J. (1981) 'Occupational mobility in Great Britain' in R. Ehrenberg (1981)

Metcalf, D. and Richardson, R. (1980) 'Unemployment in London' in Evans and Eversley (eds) (1980)

Middleton, A. (1981) 'Local authorities and economic development', Discussion Paper No.1, Centre for Urban and Regional Research, University of Glasgow

Miller, R. and Wood, J. B. (1982), *What Price Unemployment: an alternative approach*, Hobart Paper No.92, Institute of Economic Affairs, London

Minford, P. (1983) *Unemployment: cause and cure.* Martin Robertson, Oxford

Molho, I. (1983) 'A regional analysis of the distribution of married women's labour force participation rates in the UK', *Regional Studies*, Vol.17, No.2, 125–33

Moore, B.C., Rhodes, J. and Tyler, P. (1983) 'The effects of government regional economic policy', Dept of Land Economy Discussion Paper, University of Cambridge

Moos, M. (1983) 'The training myth: a critique of the government's response to youth unemployment and its impact on further education' in D. Gleason (1983)

Morrison, W. I. (1973) 'The development of an urban inter-industry model', *Environment and Planning A*, Vol.5, 369-83, 433-60, 545-54

Moylan, S. and Davies, B. (1980), 'The disadvantages of the unemployed', *Employment Gazette*, Aug. 830-32

Moynagh, M. (1985) 'Breaking the vicious circle of inner city deprivation', *The Guardian*, 18 Sept.

Mukherjee, S. (1976) 'The costs of unemployment', Broadsheet No.561, Political and Economic Planning, London

Murray, R. (1984) *From the Market to the Factory: new directions in municipal socialism*. Fabian Essays, Fabian Society

National Economic Development Council (1985) 'Investment in the public sector built infrastructure: Parts 1 and 2, Overall findings and conclusions', Jan.

Neuberger, H. (1985) 'Why is unemployment so high?', *National Westminster Bank Quarterly Review*, May, 12-20

Nicholson, B. M., Brinkley, I. and Evans, A. E. (1981), 'The role of the inner city in the development of manufacturing industry', *Urban Studies*, Vol.18, 57-71

Nickell, S. J. (1978) 'Fixed costs, employment and labour demand over the cycle', *Economica*, Vol.45, 329-45

Nickell, S. J. (1979a) 'The effect of unemployment benefit and related benefits on the duration of unemployment', *Economic Journal*, Vol.89, 34-49

Nickell, S. J. (1979b) 'Estimating the probability of leaving unemployment', *Econometrica*, Vol.47, 1249-66

Nickell, S. J. (1980) 'A picture of male unemployment in Britain', *Economic Journal*, Vol.90, 776-794

Nickell, S. J. and Andrews, M. (1983) 'Trade unions, real wages and employment' in Greenhalgh, Layard and Oswald (eds) (1983)

Norcliffe, G. B. and Hoare, A. G. (1982) 'Enterprise zone policy for the inner city: a review and preliminary assessment', *Area*, Vol.14, No.4, 265-74

Oi, W. Y. (1962) 'Labour as a quasi-fixed factor', *Journal of Political Economy*, Vol.70, 538-55

Othick, F. (1983) 'Exploring the myth that rates are a heavy burden on the business community', *Local Government Review*, 24 Sept.

Owen, D. W. and Gillespie, A. E. (1980) 'Trends in male and female unemployment in the northern region, 1971-80', *Regional Science Association Annual Conference Paper, British Section*, September

Owen, D. W., Gillespie, A. E. and Coombes, M. G. (1984) '"Job shortfalls" in British local labour market areas: a classification of labour supply and demand trends, 1971-1981', *Regional Studies*, Vol.18, No.6, 469-88

Packham, R. (1983) 'Employment subsidies: a look at East Lothian small business assistance scheme', *The Planner*, Vol.69, No.5, Sept./Oct. 161-2

Palmer, J. (1985) 'Lessons in enterprise', Letter to *The Times*, 13 Nov.

Parkes, H. and Kohen, A. I. (1975) 'Occupational information and labour market status: the case of young men', *Journal of Human Resources*, Vol.10, 44-55

Parkinson, M. H. and Wilkes, S. R. M. (1985) 'Testing partnership to destruction in Liverpool', *Regional Studies*, Vol.19, No.1, 65-9

Perry, B. and Chalkey, M. (1984) 'How many factories do we need?', *Town and Country Planning*, Vol.53, No.2, Feb.

Phelps, E. S. (ed.) (1972) *Microeconomic Foundations of Employment and Inflation Theory*. Macmillan, London

Prowse, M. (1985) 'The high tide of unemployment', *Financial Times*, 17 July

Rajan, A. (1984) *New Technology and Employment in Insurance, Banking and Building Societies: recent experience and future impact.* Gower Press

Rajan, A. (1985) *Job Subsidies: do they work?* Gower Press

Record, N. (1985) 'Time to stop the decline of our factories', Economics Agenda, *The Guardian*, 27 Nov., 26

Reder, M. W. (1955) 'The theory of occupational wage differentials', *American Economic Review*, Vol.45, 834-40

Reder, M. W. (1969) 'The theory of frictional unemployment', *Economica*, Vol.39

Rees, A. (1966) 'Information networks in labour markets' *American Economic Review*, Vol.56, No.2, pp 559-66

Rees, A. (1979) *The Economics of Work and Pay* (2nd edn), Harper and Row

Reid, G. L. (1972) 'Job search and the effectiveness of job-finding methods', *Industrial and Labor Relations Review*, Vol.25

Richardson, H. W. (1978) *Regional and Urban Economics*, Penguin Books

Richardson, J. and Henning, R. (eds) (1984) *Unemployment: policy responses of Western democracies.* Sage

Richardson, R. (1980) 'Unemployment and the labour market' in G. Cameron (ed.) (1980)

Robinson, D. (ed.) (1970) *Local Labour Markets and Wage Structures.* Gower Press

Robinson, D. (1967) 'Myths of the local labour market', *Personnel*, Vol.1, 36-9

Roper, M. (1982) 'Aspects of corporate performance in the economy of

Central Leicestershire', Leicester Economic Study Report No.3, Leicester City Council and Leicestershire County Council, Oct.

Sapsford, D. (1981), *Labour Market Economics*, Allen and Unwin, London

Scott, M. and Laslett, R. A. (1978) *Can We Get Back to Full Employment?* Macmillan, London

Seabrook, J. (1983) *Unemployment*. Granada Publishing

Seabrook, J. (1985) 'Clever talk that hides the roots of rioting', *The Guardian*, 14 Nov.

Seibert, S. (1985) 'Wage fixing loses 230,000 youth jobs', *Economic Affairs*, Vol.5, No.3, 14–18

Showler, B. (1980) 'Racial minority group unemployment trends and characteristics', *International Journal of Social Economics*, Vol.7, No.4, 194–205

Simpson, W. (1982) 'Job search and the effect of urban structure on unemployment and married female participation rates', *Applied Economics*, Vol.15, 153–65

Sinfield, A. (1981) *What Unemployment Means*. Martin Robertson, Oxford

Sirmans, C. F. (1977) 'City size and unemployment: some new estimates', *Urban Studies*, Vol.14, 99–101

Smith, B. M. D. (1980) 'An empirical study of unemployed men on the register in Small Heath, Birmingham, in 1976', Centre of Urban and Regional Studies, University of Birmingham

Smith, D. J. (1981) *Unemployment and Racial Minorities*. Policy Studies Institute, London

Spence, N. (1982) *British Cities: an analysis of urban change*. Pergamon, Oxford

Spencer, K. M. (1985) 'Changing fortunes in the manufacturing heartland', Summary of West Midlands Project for the Economic and Social Research Councils' Inner Cities in Context Research Programme, JURUE, University of Birmingham, Oct.

Stern, J. (1982) 'Job durations of men becoming unemployed', *British Journal of Industrial Relations*, Vol.20, 373–6

Stigler, G. J. (1962) 'Information in the labour market', *Journal of Political Economy*, Vol.70, 94–105

Storey, D. J. (1980) 'Job generation and small firms policy in Britain', Policy Series II, Centre for Environmental Studies, London

Storey, D. J. (1982) *Entrepreneurship and the New Firm*. Croome Helm, London

Storey, D. J. (1983) 'Local employment initiatives in North East England: Evaluation and assessment problems' in Young and Mason (eds) (1983)

Straw, J. (1981) 'Rates and Jobs', House of Commons Library Research Staff, June

Taylor, C. J. H. (1985) 'Learning lessons in enterprise', Letter to *The Times*, 26 Oct.

Taylor, J. and Bradley, S. (1983) 'Spatial variations in the unemployment rate: a case study of North West England', *Regional Studies*, Vol.17, No.2, 113-24

Taylor, S. (1981) 'The politics of enterprise zones', *Public Administration*, Vol.59, Winter

Thatcher, A. R. (1976) 'Statistics of unemployment in the United Kingdom' in G. D. N. Worswick (ed.) *The concept and measurement of involuntary unemployment*, Allen and Unwin, London

Townsend, A. R. (1983) *The Impact of the Recession: on industry, employment and the regions, 1976-1981*. Croom Helm, London

Turner, D. (1985) 'Enterprise agencies reach maturity', *Town and Country Planning*, June, 196

Tym, R. and Partners (1982) 'Monitoring enterprise zones: year two report', Department of the Environment, London

Tym, R. and Partners (1984) 'Monitoring enterprise zones: year three report', Department of the Environment, London

Vickerman, R. W. (1984a) 'Urban and regional change, migration and commuting – the dynamics of workplace, residence and transport choice', *Urban Studies*, Vol.21, 15-29

Vickerman, R. W. (1984b) *Urban Economics: analysis and policy*. Phillip Allen

Vipond, J. (1974) 'City size and unemployment', *Urban Studies*, Vol.11, 39-46

Waine, P. (1983) 'The business rates burden: a case for their reduction', *Municipal Journal*, 21 Oct.

Warnes, A. M. (1980) 'A long-term view of employment decentralisation in the English inner city' in Evans and Eversley (eds) (1980)

West Midlands County Council (1984) 'Action in the local economy', Progress Report of the Economic Development Committee

West Midlands Enterprise Board (1983) *Purpose, Policy and Procedures*, 29th April

White, M. (1983) 'Long-term unemployment – labour market aspects', *Employment Gazette*, Vol.91, No.10, 437-43

Willis, K. G. (1984) 'Local government distorts industrial development', *Economic Affairs*, Vol.4, No.3, April/June

Willis, K. G. (1985) 'Estimating the benefits of job creation from local investment subsidies', *Urban Studies*, Vol.22, 163-77

Wood, J. B. (1972) 'How much unemployment', Research Monograph No.28 *Institute of Economic Affairs*, London

Young, K. (1983) 'The problems of economic strategy' in Young and Mason (eds) (1983)

Young, K. and Mason, C. (eds) (1983) *Urban Economic Development: new roles and relationships*. Macmillan, London

Young, K. and Mills, L. (1983) *Managing the Post-Industrial City.* Heinemann, London

Ziderman, A. (1975), 'Costs and benefits of manpower training programmes in Great Britain', *British Journal of Industrial Relations,* Vol.13, 223–43

Ziderman, A. (1978), *Manpower Training: theory and policy.* Macmillan, London

Index

Page references for tables and figures are given in **bold type.**